AF683725

WITHDRAWN
FROM
UNIVERSITY OF PLYMOUTH

Between Two Worlds

This book portrays the translation of social relationships into political and economic life in the Philippines. It considers in particular the influence upon the nature and quality of institutions and practices which arise from shifts in attitude towards social relationships – shifts which might be characterised as being on a continuum with, at one extreme, an attitiude which regards social relationships as ideals or absolutes, and which emphasises individualism, institutional probity and the rule of law, and, at the other extreme, an attitude where loyalties based on kinship, local networks and places of origin are vitally important, and where social relationships, institutions and practices are often material for manipulation and the pursuit of ambition. The book argues that, whether inchoate business, powerful company, community association or central bureaucracy, its characteristics and the smallest details of its working are shaped by these movements in attitude. Regarded as material for manipulation, the translation of realtionships brings with it fission, uncertainty, instability, and an obsession with monitoring, auditing and image-play. Treated as expedient absolutes or as if ideals, their translation leads to greater stability, openness, clarity, probity, and professionalism. The implications of these ideas for material progress, social science thought, and the notion of cultural difference – East and West, North and South – are also examined.

Rupert Hodder is a Lecturer in Geography at the University of Plymouth, England, and currently holds a Visiting Professorship in the Department of Sociology at the University of Shandong, China. He writes on China and Southeast Asia, and his publications include: *In China's Image: Chinese Self-Perception in Western Thought*; *Development Geography*; *Merchant Princes of the East: Cultural Delusions, Economic Success and the Overseas Chinese in Southeast Asia*; *The Creation of Wealth in China: Domestic Trade and Material Progress in a Communist State*; and *The West Pacific Rim.*

Between Two Worlds

Society, politics, and business in the Philippines

Rupert Hodder

RoutledgeCurzon
Taylor & Francis Group
LONDON AND NEW YORK

First published 2002
by RoutledgeCurzon
11 New Fetter Lane, London EC4P 4EE

Simultaneously published in the USA and Canada
by RoutledgeCurzon
29 West 35th Street, New York, NY 10001

RoutledgeCurzon is an imprint of the Taylor & Francis Group

© 2002 Rupert Hodder

Typeset in Times New Roman by
Keystroke, Jacaranda Lodge, Wolverhampton
Printed and bound in Great Britain by
MPG Books Ltd, Bodmin

All rights reserved. No part of this book may be reprinted or reproduced or utilised in any form or by any electronic, mechanical, or other means, now known or hereafter invented, including photocopying and recording, or in any information storage or retrieval system, without permission in writing from the publishers.

British Library Cataloguing in Publication Data
A catalogue record for this book is available from the British Library

Library of Congress Cataloging in Publication Data

ISBN 0–7007–1643–2

Contents

UNIVERSITY OF PLYMOUTH
Item No. 9005483112
Date -9 SEP 2003 S-R
Class No. 302.3509599 HOD
Cont. No. ✓
PLYMOUTH LIBRARY

Figures

Preface

For the many people in Davao who have shown me great kindness over many years, much of what follows is very personal. I have therefore taken great care to preserve their anonymity. But they know who they are and how grateful I am.

The most recent periods of fieldwork for this study were funded largely by the British Academy, and by my Department in Plymouth. My thanks to both these institutions. Thanks also to Brian and Tim for the figures.

Chapter 3 contains material which appeared originally in *South East Asia Research.* My thanks to this journal and to the anonymous referee for many useful comments.

And, as always, special thanks to San – *diliko mahimo ning tana kung wala ka*!

Introduction

This book is about relationships in the Philippines and about our familiarity with those relationships: it is about how our commonality of being is translated into our politics and livelihoods, our institutions and procedures, our routines and practices, which together make up the world around us.

At the centre of this understanding of our social world is a kind of dialectic[1] that I believe is played out within each of us and among us all. It exists between the 'personal' and the 'absolute' – terms that I use to describe our attitudes towards our relationships with one another. When seen narrowly from the 'inside', other people, their relationships with one another and with me, and the practices and the institutions woven from these relationships, come to be seen as the material for manipulation, as a means to an end. Seen from the 'outside', my attitude towards the world moves away from the personal. Relationships, emotions, thoughts and desires, practices and institutions, come to be seen as if absolute, as something proper and important in themselves.

The reasoning behind these arguments and interpretations I leave to Chapter 4. I do so partly because it is not always helpful to view the world and what we read only through our academic constructs; and partly because these ideas, to some extent, arise out of the following study. Indeed, my concern in the final chapter has been to consider what these ideas mean *apart* from the Philippines and it is on this account that it could be read as a separate essay. Certainly, were it read first, the final chapter might give the impression that this book has more to do with abstractions than it has with the nuances of our everyday lives from which our social world is made, and in which the apparently abstract and the concrete come together.

The first chapter, then, moves without further preamble into an account of relationships – the tensions, the emotions, the manipulation and affection, the pose and the sincere – in a small community in the southern Philippines which I have called Nazareth, and does so in a style which I hope conveys the nature and atmosphere of these relationships with more intimacy than drier, more analytical language would have allowed. Chapter 2 considers the translation of these relationships, and of relationships such as these, into the details and the broader brush strokes of political and bureaucratic life. The personal leads, in general, to fission, uncertainty and instability, and to an obsession with policing, monitoring and image-play. The absolute, meanwhile, brings with it greater stability and openness, clarity and professionalism. In Chapter 3 it is argued that the implications of these shifts between the personal and the absolute are as profound in economic life as they are in Nazareth or in government. Whether inchoate businesses or powerful companies and oligarchies, the smallest details of their workings and characteristics are shaped by the most subtle movements in attitudes towards our relationships.

1 Mananangpot

Introduction

On the southern island of Mindanao, in the city of Davao, there is a purok[1] that I have called Nazareth. More than one hundred and twenty families live here. What follows in this chapter is an account of a Nazarene family's relationships – the give and the take, the pride and humility, the envy and generosity, the selfishness and altruism, the perfidy and openness, the manipulation and affection, the pose and the sincere. It is an account with which I think we will all be familiar. What we will also see in the relationships and emotions that were played out in the struggle to keep the family together, to meet ambition, to achieve some recognition, to capture some sense of self-worth, or merely to eke out mild contentment, is the very substance from which our institutions and practices – political, bureaucratic and economic – are fashioned.

Family and friends

Nazareth itself is like many other puroks. As you sit on the verandah under the portico of Inday and Dee's bungalow and look out, slender palm trees shoot up from the surrounding compound only to burst into jagged spikes of green against a hard, cerulean sky. The leaves of mango trees, gnarled like claws, reach up above houses of coconut-wood and concrete, only to be beaten down by the sun. And the clouds, vast spires of etched crystal which form unnoticed during the mornings around the mountains to the southwest, seem permanent, immovable, changing their shape only when your eyes look elsewhere.

Not until the late afternoon do the colours wrung out by the day strengthen and deepen for an hour or two; then even the reds and oranges of the *banderra español* blacken against a gaudy purple sky. If it is to rain, the dull, featureless, grey cement which has been oozing across the heavens for an eternity puts to sleep all movement; smoke from tiny heaps of burning rubbish wreathes up into the air, loops back down, crawls over the ground, and waits. The grey darkens into a charcoal sludge; then come the first heavy drops of water, punching craters into the earth, splattering against stones, and filling the trees with the sound of scurrying feet. The rain hardens, batters tin roofs, and settles into a steady roar. Children shriek with delight as they run in and out of the cataracts which pour from the corrugated roofs on to the soil, throwing up first clouds of dust, then sprays of mud. The odours of decay, once smothered by the heat, are now released. The colours, too, are corrupted by the yellowing shadows cast into the darkness by naked light bulbs and sodium lamps. Shattering raindrops glitter in this perverse light; rotting cables, crazily hung between the houses, glisten; flashing leaves slide against each other; and the grass stirs fitfully like a mat of shiny, scuttling insects. Soon, it is as if the world is covered by a thin film of foul-smelling oil; and even the gathering wind seems tired.

When the rain finally begins to soften, it gives way to the sharp clatter of mahjong tiles and to drifting sounds of laughter, argument, radios and televisions. Women flit here and there, chattering and scolding and throwing brittle fish from make-do woks on to worn plates. Men whose bodies are not yet ravaged by tobacco, alcohol, vinegar and salt, open small, fat bottles of beer; and, as they draw deeply on coarse cigarettes, press mustard-coloured fingers against faces burnished and rubied with drink.

Figure 1.1 A Nazarene street

It was on one such evening that Jo walked through a door into the kitchen of the bungalow and stood there swaying slightly. To his left, set high on the wall, just above a large fridge, were wooden cupboards stuffed with canned goods, dried coffee and milk; to his right was a small, shining enamel stove; in front of him a smooth, long, concrete worktop divided the kitchen from a large central room into which three bedrooms and a bathroom debouched. The floor of the room was a deep, shimmering pool of wooden mosaics. Across its surface young women would skate each day, coconut husks tied to their delicate feet. To one side of the ebony dining table which dominated the room three small, uncomfortable bamboo-framed chairs were grouped stiffly around one another. To the other side rested an enormous sideboard, filled with the best, but never-used, cutlery and plates, glasses and towels, sheets and tablecloths. Scattered on top of the sideboard were family photographs and empty bottles of Scotch whisky. At the far end of the table, and just to one side of the front door, stood another smaller sideboard bearing an old radio and cassette player. And in the corner of the room, between the two sideboards, was a television placed high upon an octagonal stand. The front door, heavy and ornate, opened onto a large verandah. From the verandah, a stone path, cut with drainage channels, wound its way past a *nippa* hut, across the foundations of the old house, to a barbed, rusting, iron double-gate. The gate was set in a high wire fence. A wall of breeze blocks, its coping crusted with glass, made the other three sides of the compound.

Jo, small and wizened, his thick hair streaked with grey, his head and hands too large for his body, remained standing in the kitchen. He worked for Inday and Dee on their farm and, unless invited, rarely used the front door or ventured into the central room. He usually approached the bungalow through a thin grove of coconut palms which gilded the west side of the compound wall, and entered the back of the house through a white iron-grill. The gate opened into a long room where another table stood. At the other end was a doorway which led into the back kitchen with a grimy stove, gas cylinder, washing machine and running water. Here, most of the preparation, cooking and washing took place. The unpainted walls of the purely functional long room and back kitchen were lit by a single neon strip. A second doorway, filled with a greasy wooden mass, led from the back kitchen into the front one, from the practical to the theatrical, where the Bacchian Jo now stood and performed. He asked everyone to listen to him: '*bantug gra pobre ko, gi daug-daug mo ako*' (I am abused because I am poor). But though *daug-daug* meant abused, he said, did not *daug* mean morally victorious? And if he was morally victorious twice over because he was poor, then could it not be reasoned that he was abused because he was moral? The four women sitting at the table seemed to enjoy listening to his play on words; and so he explained his joke several times. He then seemed at a loss and returned to the back kitchen. As he left they called after him, saying that from now on they would call him 'winner-winner me'. They laughed all the more loudly and returned to their meal.

It was the second sitting. The old man, Dee, waited on by the four women, had eaten first: rice, meat, fish and mounds of slippery vegetables. When finished, he retired first to a rocking chair in front of the television, and then to his bedroom. Inday, his wife, who had organised the shopping, the cooking and the service, now sat at the table with Sal, her daughter, and with Ellen and Bing. Their food was freshly cooked, but Dee's leftovers were passed down to them; and theirs in turn were passed to the back kitchen where two of Inday's sons and 'winner-winner me' ate their meal.

Ellen had been with Inday for nearly thirty years. Her great-grandmother and Inday's great-grandmother had been sisters, or so it was now said. At the age of nineteen Ellen had become pregnant. At the time she was living with Pitant, her aunt, who regarded the pregnancy as an insult to herself and her family. She took to beating Ellen's arms and legs and, one day, in an explosion of temper, banged her head against a wall. Afraid that the unborn child would be harmed, Ellen had turned to Inday who took her in. Inday paid Ellen's medical costs, and persuaded the parents of the unborn child's father to pay for a maid to look after Ellen during the pregnancy. After delivery of the baby boy, Ellen fell into a black depression and on medical advice the child was removed from her and left in the care of the father's parents until she had recovered. She had been in Inday's debt ever since. She apportioned her time between her own small house near Binugao, where she lived with her son, and Inday's sprawling family and properties in Davao, Cebu and Manila. She ran errands, shopped, ironed, cleaned and cooked for them. And for this she received little or no money. But Inday would secure her work for her. At the moment she worked for one of Inday's immediate neighbours, the Gutierrez, who in their family compound had set up a small noodle factory.

Ellen was just one of a number of women who had worked for Inday in this manner in return for her patronage. Elly's story was more tragic. She had been born in a poor mountain village in Agusan, many hours drive from Davao. She first came to work for Dee who travelled the provinces for the Bureau of Internal Revenue. He found her reliable and honest, and recommended her to Inday who trained her to cook and keep house; and though barely their senior she had looked after Sal and her sister and brothers through much of their childhood, adolescence and university days in Manila and Cebu. In return Inday paid for Elly's school and university education and, once Inday's youngest child had graduated, she encouraged Elly to seek a life of her own. Elly married an Indonesian who worked as driver and cook for a prominent official in the Indonesian diplomatic core stationed in the

Figure 1.2 The noodle factory

Philippines. Elly and her husband remained with the diplomat: the pay was good, and they travelled; and when their employer returned to work in Indonesia they moved with him. Elly had written to Inday regularly until three or four months ago. Then silence. Then a 'phone call from her employer. Elly had stomach cancer. She wished to return to her village in Bukidnon. Inday thought the long journey home would finish her the more quickly. Words of comfort and sympathy, and tears, were passed down the phone. Now she was gone.

Bing was a recent addition. Her husband had worked for Inday's eldest son David in a gold mine in Davao del Norte. The mine in which David and his in-laws were the main shareholders had lost money and then closed. Inday had agreed to take Bing on. The money was not good, but it allowed Bing and her five children to eat something; and for Inday the arrangement provided some relief from Dee. Three days ago Ellen and Bing had been sent to the farm in Binugao – at best nearly a two-hour drive by Jeepney – merely to feed corn to Dee's precious cockerels, a task it seemed that he would not trust to Jo. Bert had, for many weeks, been driving his father there and back each day in an old and battered jeep so that he could prepare his animals for their fights. And each day, there and back, his father would instruct Bert how to drive safely and correctly, and how to change gear without wearing the machinery. Bert had grown tired and had asked his father if he would like to drive. Dee was silent until they had reached the compound. He then declared that until such time as he saw fit, Bert could no longer drive the jeep. Bert retorted, saying that he did not in any case want to drive what was no more than a pile of junk. His father had then sworn that Bert would never drive the jeep again. Bert left the bungalow, vowing that he would never return; and as he left with his daughter in train Dee ordered him never to enter the compound or eat his food again. Inday cried symbolically, asking why he treated her children in this way? During the first five years of their marriage she had been without child. She had then borne nine. Where was his gratitude for this blessing?

Dee said nothing. He was resolute. His decision stood. There was more to this than just Bert's driving. He had given Bert every opportunity. He had sent him and all his other children to the best schools in Davao; and then to universities in Cebu or Manila. Bert had met all his efforts with ingratitude and recalcitrance; and though he had won a degree, he had stubbornly resisted entry into any of the professions. Dee had then arranged positions for him in his friends' businesses. All Bert had had to do was turn up for work on the first day; but he had not done so. And Bert had, on no less than nine occasions (Dee had counted), answered him back. Had any of his other children ever been so disrespectful?

There was no hope that either man would apologise and make amends – and so it remained for more than a year. Dee was left with Ellen and Bing, and, the day after Bert's expulsion, he had sent them to Binugao. But could he rely on them to care for his cockerels properly? Shortly after they had left, Dee shouted for Jun, whose own small bungalow and tiny plot of land abutted Dee's. A few moments later Jun appeared. He was in an invidious position. It was to his house – in which he, his two daughters and his grandchildren all lived – that Bert had banished himself and his daughter. He was friends with Bert, and also owed much to Inday and Dee. His estranged wife worked in Hong Kong, and he had a daughter in Japan. Even so, the income was small; he had had no regular job for more than fifteen years, and had no skills or education to speak of. One son-in-law had work but he was unreliable; the other had already abandoned Jun's daughter and grandchild. Inday helped out when money and food was short, and David, a surgeon, would always be available for diagnoses and – if he had on him samples garnered from the salesmen who plied their trade – free medicines, too. And Jun enjoyed Dee's cock-fighting vicariously. So Jun went when he was called; and the next day he would, as requested, collect Dee's cockerels from the farm and bring them back to the compound. Only then would Dee feel at ease.

When Jun returned with the animals he tethered them to small stakes, each a safe distance from the other. That same afternoon one cock managed to free itself and set about another, tearing its feathers and drawing blood. Bing had made an effort to separate the two, but as she approached, one flew into the

Figure 1.3 Jun's house

air, its claws flailing wildly. She turned and fled, clutching her head in mock terror while Sal and Ellen looked on in amusement. Inday seemed not to notice. Dee, in his bedroom, woken by the noise, let out a yell for Jun, and, still shouting, rushed like a maenad onto the verandah. Jun dutifully appeared, separated the animals, calmed them and, under Dee's instructions, placed them in their separate boxes in the coup at the back of the compound. The women laughed up their sleeves, but giggles quickly surfaced once Dee had returned to his room. There he stayed for the rest of the day, emerging only for his evening meal.

Figure 1.4 Looking east from Jun's house

The next day, some four days after Bert had left, Dee turned on Sal. He asked her if he could talk with her in private. Sal immediately knew what this would be about. Dee had long suspected Inday – large and rotund and now in her early seventies – of seeing a young man of twenty-five years and a father of three. When Inday went to visit the sisters at the Redemptorist Convent, no more than a five minute walk from her door, and when she attended mass there in the early morning or late afternoon, Dee would hover at the entrance of the compound. Occasionally he would even make his way down to the basketball court from where he could see the gate to the convent. Any car which he did not recognise he took as a sign; and if the young man's dog should happen to wander by, then that, too, was a sign. No-one said anything, but all the neighbours knew what he was up to; and when Inday passed by on her way home they would ask 'is the Barangay *Tanud* [spy] out again today?' She would laugh, but his foolishness wore her down, and that hurt Sal. Now he wanted to talk to Sal. If she said nothing then he would very likely interpret her silence as support for Inday. If she spoke to defend her mother, there would be an argument. She therefore decided to put the matter to rest as quickly as she could, and to do so while others were around them. She said that she did not see why they needed to talk in private; she observed, casually, that her mother had, as usual, been to church today and nowhere else; and she said that she was now going into the back kitchen to prepare his supper. Dee said nothing and gave away no hint of his thinking.

But the following day Sal's graduation picture had been laid down on its face under a plastic bag. In its place was a picture of Dee in naval uniform, taken shortly after his return from West Point. He had told Bing to make the adjustment while Sal was out, and had confided in her his belief that if his own picture was removed, this would mean that Inday no longer cared for him. The convoluted thought behind this symbolism caused the women much delight.

That afternoon, before the rain came, and before Jo was to give his performance, Sal urged her mother to be more forceful and assertive. Inday listened quietly, but her concerns were necessarily wider. Although the titles to the land (and property) which she and Dee had acquired in Manila, Cebu, Davao, and in other parts of Mindanao, the Visayas, and Luzon, had been transferred to their children in name, these possessions still belonged, in everybody's mind, to Inday and Dee. In practice, most of the land belonged to Dee alone, and was his to dispose of as he wished. And he had made it very clear to his tenants that if they did not pay their rents directly to him, they would be turned out. The amount of income flowing in from these assets was not known to Inday precisely; nor did she know how much tax was owed. Worse still, Dee had threatened to cut off Inday and their children, and hand over all his property to his relatives in Abra.

Yet it was Inday who held the upper hand, and she knew it. She had, over the years, won control over some of the land so that she might keep house and pay tuition fees and other incidentals without constantly having to request money from Dee who, when in the Bureau, was always being moved from one province to the next. She also had her own land in Cebu, which had been left to her by her parents. And, as a last resort, she could always threaten to entangle Dee in the courts, for the land was owned legally by their children. Above all, who would be tolerant enough to look after Dee? Over the last two years, while staying at his house in Manila and at her house in Cebu, he had successfully isolated himself from his own relatives and from her's, and so had been forced to return to Davao. Who in Manila or even Abra, his home town, would tolerate his intolerance? Her relatives would not do so, nor, she suspected would his. If she withdrew her support, he would have nothing except his income. How long would that last if he had no-one else to rely on except himself? Even the best-paid maid would not last more than a month or two.

She also knew, though the accusations he constantly threw at her made this difficult to appreciate, that he was not entirely himself. She suspected that he had in his own mind transformed her into a reflection of himself upon which he could hang his own feelings of guilt. And there was no doubt that the more tiresome aspects of his personality had been accentuated by age and illness. He had suffered with diabetes for many years; tuberculosis had been cleansed from him only recently; and a mild stroke seemed to have weakened his capacity to ward off those imaginings and delusions which pray on all of us and which, without conscious effort, often lead us to deceive ourselves and others. More than all this, she held great affection for him; and in the preservation of marriage and the unity of family she saw her own self-esteem and the respect and admiration of those around her.

Together they had achieved much. Inday had been a maid in the service of the Aboitiz – a prominent merchant family – in whose company her father had worked as an engineer in Cebu. Dee had been a naval officer. They had married quickly under pressure from their parents who, in those more prudish days, had worried about the lateness of their return from a date without chaperone. In the first few years there had been hardship and arguments, and no children. But the marriage had worked; to Inday's mind it was a great success; and she knew that it was widely recognised as such. They had both worked hard, earned money, saved, bought land and built houses. They had carefully selected the right private schools for their children. With an imperious hand they determined the profession that each child would enter. They had brought up their children firmly but compassionately. They had taught them to respect their parents, God, each other and the honour of the family. And they had inculcated in them the strong belief that, as far as their relationships outside the family were concerned, those who appeared conscious of their superiority or inferiority could never win the respect of others. They taught their children well, trusted to their common sense, tolerated their friendships even with those families of whom they were dubious, and they strongly encouraged their friendships with those families of which they approved. Parties were always given and had to be attended; the children were rotated among their friends as house guests; extra-curricular activities, such as ballet and music, were paid for; and they entwined their children's expanding networks of relationships with their own more established networks.

Dee's career as a naval officer and then as a ranking official in the Bureau of Internal Revenue afforded him the standing and opportunities to cultivate a broad range of relationships. Dee and Inday had known the Cabreros family since their first arrival in Davao in the early 1960s. Juan, the head of the Carbreros family, had also worked for the Bureau. His wife had been born into the Castillo family, which at one time had owned large tracts of land in Davao, and had enjoyed considerable influence. Her brother's daughter, Bee, had been Sal's classmate at Assumption College, a school commonly thought of, then as now, as one of the best for girls in the city. Other contemporaries of Sal and Bee at the school were Ruth and Jenny, who, with Bee, came to form part of Sal's *barkada*. Ruth was from a large, landed family, and related by blood and through marriage to a string of influential families – the Palma-Gil, Hizon, Pichon, Rita, Bangoys and Villa-Abrille, whose names now decorate the streets and monuments of the city. The four girls – Sal, Bee, Ruth and Jenny – also studied at ballet school together and went to the same parties; they had known each other's boyfriends and, at a later date, each other's husbands. Another member of Sal's *barkada* was Yvonne, whose family owned a chain of pawnshops in Davao. Yvonne's parents were the *compadres* of the Montilla. Both these families had originated from Cavite in Luzon. The Montilla's – a professional family of doctors, engineers and managers (for the merchant Alcantara) – were introduced to Inday and Dee through the Cabreros, and they and their children became life-long friends.

It was partly by virtue of Sal's attendance at Assumption, and partly because of Inday's voluntary work for a religious organisation, that Inday and Dee came to know Noy, the head of a once-landed, now-merchant, family. He was very active in that same organisation and held Inday in high regard. He had even gone so far as to arrange for his relatives' friends in the United States to look after Inday on her one and only visit there. His sister had taught Sal at Assumption and later became the school's headmistress.

Sal left school in Davao for college in Cebu, where she lived with her grandmother and her grandmother's adopted son. Until the age of nine he had been forced, because of the family's straitened circumstances at that time, to wear Inday's clothes. This, it was said, had had its effect and, though he was now married, explained his rather effeminate behaviour. When Sal graduated with an arts degree she left for a dental school in Manila. There she lived in her parents' house; next to it, and in the same compound, stood her father's sister's house. Inday or Dee visited the children from time to time, and Sal's father's sister acted as their informal guardian. A second Aunt – a fictional title rooted in the assertion, probably true, that, when infants, she and Inday had shared the breast of Inday's milk nurse – was also asked to keep an eye on Sal's wellbeing. She was the captain of a nearby barangay. This position, together with her strong personality, and her ties of fictional kinship, made her an excellent choice as both guardian and chaperone. But it was Sal who was made responsible for managing the income from their lands and properties in Luzon, for returning a portion of that income to her parents, and for sternly metering the rest to pay for tuition, transport, books and food, and for the general upkeep of her parents' house where she lived with a number of her brothers, all of whom were at various stages of their studies.

After Sal had passed the school's requirements for dentistry, and had succeeded in the government exams (the latter are necessary before one can be licensed to practise and acknowledged by the world as a true professional), she returned to Davao Medical School where she taught dentistry. It was also here that her eldest brother, David, had read medicine and where he had met his wife, Maria. Her mother, Audrey, had over sixty years built up extensive property and commercial interests from nothing. Both David and Maria went on to compete their residency training at Davao Doctors' Hospital, where two of Maria's nieces worked, one as a nurse and the other as a midwife; and where one of her many nephews worked as a medical technician. The *ninong*, or sponser, at their wedding was Congressman Garcia in whose district Audrey had served as a barangay captain for a number of terms. As *ninong*, the congressman was therefore Audrey's and Inday's *compadre*.

At Davao Doctors' Hospital, David worked under Belisario, a member of a prominent merchant family for whom Inday came to work occasionally as a land-sales agent. Also working as a doctor at the hospital was the brother of the Chief Mason of one of the lodges in Davao. David joined this lodge temporarily; and Martin, one of Maria's brothers who later became one of David's business partners, became a permanent member.

David's marriage to Maria also opened up opportunities for Sal. Another of Maria's brothers sub-let his clinic in another private hospital (the Ricardo Limso) to Sal for a few hours each week. There she would see private patients in order to help subsidise her lecturer's salary. It was his intention to run as a city councillor. He therefore spent as much time away from the clinic as in it, and because his political ambitions were funded largely by his mother, Audrey, he could afford to rent it to Sal at a very low rate.

Not more than two minutes walk from Sal's clinic, and not more than five minutes walk from Davao Doctors' Hospital, stood a mahjong parlour owned by a Filipina whose Chinese husband had died many years ago. Inday, who enjoyed mahjong, spent much of her time here while Sal worked in the clinic; and when both had finished they would return home to Nazareth together. Inday had met Mamay Wong through Alma, whose grandfather had been Mamay Wong's grandmother's brother. Alma lived a few minutes walk from Inday in the neighbouring purok. She and Inday were members of the same religious and funeral organisations; one of Alma's daughter also worked in the Bureau; and both Inday and Alma were keen mahjong players. And so was Bert. Regular players at the parlour, all of whom came to form one of Bert's many and extensive *barkadas*, included Jun (of Nazareth); the son of a powerful land-owning family in Davao with political influence in Manila; Roger whose brother was, for a time, the National Director of Immigration, and who had been involved in various business partnerships with Martin; and Linda, Bert's fiancé. Little more than two hundred yards from the parlour, Bert and Linda ran a food stall outside what was then a large department store owned by the Gaisano brothers (a Chinese merchant family from Cebu), one of whom became a *ninong* at their wedding. Another member of Bert's *barkada*, and another regular player, was Gary, a doctor of Chinese descent, who also rented a clinic in the Ricardo Limso.

Yes, Inday was right to be proud of her and Dee's achievements. Land and buildings provided income, collateral and security: Inday and Dee had accumulated land and property in various parts of Davao and in other places across the Philippines. Education and a profession meant a reasonable and relatively assured income, and created opportunities for widening one's social contacts: Dee had been a naval officer, a ranking official in the Bureau, all nine of their children were educated, and eight of them had become professionals. Bert, it was true, had not entered any of the professions. But he had graduated with a degree which, had he followed his father's instructions, would have secured his path into law; he would perform for his mother any job no matter how troublesome; he kept her informed about what his other brothers were up to; he was known widely to be honest, sagacious and politic; and he had, with quiet intelligence, built up an irreproachable reputation as a giver, which would be to his advantage financially now and in the years to come. Indeed, all her children were capable of weaving complex webs of relationships, and were skilled performers in their social duties. These webs were of vital, even paramount importance. With those relationships came influence; with influence came power, opportunity and money. Without those networks, education and profession meant little, and land, property, income and power could not be protected, made secure or built upon.

Neighbours

It was only natural that, with their land, educated children and extensive networks, Inday and Dee should also be regarded highly within Nazareth. It was natural that they would be acquainted with other notables within the community, such as Lagdameo (whose daughter had attended Assumption, and whose wife had worked in the Buhangin Association alongside Inday), and with Applicador at whose golden wedding anniversary Inday and Gloria, the barangay captain, had been appointed sponsors. It was natural that Inday and Dee should also count among their *barkada* other respected Nazarene families such as the De Venecia, the Siason, the Dagohoy – whose fathers had all worked for the Bureau – and the Serapio, whose father had (along with the Montilla's in-laws) worked for the Alcantara. It was natural that Inday and Dee should not only entwine the networks that they formed within the community with those established by their children, but, as with the relationships which they formed outside Nazareth, hand those networks down from one generation to the next, so that the children of Inday's and Dee's friends became members of their own children's *barkadas*. And it was only natural that, as with the relationships they formed outside Nazareth, Inday and Dee and their children would lend their relationships to each other. By entwining, lending and passing on to each other the relationships which they formed outside the community, they expanded one another's opportunities immeasurably; by repeating this practice within the community, almost every

Nazarene was drawn into Inday's and Dee's and their children's networks. At the centre of the family, Inday and Dee thus found themselves with considerable influence over their neighbours.

More than twenty years ago Inday and Dee had allowed Perez and his sons, immigrants from the mountains in the southwest, to build their stilted houses on a small plot of land in the corner of the compound. The wall which now marked the edge of the compound and divided it from the Perez's shacks had been built only recently. Though populated by many professionals, civil servants and a few successful businessmen, Nazareth had grown up over more than forty years on squatted land: it was only a few years after the arrival of Aquino that the land was bought by the National Housing Authority and sold on cheaply to the Nazarenes. The housing authority had sent in their officials to determine the boundaries of each plot and drive in posts to mark the boundaries. The posts were then moved by the residents. But Inday and Dee had already begun their wall. Although his children had become members of Henry and Bert's *barkada*, Perez had always been trouble.

Father and sons had been involved in petty thefts outside Nazareth and had brought their spoils back to their shacks where they, and occasionally their associates, would squabble loudly. More than once the police had been called to stop the fights which broke out among them. Petty criminals such as they, and others who were simply poor, were the kind of people from whose ranks the New People's Army (NPA) would recruit their informers. They would be expected to tell the guerrillas who lived in Nazareth, what these people did for a living, who lived with them, and what their routines were. The guerrillas would then decide who their enemies were, and send in the 'sparrows' – groups of young men – to kill them. In response, the *Alsa Masa* had been formed – a small band of men who, in the case of Nazareth, were mostly purok officials armed with handful of rifles and revolvers lent to them by the AFP (Armed Forces of the Philippines). Inevitably, they, too, became targets. Attempts were made on the lives of Simon, the purok leader, and Jojo, a special constable. Both were good friends of Henry. Partly because of that relationship, and partly because he had joined the army as a lieutenant for three years immediately after graduating in agricultural science, an attempt was also made to kill Henry. A group of nearly a dozen teenagers gathered outside the main gate of the compound as if they were summoning their courage. One stepped forward and casually asked if Henry was at home. Inday poked her head outside the door and replied dismissively that he was not. (Having received warning of the approaching gang a few minutes earlier, he had disappeared with his father's pistol into the maze of paths and alleys at the back of the compound.) For some reason the sparrows decided not to enter the house to see if she was telling the truth, perhaps because they would have felt too exposed covering the ground between the gate and the house itself. Meanwhile, Sal, with two maids and a visitor, lay on the floor in silence. Henry escaped with his life to Manila and there rejoined the army. Others in Nazareth were not so lucky that day. The teenagers soon organised themselves more effectively, and Pusan, who lived down the track twenty metres from Inday's compound, was shot in the head in front of his wife in their kitchen; a policeman who lived to the north of the community met a similar fate; two other young men were carried to the local government hospital, their legs shredded into jellied ribbons by automatic fire.

The reputation of Nazareth had by now reached a very low point, and the uncertainty of life had become intolerable. There was little that could be done about the NPA, and they would continue with their threats and murdering until they made their truce with Aquino. But petty criminals and suspected informers could be dealt with. Simon and the other officials had asked Perez to mend his ways, but he only brought his thieving closer to home. When he was killed it was not thought that Perez worked for the NPA, at least not regularly, nor that he had been killed by the guerrillas. Criminals outside Nazareth were blamed; yet there was at the back of every mind the *Alsa Masa*. Whether true or not, it was a useful thought to let run. If it appeared that a big stick had been used, then even a small carrot would look tempting. Now that Perez was dead it was certainly easier to bring his sons into line. His eldest son, Luis, had no money or job. Through her *compadre*, Congressman Garcia (in whose district Nazareth lay), Inday arranged it with the city authorities to recruit Luis as a traffic policeman. It paid little, but enough for him to provide the bare minimum of food for his wife and children. Inday would also supply rice and coffee. And she took on his eldest daughter, Louisa, as a maid. Louisa, who was nine years old, attended school during the afternoons, but spent her mornings (from about 5.00am until midday) sweeping, cleaning, buying drinks or rice from the local *sari-sari* stall, and carrying messages for Inday. Inday fed Louisa, paid for her pens and papers, and for her school books and clothes. Occasionally Louisa would receive a bowl of ice-cream, or a slice of chocolate cake as a treat. But Inday was reluctant to give her money because she would almost immediately hand it over to her parents.

There was no sentimentality in the relationship between Inday and the little girl. Louisa was not comforted when she cried; she was not lavished with presents, clothes or shoes; there was no demonstration of affection. But she knew order: Inday told her when to eat, when to do her homework, and gave her spot tests on her spelling and mathematics. Inday visited her school to ask about her progress. The tasks given to Louisa, though numerous and repetitive, were light. She was taught the difference between acceptable and unacceptable behaviour. And in the evenings, over a meal, she would share in conversation dominated by the lull and sway of current and past relationships. She was, in effect, being presented with clear goals from which she could extract self-esteem. Marriage and children would signify her entry into an adult world. The further expansion of her social networks, a publicly successful marriage, children who proved capable at school, and perhaps even a profession for herself, would all add to her worth, status and self-confidence. The 'sisterhood' into which Louisa was being pulled, the order that she knew, and the domestic and social practices she was being taught by a prominent family, amounted to a compassion she had not known in the chaos of her own home. And should Louisa prove honest, Inday would help her achieve professional status as a nurse. She would then be in a far stronger position to assist her parents and younger brothers and sisters.

But there were tensions between Inday and the Perez family. David had administered treatment to Louisa's mother's father, who suffered from tuberculosis but had sought help only when it was too late. When passing Inday's compound one day he collapsed in a pool of dark, frothy blood. Inday made available Dee's jeep as a hearse, which, although too short (the foot of the coffin stuck out of the back), served its purpose. During the vigil over the body, Inday also provided a lamp and an extension plugged into her house, and Henry, now a lieutenant in the army once again, supplied the bananas and coffee. After one week of vigil, and despite the heat, the body had not yet been buried. Louisa's parents were still holding 24-hour mahjong sessions (for every winner paid a five pesos *tong* which went to the bereaved family); and since they had been unable to secure the barangay captain's chop, a wooden seal (for he was away at the time), they had been making good use of Inday's signature on a sheet of paper which they presented to every Nazarene in order to collect donations. There was a humorous side to this which Inday appreciated. Yet her sense of propriety was now being offended. Her objections were partly that they had used her reputation to collect donations cynically, and partly that the funeral was not the demonstration of respect that it should have been. To her mind, the ritual marked the status of those who were dead and those who still lived. A cheap coffin would quickly become a matter of gossip. The money spent on the funeral, the number of people who attended, and the right atmosphere, created, first, by the public wailing, into which genuine feelings of despair are channeled, and then by the more relaxed, cheerful wake, were part of a performance which confirmed the achievements and purpose of being. In common with most women in Nazareth, Inday was a member of the *dayong* – a funeral association. And she had, as a gift, paid for Sal's membership, which Sal accepted with a wry smile. In death, as in life, things had to be done properly.

Another incident heightened the tension between Inday and the Perez family. Louisa had four brothers and sisters. Three other children had died from dysentery, measles, bronchitis, poverty and ignorance. Their lives might have been saved had their parents sought help quickly from Inday or from the government hospital outside the entrance of which their grandmother often sold fruit. It was all the more aggravating when it was discovered that Louisa's brother (who was four years old) and sister (a two-year-old) were afflicted with sores. The girl's mosquito bites on her feet and legs had become infected; and an untreated cut between the toes had caused the boy's left foot to become swollen and extremely painful. Sal took the initiative to clean the wounds, hoping to shame the children's mother into doing something to alleviate their discomfort and perhaps avoid another death. As she cleaned the girl's bites and the boy's foot, now covered with flies, both children cried pitifully. Their mother's reaction at the sight of ugly sores she would not touch was merely an expression of disgust. When Sal had finished, the boy's six-year-old brother carried him back to their hut. Within two hours the boy, again barefooted, limped out onto the poorly drained soil of the compound. Inday would not arrange for the children to be vaccinated against tetanus, nor would she herself, nor through her son, dispense any medicines or attempt to persuade the parents to consult a doctor. She was not prepared to be blamed should anything subsequently happen to the children; and she suspected that the parents were deliberately neglecting their children in order to play on her emotions and charity.

When Luis returned home, Inday was angry and indignant. Luis blamed his wife, and then asked Inday for twenty pesos to buy rice. Inday shuffled away muttering, and returned with her purse and handed a bank note to him – a performance full of irony and futility which raised much laughter in her household. Louisa's mother then appeared and began sweeping the compound – a ritual she went through whenever she wanted a few pesos, ostensibly for food, but always spent on tobacco. A short time later, Luis, with a cigarette hanging from his lips, ostentatiously paraded his concern for his children by sitting his two-year-old daughter upon a wooden stool in the middle of the compound in plain view of all, and began to shave her head. Earlier that day she had made a bald patch with a razor she had found in the midden.

Another incident, however, prompted Inday to intervene directly in the affairs of Luis and his family. She learnt that Luis was suspected of taking bribes. His behaviour might reflect upon her as she had secured his job for him. Henry asked his mother to intervene through Congressman Garcia, but she refused: if Luis offended again, her own reputation for her ability to judge character might be sullied. It was then brought to her attention that Louisa had missed school for two consecutive days. Louisa had been ordered by her mother to stay at home and wash her father's clothes. Her mother would no longer do his laundry. Most of her husband's salary was being spent on palm-wine and another woman. Inday was furious and threatened to withdraw all her help and support. To show his contrition, Luis and his daughter walked slowly across the compound hand-in-hand on their way to church. But the following day, matters seemed to worsen. Luis refused to sleep at home, saying that he feared his wife would kill him while he slept. Inday ignored these histrionics and said only that she wished Louisa to attend school the next day. That same night, Louisa ran crying to Inday. Her mother had whipped her out of jealousy over the special treatment Inday had shown her. Inday then told Luis and his wife that they had been abusing their relationship with her, and she made it clear that if they continued to take advantage of the generosity she had shown them, she would release Lousia and break off all contact with them. The mother was chastised for her inadequacies, the father for his deceit and infidelity.

The final straw, however, was Louisa herself. She was suspected of stealing a few pesos from Inday. Inday no longer cared whether or not the child had done so on the instruction of her parents. She threw the child out and washed her hands of the whole family. Inday was aware that the relationships which brought her influence also made her vulnerable. In forming those relationships, one took on, used, and was seen by others to possess, a particular character role. Henry was quiet and diffident in his manner, and slow in speech. He would not womanise, he was a font of gifts and money to his *barkada*, and he was especially kind and generous to the Nazarene children. Yet despite this soft shyness, he had been decorated in actions against NPA and Muslim insurgents, mentioned in despatches, and would drink and smoke with the lowliest of them. Bert, too, was just like them: he enjoyed drinking and gambling, and seemed free of all the pretensions which might be expected from a family of such standing. He would do what he could for them through his sister, brothers and parents, and this often proved to be more than was hoped for. Al was a chancer who would lavish those around him with money and whisky, meet the vicissitudes of life with a smile and a laugh. David was solid and responsible, perceptive and politic, occasionally secretive and ruthless, always measuring his words, and never indulging in gossip. He was always ready to make a diagnosis without asking for anything in return. There could not be a daughter more dutiful than Sal, no one more scrupulously fair and balanced in her treatment of others regardless of rank or status. Inday was vivacious, talkative, gregarious, and saw in her God humour and forgiveness; and she was above all generous and willing to help anyone who asked. But character roles had the danger of becoming public expectations which others could use to their advantage. A steely harshness which could make the genuine seem more like artifice was a necessary defence, even in the face of the most prosaic and ordinary events.

On the west side of Inday's compound lived Julie, a large and lively woman who had, for the last two years, dressed herself with great care in gaily coloured clothes. She had produced four boys and was now hoping for a daughter, and no superstition need be overlooked. Inday had lent her a pan

– a rather good one made of stainless steel – shortly before one of her numerous visits to Cebu, where Dee was quickly making himself unpopular. Inday had forgotten about the pan until she happened to see it hanging there in Julie's kitchen. She asked for it back. Julie said that the pan was hers: she had already returned Inday's pan several days ago when she was in Cebu, and bought one of her own. Inday was incensed: until the pan was returned she would not talk to Julie again nor allow her children to play in her compound with her grandchildren. There had been no friction between them before this incident, no inkling that there would be trouble. But Inday would not be taken for a fool. It was only after a suitable period that Julie relented and handed the pan back. Whether or not she had intended to keep the pan, it had to appear as if only her memory had been at fault.

On the eastern side of her compound, just to the south of the Perez compound, was another troublesome neighbour. Lalay's house and the land on which it stood was hemmed in on all sides. The only path from house to the main track was across Inday's land. Lalay claimed this path was hers, if not by right, then by common sense. But Inday would not give it to her. She feared that if she did Lalay would claim as hers ever-increasing slices of land on either side of the path. After all, to Inday's thinking, Lalay's character role was highly suspect. Was she not a bad mother? She did not merely argue with her children she shouted at them so that all could hear, and she had often come to blows with them. On one memorable occasion, Inday had found Lalay rolling around in the mud locked in combat with one of her own daughters.

And so the wall, crusted with glass, was built, defining Inday's and Dee's compound. Henry asked Luis and Guhilde (a relative of Luis) to lay the rough, grey blocks for a small consideration. Lalay cursed the two men as they built the wall, confirming what Inday and Dee long suspected – that she was a witch. Perez and Guhilde smiled through their cigarettes at her spells. Luis would keep his job, Lalay would still be allowed access, and Julie would still ask David to examine her children whenever they became ill; and just as Inday found advantage in her influence over them, they too would continue to find advantage in her.

Family and in-laws

Inday's reputation and the reputation of her family were one and the same. And that reputation was sound enough. Dee was not making life any easier, and there was always the possibility that in his dealings he might squander or give away land and money. But she found solace in what they had achieved together, in their reputation, and in their luck. As she looked around her she saw, both with sorrow and a certain exhilaration, many of her contemporaries drop by the wayside. Dee also wondered with a smile whether those who were falling around him were his unwitting shields against fate. Teano's death had been curiously grotesque. He had decided to cut the branches of a mango tree which stood at the front of his house. The tiny grubs which lived in its leaves often fell like rain on to his bare back, sending a raw, angry rash streaking across his body. He would not pay a younger man to cut the branches, and had climbed the tree with a hand-saw on a particularly hot morning. His house lay on the edge of the basketball court on the track which led past the convent and out onto the main road. People walked by all the time, and in the morning they had seen him busy in the tree. At midday he was still there. His maid had asked him if he wanted to eat, and she had been told to go away. He was still there in the afternoon: passers-by had noticed a sleeping figure, pointed at it, and laughed. His wife, who had been attending to her social rounds, returned to see his wallet full of money lying at the foot of the tree. She and the maid, with the help of Simon and other neighbours, pulled him down only to find that he must have been dead for several hours. De Venecia had not been so lucky. He was still bed-ridden with a stroke which had left him speechless, able to move only a few fingers, and yet, as far as one could judge by the way in which he squeezed your hand in reply to your questions and the pleading light in his eyes, tragically clear and lucid in his mind. He was placed in the central, air-conditioned part of his house, on a bed of fine cushions. Around him the life of his family and the entertainment of their guests carried on as normal. In this, perhaps, he found comfort. Dee had come away from one of his visits, though, radiant with vindication and a spring in his step: less than a year ago De Venecia had been making fun of his walking stick. Now he no longer needed what De Venecia was not even able to use.

But there was no humour to be found at the end of Alma's life. Her daughter had died of breast cancer less than four years earlier. Alma's son-in-law had re-married within a few months; he never came to visit her; and he never sent money to her. For him, she felt, her daughter had never been. When Alma discovered that she too had breast cancer, she seemed determined to let go as soon as she could and refused all treatment. She continued to play mahjong regularly with Sal, Inday and Jun, always fidgeting with her dress as she tried to cover the lump. It was not long before the growth began to rupture incessantly. A few months later she took to her bed. Her skull, jaws and teeth soon found precision through her yellowing, morphine-dried skin; and as she emptied of life her eyes turned into inky-black hollows. She spent the last few weeks blinking wide-eyed at the half-closed wooden slats of her bedroom window, and listening to her remaining daughter's five-year-old grandchild totter about the small, cheaply furnished house. Inday would no longer visit her. If she did, they would only cry, and that did neither of them any good.

Two-and-a-half years after diagnosis, and four years after the death of her daughter, Alma died.

Yes, Inday had her troubles with Dee but, so far, luck and God had been with them. The more she martyred herself to his unreasonableness, the more those around her would admire her self-sacrifice. And by giving way time after time, Dee would occasionally melt. On their forty-ninth wedding anniversary a dozen old women gathered to celebrate their achievement and his continuing recovery. Dee stepped on to the porch where he was asked to give a speech. He gave thanks for his life and for his marriage, and said that his speech was proof enough of his return to full health. Inday linked her arm in his and kissed him on the cheek. Gazing at no-one in particular and looking as demure as it was possible for a woman of her mettle to do, she wondered aloud if her kiss would be returned. His eyes sparkled with mischief and immediately he replied that they had not gathered to pray for her to receive a kiss from him. She chuckled and their audience laughed at the transformation of tension into humour.

Yes, Sal might well enjoin her mother to be more assertive, but Inday had other things on her mind. As she saw it, the main problem lay not with Dee but with the relationships among her children and between them and their in-laws. With the exception of Bert, who seemed content with his lot, each child wanted to make something more immediate and concrete of their lives; and with these ambitions came envy. Their wives, too, she believed, made things worse, egging their husbands on, encouraging them to compare her sons with each other, to wonder who among them would, in the end, inherit land and property, and who would, in the meantime, benefit from their parents' favours.

For the most part, these tensions were remnants of childhood periodically revived to give weight to some new indignation. David, the eldest child, had always been favoured because he was the eldest. And because he was favoured he was given authority and responsibility. Even now his brothers and sisters treated his advice more like instructions. But much had also been expected of him. After school he had, under his mother's influence, entered a seminary in Cebu. He found temptation and his father's opposition too great, and was pushed with great ruthlessness into medicine. He had obeyed because he was the eldest; and he had succeeded because his father and mother and his brothers and sisters and, it seemed, the rest of the world, expected him to succeed. Sal, the eldest daughter, had also found her life mapped out for her, and in return for her compliance and success, she too was accorded responsibility, authority and favour. But when her name had not appeared in the list of candidates who had passed the government board examinations, and her father had dismissed her publicly as a failure and a disgrace, she was destroyed. Two days later it was a glorious relief to find that her name, together with those of several other candidates, had been omitted accidentally from the newspaper. With her status as a professional confirmed, and her estimation in the eyes of her father and the wider world now assured, her self-confidence was restored.

Sal still felt subordinate to David even now, but she too was treated with deference by her younger brothers – all the more so because she kept her opinions of the way in which they lived their lives to herself. Only Mary did not see why she should have to take second place to her elder sister. And for these feelings she blamed her parents. Inevitably her resentments affected the way in which she looked at Sal, and, in return, how Sal looked at her. Mary had studied in Manila where she had lived in her parents' house, keeping it in order much as Sal had done. Now that only she lived there permanently, her parents let part of the house, and had asked her to collect the rent from the tenants there and at their other properties in Luzon, again much like Sal had done. Unlike Sal she had not yet passed her board exams; unlike Sal she had siphoned off much of the rent and lavished it upon her own friends in Manila; and unlike Sal she would not accept any supervision. It was also fairly certain that she enjoyed other women. Her use of the rent had annoyed Inday. That Mary had provided Dee with an easy excuse to funnel their tenants' rents directly into his hands annoyed Inday even more. That Mary's preference for other women was regarded by Inday and the rest of the family as a mildly amusing foible annoyed Mary. Had they taken her more seriously, she thought, they would have had a very different view of her behaviour. Through her parents' eyes, she believed, she was seen as hard-headed, argumentative and difficult: what else could be expected of her?

Only in Mary was there doubt of the legitimacy of Sal's position; but only Sal accepted David's authority largely, though not entirely, without question. When Dee bought a new four-wheel-drive pick-up truck and made it over to David for use in his work, Henry was told explicitly by his father that he could not drive it. Henry believed this was unfair and unreasonable: he had the greater need since it was he who was managing Dee's farm at Binugao. Dee had replied that Henry was a careless driver who would tinker with machines about which, if the truth be known, he knew very little. The run-down jeep (the same jeep from which Bert was to be banned a year later) was in its sorry state largely because Henry, rather than take it to a proper mechanic, had always been trying to fix it. This dispute had come on top of another. Henry had wanted to turn the farm at Binugao into a proper business and register it at a corporation; and David had quickly put a stop to that. Henry's frustrations were difficult for him to bear. He was a professional. He was a graduate in agriculture, much like his father. He had joined the army (twice) as an officer, and during his second term of service he had risen to the rank of captain. In the army he had been made responsible for the lives of hundreds of men (regulars and militia), and been charged with the peace and order of large areas of western and southwestern Mindanao where communist and, more recently, Muslim guerrillas operated. Twice he had been decorated for his bravery and presence of mind in combat. He had married, resigned honourably from the army, and now had fathered a child. He had helped Dee in many ways, and he was much respected for his generosity, for his gentle, shy, self-effacing manner, and for his valour. Yet still his father and brother treated him in this way. It was partly for these reasons that he determined while still in the army to buy his own land and set up his own farm in Lanao del Norte.

These disputes over the truck and the farm brought him into an open argument with David. This was, as everyone knew, quite futile. Henry might as well have argued openly with his father. Whatever his justification and however righteous his cause, David held authority over him and that was the end of the matter. David's authority, and the favours which his parents had shown him, may have been justified by his success as a surgeon (which had in any case been demanded of him), yet that authority existed not because of his achievements nor even because he was merely their first-born. He owed his standing merely to his parents' need for a chief assistant, for their own righteous hand to rule among their children. And if, because of this, resentments among their children strengthened, then that, too, was taken as further justification for David's authority. Unable to escape from this gyre of injustice, as he saw it, Henry threatened violence. David treated this as a smutty joke. Henry, now embarrassed as well as angry, would not be in the same house as David. It was to be nearly a year before Henry's wife, Christine, brought the two brothers together, using her daughter Sarah and a very complex play of emotions.

Bert and Linda had lived together either in Inday's house, or in her parents' house, for at least ten years before they were married. The relationship had been tempestuous, and more than once Inday had thrown them out for arguing and flinging chairs at each other. The marriage itself was a strange affair. The ceremony and party was well attended; one of the Gaisano brothers agreed to become a *ninong*. Yet within a week of the ceremony Bert declared that they had never been married. The proper documents had never been signed, or had mysteriously disappeared. The source of the problem, or justification for the sudden change of heart, was that both accused the other of not being able to produce children. Inday had then tried to repair their relationship. She had for many years opened her house to Sister Mayon who, funded by donations from the owner of a large oil company, brought from Bukidnon and other provinces children and adolescents disfigured with hare-lips. Here David and a number of other surgeons would operate on them without charge. Once every month or so twenty or thirty children and teenagers would litter Inday's house and compound waiting for, and recovering from, their reconstruction. Inday asked Sister Mayon if she also knew of any children who might be available for adoption. Sister Mayon did indeed know of such a child from a poor Muslim family in Bukidnon: the child was five, or so Sister Mayon thought, for there was no birth certificate. No formal adoption was ever made, but the child's family agreed on the settlement, and the child was duly brought to Davao where Bert and Linda took possession of her. Almost at once there was a dispute. Linda had arranged through her sister to have a birth certificate issued, but she did not name Bert as the father and she gave her own surname to the child. Bert immediately ended his relationship with Linda, and Inday threw up her hands at the perfidy of the woman. Linda's sister tried to bring the two back together and two summits were held in the compound between Linda and Bert, their parents and an assortment of brothers, sisters and on-lookers. Bert was adamant that there could be no reconciliation, and Linda produced tears of regret. The two did agree, however, to share the child. Inday came to suspect this was merely a convenience. Linda was busy running a mahjong parlour and sari-sari stall which she had recently set up near her parents' house with money given to her by her sister who, when she was not dealing with Linda's affairs, worked in Germany. At the weekends, when the parlour became especially busy, the child, who was already exhausted by one late night after another, could be sent to Bert in Nazareth. But it was a convenience that brought much pleasure to Bert. He was a good father, though he was not always demonstrative in his affections and would often leave the child with others to look after while he lost money at the Galleria or performed all those other social duties that occupied most of his time. When he returned she would wrap her arms around his thick, shirtless girth, allowing herself to be dragged about. And he would keep her clean, make sure she was properly rested and fed, encourage her to work hard, praise her for her efforts, and let others know that she was a very intelligent daughter.

She was not Inday's only adopted grandchild. David and Maria had three adopted daughters of their own. Audrey had borrowed the children from a couple who managed one of her ranches. The mother, who was related to Audrey (the two women's grandparents had been siblings) had eight children all told. Handing three over would make things easier for her, and she knew that she could never give the children all the advantages which would be open to them as Audrey's grandchildren. The three girls took David's surname and the adoption was made formal, but the mother would be able to see her children whenever she wished, and her daughters would always know who their natural parents were.

Inday and Dee were proud of all their adopted grandchildren, they treated them as their own, and both sets of children would carry their adopted father's respective positions within the family. Yet there was no denying that David's children were of Audrey's blood, and that Bert's child was of very different stock. Between themselves and Tommy's children, too, there was not quite that immediacy of the senses which brings one close to another in a way that defies words. Tommy and his wife, Joy, worked in Saudi Arabia and were fortunate enough to have their children live with them. She was a doctor and he a nurse. When home on leave he would always visit Nazareth, but Joy and her children rarely did so, and even then they would stay for only a short time. She seemed to find the compound and the house rather distasteful; and Inday found her rather precious.

Al's children, however, fared the worst. His first marriage to Zoe had lasted nearly a decade. But no children came out of it, and there were other problems which strained the relationship. Dee had lent much of the money paid to him on retirement from the Bureau of Internal Revenue to Al and Zoe who used it to buy a house in an expensive subdivision in Davao. Al worked overseas and he agreed to pay his father back from the salary which he sent home to Zoe each month. Zoe, however, channeled much of the money to her brother who lived a few doors away on the same estate. This he used to set up a jeepney firm. Zoe secured a licence and a route; her brother and his wife drove the jeepney; and all three of them shared in the costs and profits. Zoe also took over Bert and Linda's food store outside the Gaisano's department store to whose sales girls Zoe's sister-in-law lent money. Zoe's food store collapsed, however, when she was abandoned by her cook. Not only had he to cook for Zoe and her maid and very often for her brother's family and occasionally for Dee, Inday and Sal, but for her business too. Yet he was paid only a domestic's salary; and this he often received several months late. When that business, too, ended, Zoe bought three trucks and attempted to gain a foothold in the construction trade, hauling sand and gravel. This business also failed: her drivers were difficult to handle and she found herself being constantly undercut by the larger trucking companies. This enterprise was followed by another unsuccessful venture – a mahjong parlour. Meanwhile, Dee, who had not yet been repaid in full, watched her businesses rise and fall; and when he visited the house, he felt that she treated him coldly.

The marriage was eventually annulled on the grounds that no children had been produced. To end things quickly, Al gave Zoe the house, provided she released him from all other ties and obligations. She agreed and set up a workshop turning out *nata di coco* for Dole. In the small bedroom which she and Al had once shared, she put a small fridge and microwave oven. The rest of the house was ripped out to make way for noisy machinery, tangled hose-pipes, and barrels of rancid water. The business proved more successful than her earlier attempts, but it was technically illegal and soon she was paying out money to various officials whose responsibility it was to monitor business licences and land use. Dee had still not received all his money back, and the house in which he had sunk a large part of his government pension was being destroyed in front of his eyes. But worse was to come. He learnt through Bert that during his last period of leave, Al had taken up with a woman who worked in a bar in the city. The next they knew of it, Al had married this woman. She had then borne one child after another – four in all. And it was to them, and her parents, that his salary was now being remitted. Dee refused to see Al and would not recognise or meet with his new wife. When, quite unexpectedly, Al turned up in Nazareth with suitcases full of whisky, tobacco and other luxuries, hoping that his father might now be in better humour and more willing to accept his new family, he was met with a stony face and steely intransigence. Dee said that he would not even recognise Al's children. Inday was more sympathetic. Al's children were entirely innocent, and of this she and Sal tried, unsuccessfully, to convince Dee. Still, she would not allow their innocence to influence her belief that her new daughter-in-law's fast clothes and finery were exactly what a cheap gold-digger would wear. As if to emphasise her disapproval, she and Sal continued to see Zoe and treat her with respect. Zoe was loyal and her faults were merely those which derived from her inability to manage openly that loyalty to her own family and to her in-laws. Inday understood Al's desire for children but it was his duty to support his wife, and since it was he who had borrowed money from Dee, it was his loan to repay. Whereas Al had, in Inday's view, behaved improperly, Zoe was merely awkward in her relationships. As a consequence, she had allowed others to build up an unflattering impression of her own character – an impression which could then easily be strengthened by prejudice: she was a Tagalog, not a Bisayan, and this was enough to explain, and to confirm, her parsimony and coldness.

For all these reasons, Sarah had a special place in Inday's and Dee's affection, and of this Henry and Christine were aware. They also gave every opportunity for these affections to grow. During the two years when Henry was building up his farm in Lanao and Christine worked her profession as a government engineer, they had left their daughter in the care of Inday and Dee, often for months at a time. The child, whom Inday spoilt shamelessly, came to see the world as her stage and her grandmother as her most loyal acolyte. Christine had later taken the child in hand, disciplined her, and changed her almost beyond recognition. But the bonds which grandmother and granddaughter had formed remained very strong. With Sarah's sixth birthday approaching, Christine saw this as an excuse to visit the compound, and, under her gentle pressure, Henry found himself patching up relations with David with a simple, quiet apology. Inday did not say anything directly to either David or Henry, but all knew her desire for tolerance and harmony well enough not to wait for her to show her hand, especially on the occasion of her granddaughter's birthday.

Henry's threat to do David physical harm a year earlier had not been an idle one. David's authority made even the thought of it seem ridiculous. But violence was always a possibility in the heat of the moment. If that personal authority was lacking, and if restraints had been loosened by alcohol, then it became a real possibility. And Henry's threat had come not long after a fight between him and Bert. The two brothers had been drinking one evening in the *nippa* hut when Henry had asked Bert why he objected to his friends entering the compound? And why, still more, did their father seem more prepared to let Bert's friends into the compound? Bert had replied that both he and Henry already knew the answer to the second question. Their father had said that many of Henry's friends were thieves and cut-throats. Henry cared nothing for this exaggeration: they were rough-hewn, certainly, but there was nothing wrong in that; and his *barkada* within Nazareth, and those of Bert, were not mutually exclusive. They shared many of the same friends. Bert replied that Henry had no right to question whether or not his friends came into the compound, especially after everything he did for their parents. And in a demonstration of his firmness in his belief he slammed a glass on to the table, breaking it. Henry, fearing that this was a prelude to an attack, had struck first with his fists, and Bert had counter-attacked in kind. Inday ran out and threw herself between the two, throwing her arms round Bert, shielding him with her body and a stream of platitudes about family, children and filial piety. Sal followed, placing herself between Henry and her mother. With tempers fired by alcohol, and with broken glass scattered about, this was a brave thing for mother and daughter to do; and gave Jun time enough to bring into the field Jojo, a compadre of Henry, and a former member of the *Alsa Masa*. He separated the two men, placing one inside the bungalow and leaving the other lying on a bench under a mosquito net by the *nippa* hut. The next morning Inday made it clear through her silence and her funereal, but artful, mien how upset and disappointed she was at their behaviour. Without saying a word she shamed them into sheepish apologies to everyone.

There is no doubt Inday had saved one or the other from serious harm. But the more damaging, ever-present danger to the unity of her family were not the flashes of anger, nor the minor disagreements and envies. Criticisms which struck at the heart of what each felt themselves to be were, to her mind, still more baleful. Within a few days of his return from the Middle East, laden with gifts, and with his wife and children in train, Tommy had asked Robert in an off-hand, throw-away fashion what he intended to do with his life. Why had he not made provisions for the future? Bert at first ignored the jibe, and merely replied that he gave those kind of matters only such thought as they deserved. Tommy kept on over a period of some days with the odd comment here and there, gnawing away, comparing his own material success and his bright shiny family with Bert's lot. To silence him without a direct confrontation,

Bert put it around to his friends (some of whom were also part of Tommy's old *barkada*) that he would strike. Tommy wisely left for Manila, only to be summoned back by his mother. He returned to find that news of the rift between himself and Bert had reached Inday. She had words with Tommy, whose remarks, she said loudly for all to hear, were unfair and misconceived. Did he, Tommy, think that they really cared for the baubles he brought them? Look at her house, look at her simple furniture, look at the way she dressed! She and Dee had done everything for their children: all of their money had gone into land and their children's education; and they had done everything to show their children how to live. Where had Tommy been when Dee had been ill? Who was there, in Nazareth, helping them? Which of her children was generous to a fault? What kind of person was it that cared only for trinkets and money? There was a certain amount of pose in the phrases which poured from her lips. Yet much also that was genuine. Tommy's display of material wealth would have been no fault had he been generous with it, and had he not used it to imply, let alone say outright, that he was doing better than his brothers. Inday and Dee were not completely indifferent to their surroundings. But their relationships with the people around them were the only true measure of wealth and the means of power and influence through which money, land and things would flow. As far as they were concerned, the cheaper, the more practical, and the fewer the trinkets which she and their children possessed, the better. Such luxuries as they had allowed themselves – the television set, the gleaming stove, a washing machine, the cutlery and linen in the sideboard, and her jewelry – were to them luxuries only in part: such things were first and foremost objects for display, symbols that were, to Inday and Dee, transient and superficial when set against land and concrete. In his criticisms of Bert, Tommy had, to all intents and purposes, dismissed all that she held dear; and in dismissing such basic values, he seemed to allow no room for compromise. There was, from this time on, always a distance between Bert and Tommy. And in Tommy there was a growing feeling that he would not be recognised for what he was and what he had achieved – a feeling made more intense by his desire to show that he, no less than his wife, a doctor, could provide equally well for his family.

It was not just Tommy's callous one-upmanship that had irked Inday. He was thought by a number of his brothers and sisters to be parsimonious and judgmental, and obsessed with keeping everything spotlessly clean and just so. His wife, too, they found rather affected and neurotic; and under her influence his children seemed remote. There was also the question of land. Inday was determined that if large sums of money were needed, and if there was no alternative, it was better to sell land within the family. Inday had agreed to sell to Tommy land which she and Dee had titled in his name. As he understood the deal, Inday had sold the land to him at less than the current market value precisely because this was a transaction within the family. When he next returned to the Philippines, however, he discovered that the money which he had sent back to his mother with the expectation she would use some of it to begin construction on his house had, in fact, been used to pay back her debts and his father's medical expenses. Inday explained that Tommy had only now finished paying for the land; he had yet to return enough money to begin his house. Tommy was furious at what he saw as deceit. Inday replied that it had been agreed all along that Tommy should pay the full market price for land. Tommy then argued that he was being asked to pay for land which she had already paid for, simply in order to cover miscellaneous costs which would not add to the value of the land. Inday disliked the implication that her debts and Dee's medical costs were less important than Tommy's book-keeping. She had given Teddy life; she had educated him; and the money had been needed to pay for his father's treatment – the kind of eventuality for which she had originally bought the land. There were economic arguments, too. The 'full' market price she had asked him to pay was no more than 60 per cent of its true market value, and this for a plot of land which would rise substantially in value over the next ten or twenty years. Why did he not trust her? Tommy then foolishly mentioned that Inday had, or so he had heard, also been attempting to elicit a proportion of Maria's and David's savings. The source of the rumour, he said, was Maria herself. David denied it, and Inday contemptuously ended the negotiations. But Tommy had scored a hit.

It was undeniable that David's marriage to Maria had been a good match. Maria's parents were from humble beginnings. Her mother had started her first business in 1937 after marrying the suitor with the largest wage packet and thereby escaping an unhappy stepfamily. She bought an army-surplus jeep, renovated it and sold it in Manila for a profit which she then used to buy others. She continued with this circuit even during the war until she had built up her own fleet of sixty vehicles. After the war she diversified into gasoline stations. The profit margins from the transport business were small, but there were few competitors and her turnover was large. Always diversifying as competition intensified or as other circumstances changed, and always maintaining a high turnover, she created a business empire which eventually came to revolve around a real-estate company. She and her husband had an equal part of the majority of shares in the company: the remainder were divided equally among their children. Yet she alone made all the decisions concerning this core asset. Her remaining gasoline station was handed to one of her sons, James, and his wife Betilda, who together also owned and managed a construction company.

Audrey would always retain a strong influence over their affairs, and those of her other children and grandchildren. She had educated them, provided them with introductions into professional institutions at the start of their career, or set them up in their own private practices; she established extensive lines of credit (which she had underwritten) for those of her offspring who had ventured into business; she funded their political ambitions; and she integrated them into her business empire. And if her children and their families did not live in the houses she built for them, one next to the other on strips of land which she owned, then they would live with their parents in a huge, chalet-style mansion. The monopoly of power she had over her core assets, the dependency which she fostered, the networks of relationships she drew upon herself, and, through these networks, the influence she wielded over her family's various business, professional and political interests, were deliberately engineered largely in order to limit family squabbles which might otherwise spill over into the core of the family's trading interests. There was, after all, much to play for. Audrey's lands and properties were abundant, she and her husband were old, and her children and grandchildren were many. On Sundays, before the death of her husband, she would hold court, sitting on a large, heavy, ornate mahogany throne, her legs resting on a foot-stool; and as her grandchildren and great-grandchildren gambolled about her, she would dispense her favours, and shower them all with crisp bank-notes from a large bag hung over her wrist.

This cloying atmosphere, into which David was drawn, weighed on both his ambition and his loyalty to his own parents. His life was less his own than it was his wife's parents. He was their own personal surgeon, and though he had standing within her family, there was, as his in-laws jostled for position and a share of the inheritance, suspicion of him and even of his adopted daughters. The closeness of this court of which he had become a part, and the wealth of the courtiers with which he was compared, could not but strengthen his desire for independence, money and greater status. This led him into various business ventures (some connected to his profession and some not), and to consider political office – ambitions which brought him into conflict both with his own family and with his in-laws.

Shortly before Dee had lent him the new four-wheel drive, which had added to the trouble between David and Henry, David had decided to renovate and then sell an old Toyota jeep which Dee had given to him many years earlier. A share of the proceeds was to be used as a down payment on a new car; and part would go to help pay off his mother's debts to the Credit Union. The Toyota was renovated by Andrew, who was Maria's nephew and a member of one of Bert's numerous *barkada*. Andrew's business was supported by his mother Judy, whose business was in turn supported by Audrey. The estimate for the job was P80,000. Once the work had been completed, a buyer for the jeep was found through one of Andrew's uncles. The buyer agreed to pay P270,000 for the renovated Toyota – some P70,000 more than David had expected. Andrew then presented David and Maria with a bill for P110,000. Not only did this exceed the original estimate, but it also included charges for parts which David had given to Andrew. Andrew's creative billing was motivated not so much by greed as by the opportunity to pay back a debt to his mother. At this point Maria learnt by chance that Audrey had, on Maria's earlier instructions, managed to sell a ring which had belonged to Maria for P25,000. Maria requested that Audrey should give the money to Judy, Andrew's mother. By repaying Andrew's debt to his mother, Andrew would be paid off indirectly, and Maria and David would only need to pay Andrew the amount originally agreed for the jeep's renovation. Audrey, however, chose this moment to recall an old loan which she had made to her daughter Judy, and kept the proceeds from the sale of the ring for herself. Judy and Andrew redirected their anger at David.

The distrust which Audrey and David felt towards each other deepened. Audrey had bought several large plots of land which she had wanted to register in David's name in order to mitigate her own tax burden. At first he had agreed, but then he was advised by his father that his own tax burden would rise. David pulled out of the arrangement with Audrey at the last moment, much to her chagrin. It annoyed her even more when, sometime later, she heard that David had sold a plot of land for more than three times the amount he had paid when he bought it from her eighteen months earlier. Audrey suggested that he should pay 'interest' on the difference even though there had been no loan. David would not have been able to make such a profit, reasoned Audrey, if she had not agreed to sell the land to him at the time and at the price that she did. But David refused to make any money over to her, and would not be bated. These incidents were, he knew, but small plays in a drawn-out series of much larger games. Audrey was merely doing her best to foster dependency in David and Maria upon herself by manufacturing financial or moral obligations in them and by exercising moral claims over them. The more he made plain his frustrations, and the more he showed his determination to escape the court, the more determined Audrey became to hold David and Maria there.

Eventually the opportunity came for David to set up a private hospital in a small market town in South Cotabato, some two hours drive from Davao. Maria went with him, but her resentment was fed by her mother who would make sure David's impending move would be brought up in every conversation she had, and then ask, with a sigh, what sort of life could Maria hope to have in such a small town? Maria made no effort to foster relationships there. To the contrary, she allowed her cold and dismissive manner free reign. She became unpopular, her practice suffered, and this she used to vindicate her resentments. Audrey took this behaviour as a signal for her to step in. The maid whom Audrey had sent with Maria and David when they left for South

Cotabato had been reporting back to Audrey on her life with David; and Audrey reported that she had heard, through her agent, that Maria was being mistreated by David. This, however, proved to be a serious misjudgment of her daughter's character. For all her faults, Maria was entirely loyal, and despite her rather cold exterior, dismissive manner, directness and the disdain with which she seemed to view the social arts, she would do as she said, and she would do all she could to help those for whom she cared. Neither she nor David would talk to, or receive, Audrey for more than a year. Only then did Audrey finally made the journey to that small market town once again, this time to apologise.

It was not long after that Maria's father died. Her mother, with prescience and judgment and a certain unselfishness, acted to ensure that her empire would not be the cause of her family's disintegration. She sold the smaller businesses, much of her land, and even her grand mansion with its cool, sprawling verandahs lined with wicker chairs, and its broad, flowing rooms heaped with outsized Chinese vases glued to the floor, and with furniture of teak and mahogany. The money she divided evenly among her children and their children. The core of the empire, the real-estate company, would be left intact. Each of her children were given equal shares in it, and the presidency would be rotated among them. Maria, however, was made the company's permanent treasurer, and no cheque could be spent without her agreement and her signature. A smaller, though still spacious bungalow, was bought into which she moved with Maria who ministered to her; and only then did she allow herself to lose her grip on the world. There would no more Sunday gatherings now, and few of her children would visit her. Maria's adopted daughters would play around the old women, tattooing her, styling her hair into outrageous forms, apply various kinds of make-up, and giggle, while she smiled benignly and flitted in and out of clear thought.

Maria remained with her mother and set up her own practice and a pharmacy in Davao, and David stayed in South Cotabato. When he returned to the city at the weekends he would go first to Nazareth, and then look to his own dealings in Davao. His position as a surgeon and as the director of a hospital, his charity work, his personality, and his parents' and in-laws' names, gave him the opportunity to meet businessmen and politicians in Cotabato and Davao and build valuable relationships. Now he also had greater freedom and, through Maria, a share of Audrey's estate, or so he thought. Of these hopes he was quickly disabused. He was asked to run as vice-governor of South Cotabato. Maria objected, and so did his father who was adamant he should concentrate on his profession and forget his fanciful business projects and political ambitions. Then he was asked to invest in a gold mine in Davao del Norte with James and the owner of a large security company and a luxurious hotel in Davao who was well-connected with a number of rising political stars in both local and national governments. He turned to Maria for money. She refused him: the mine was in an area where banditry and guerrilla actions were commonplace; finding gold in large enough quantities was always a risk, especially for small operators; and selling gold profitably in a market ostensibly controlled and monopolised by the state was a corrupt and uncertain business. But he was not to be stopped a second time and he took out a loan from a bank opposite his hospital in South Cotabato. He had borrowed money from this bank once before when he and a handful of young surgeons from Davao had first set up the hospital. Collateral was still needed, but the manager was a friend, and so he signed over land which, though titled in his name, still belonged to Inday and Dee. It was only when the mine folded (Maria had been right) that Inday and Dee were told their land might soon belong to the bank. To soften her anger when he told her the news and asked her for money, David let her know that he had arranged for Bing, the wife of one of his former employees at the mine, to work with Inday in Nazareth. She accepted the help, but she was not placated in the least. David was ordered to ensure that he made his payments to the bank: she would not bail him out. He had not been straight with her, and she saw no reason why Maria could not help him. When David then reported that James had asked to borrow the new four-wheel drive which Dee had lent to David, and which Inday and Dee also had need of at that time, Inday suggested that David should tell James to ask Maria for the use of her land cruiser. Had Audrey and her family ever cared for anything other than money? That Audrey now only had Maria to look after her said it all.

* * *

It was that same evening, only a few hours after Inday had given this lecture to David, and Sal had enjoined Inday to be more assertive with Dee, that Jo gave his performance. Still laughing at 'winner-winner me', Inday retired to the chair vacated by Dee in front of the television, tuned to a karaoke channel, and in her high-pitched, wavering voice sang the words that ran along the bottom of the screen. Outside, high above, a small orange light flickered in the darkness. It was the *manananggot*. Moving with extraordinary grace, and with barely a word or a look or a sound, he climbed coconut palms to bleed them of their wine. Caught in the rain he had stayed in the tree, at its gently swaying heart, smoking cigarettes and watching. Each in their own way had found some relief from the heavy musk of relationships that clung to them all.

In the early morning of the new day, the light was clear once again, the colours balanced, and every precisely defined leaf radiant. Bodies began to shuffle about, still bemused by sleep, hawking loudly, their lungs covered by the night's dampness. The air filled with the acrid smell of rice-coffee, the cries of cockerels, and throbbing music. Jewelled-eyed children, black hair rust-reddened by the sun, swept floors, pushed fish and rice into their mouths, stuffed their satchels with dog-eared books, and, through fleets of rasping tricycles smothered in blue fumes, scampered off to school.

2 Making politics

Introduction

We turn now to the translation of the Nazarenes' relationships – and of relationships such as theirs – into the institutions and practices of political and bureaucratic life. This translation was shaped by attitudes towards our relationships that I have characterised as 'personal' and 'absolute'. With the personal came manipulation, instability, fission, an obsession with monitoring and image, and a need for authoritarianism. With the absolute came simplicity, stability, direction and quiet authority. These two attitudes do not exist one without the other. They are at the core of what we are, creating within us and among us all both tensions and complementarities, and finding expression in the world around us.

Shadows of community

As we saw in the previous chapter, kinship was at once a strong and loose concept which embraced relationships so distant and vague as to be more fictional than real. Once the mutual need for a relationship was recognised, kinship could be 'telescoped' or 'discovered' much as it was among the Creole of Sierra Leone and the Overseas Chinese.[1] Or it could be offered and accepted as a symbolic accolade for a relationship stretching back many years or for some act of sacrifice or intimate service. But whether true or fictional, kinship provided each individual with a strong entrée into another set of relationships established independently by a relative around some other kernel, be it place of origin, profession, or attendance at the same class, school or college. These webs were even handed down from one generation to the next: a child's *barkada* (or group, or gang, of friends), for instance, comprised the offspring of the child's parents' *barkada* or *compadre* (or godparent); and these relationships bequeathed to the child were carried far into adult life.

Although these relationships were strongly affective, especially if cemented over the years through repeated contact and the constant exchange of material items and the most subtle obligations, and enhanced by notions of *compadre*, *pakikisama* (or keeping in with the group), *utang na lo'ob* (or debt) and *barkada*, they were also strongly pragmatic and instrumental. They were a sanctuary, an emotional refuge, a defence against gossip and criticism as well as a means of launching such criticism; they were channels through which money, information, news, advice and material goods could flow, and through which employment might be secured, children adopted or farmed out, and assistants, workers and maids recruited; and they opened up direct and untroubled access to institutions and to the services or authority which those institutions offered. The extent and reach of these networks – by which I mean the sheer number and position of those people who were placed under an obligation by the favours they received, in whom a dependency was created, or to whom something was owed – were the symbol, the measure and the means of control, power and social prestige. Those who were able to read and judge characters accurately, to foster trust and loyalty, to handle the maze of conflicting personalities, emotions, interests and obligations, and so with a natural dexterity to wield the webs of the relationship to their own or another's advantage, were to be admired greatly.

For each person the true community would expand, shrink and float with these borderless networks. Places such as Nazareth were but a haphazard composite of fragments, a mosaic of those true communities. It was those who looked further afield, whose networks were the more expansive and who, in consequence, had the greater power and influence, and who, quite incidentally, brought a greater sense of cohesion to that mosaic. Those who looked inwards, preoccupied with their own immediate neighbours, lay in the shadows of larger, brighter worlds. Those who lived beyond even these shadows, who had no community, would expect to be treated at best with indifference or condescension, and at worst with hostile suspicion or dismissive contempt.

Nor, then, was community defined by the civic institutions which constantly bubbled up from these networks. Across the city, the number of new associations formally registering with the Department of Trade and Industry averaged nearly seventy a month;[2] more than four-fifths of the poor belonged to an association; and most Nazarenes were members of a funeral association (*dayong*), or credit circle (*bot-bot-ay*), a dance troop, a market association, youth movement or some other kind of organisation, such that if they were not linked by kinship, *barkada*, *caba-bata*, class, school or college, then they were linked by their membership of an association (see Figures 2.1 – 2.3). The associations were shaped from the stuff of the everyday and, as we have seen, the everyday was intensely political. Most of the people who moulded these

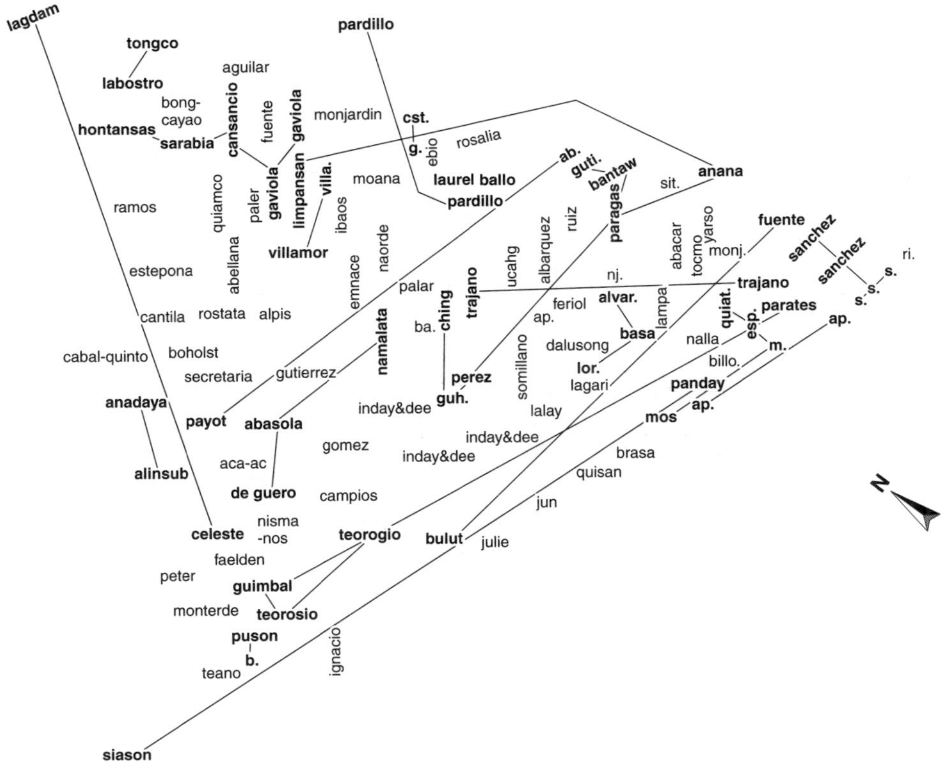

Figure 2.1 Networks of kinship in Nazareth

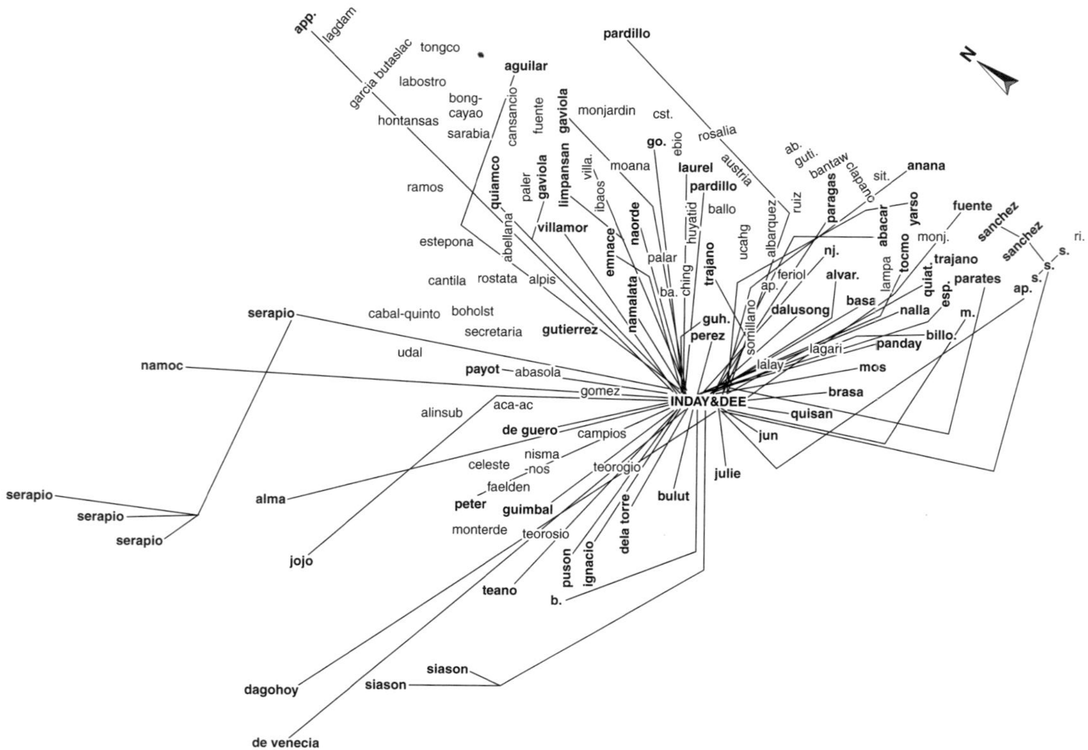

Figure 2.2 Networks of *barkada* in Nazareth

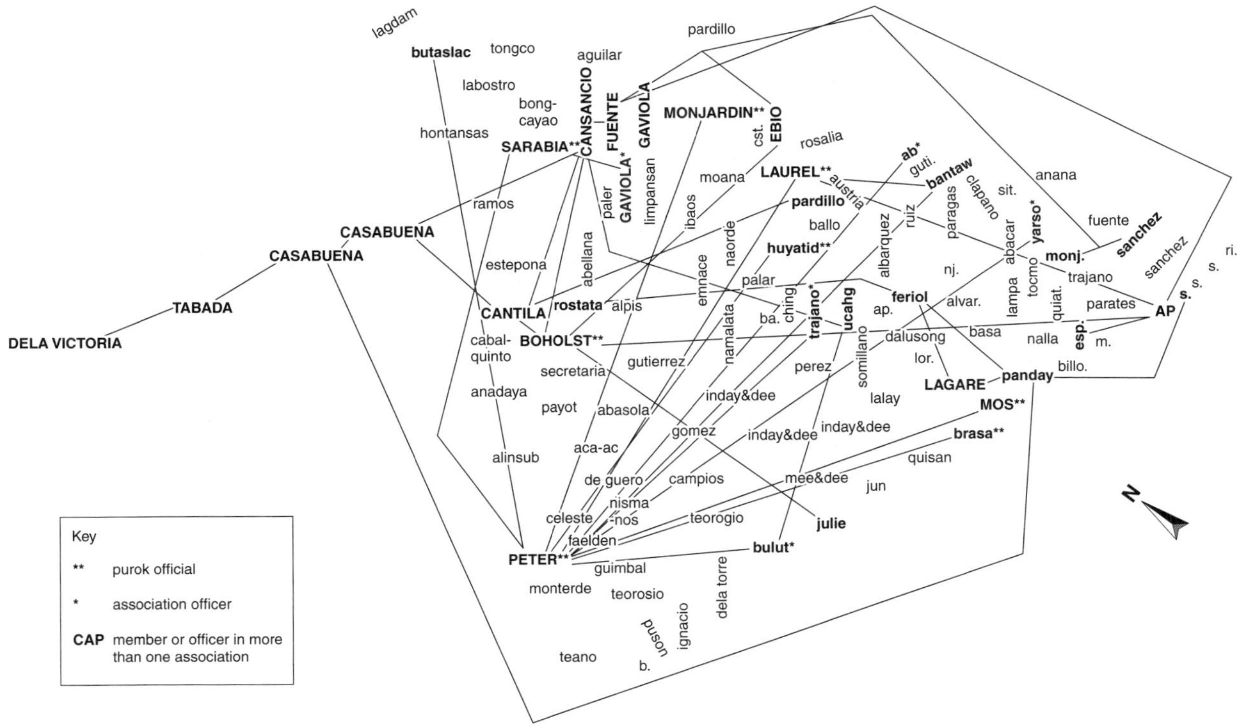

Figure 2.3 Networks of association in Nazareth

organisations from their personal relationships were still part of wider social networks and, therefore, part of wider and often conflicting interests, obligations and pressures; and their power lay not in the pargeted shell of the institution, but in the ever-changing relationships upon which it rested. There was, in consequence, no clear fit between authority and institution, formal position and status, image and substance; and as easily as they were formed these loose corporate bodies fell apart.

Even if the organisation held together, the kernels around which relationships were formed would often lose their meaning and purpose, leaving the association to wither. In earlier days, after the Second World War, as migrant entrepreneurs from Luzon and the central Visayas moved into Davao, these associations were formed around place of origin, language and other 'markers' of ethnicity, and were segregated broadly into those who held themselves to be true Dabawenyos and those who did not. But in the absence of a clear threat or advantage and, as we shall see, with attitudes towards relationships shifting in so many spheres of life, ethnicity gradually came to be seen more clearly for what it is and has always been – a common-or-garden prejudice that is drawn on fitfully and absent-mindedly. In Nazareth the only successful *sari-sari* stall was run by a family that had only recently moved in. Their businesses were many and include a piggery. The profits from that had been used to set up the stall and a bakery – by far the finest in the purok. They were Chinese, though their grandchildren no longer spoke the language. Yet no-one recognised them as such. Chi'ing was as poor as a church mouse; that he was Chinese did not register either, despite his name. Neither was Gutierrez thought of as Chinese, though he spoke it and owned a small noodle factory in Nazareth where Bing and Ellen would sometimes work hanging out the yellowing strands to dry a little before packing. His wife also spoke a little of the language. She was, she thought, Chinese on her mother's side, though her husband was sure of it. Their children had all entered the professions and spoke their father's tongue barely at all. The Angs, too, were Chinese, though it was of no interest to anyone, and they could not be entirely sure about their name. It had been taken, or so their grandfather said, from a young Chinese man who had died at sea during the crossing to the Philippines. Inday, too, was part Chinese. Her father had been northern Chinese, a remarkably tall, kind and patient man, who neither drank nor smoked. His virtues were made all the more virtuous by his wife, a tiny Malay from Cebu with a foul temper who ruled her children and her grandchildren with a bamboo cane in one hand, and a bottle of red palm-wine in the other. Yet no-one thought of Inday as being Chinese, even remotely. The only person who was recognised by nearly all Nazarenes as 'being' Chinese was Yap. His dapper house, with its newly painted walls of blue and white, was always quiet. He was seen rarely, and only occasionally would his air-conditioned cruiser with its impenetrable black windows and shiny chrome rumble along the tracks of Nazareth. It would come to a stop in front of his blue metal gate and there it would wait, grumbling, until a shy young woman in a dustcoat let it into a driveway lined with bougainvillaea and orchids. She was his woman, his mistress. He was, everyone agreed, 'Chinese'. This was not because they disapproved of his behaviour. James, Maria's brother, had set his own woman up in the neighbouring purok. Everyone knew of her, including his wife, and though she did not like his philandering she would tolerate it as would many women in her position: she was number one and everyone knew that she was being wronged. Her esteem would only gain from her forbearance; and that was a mighty weapon she could use against him if she should have need of it. The other woman was, she knew, no better than a whore who lived in shame without future or respect. No, Yap was Chinese because none of his communities reached among the Nazarenes. He had no relationships there, and so, like his own whore, he had no status. He was Chinese because they did not know him.

Of all these people, even of Yap, 'Chinese', if it was recognised at all, was a vague, mostly inconsequential description. It carried with it a sense of playful admonishment and pride. Though Diday's stubbornness and Al's waywardness were Chinese traits, Inday would attribute her own sterling qualities, her hard work and selflessness, and her modesty, to her upbringing, her common sense, her religion, and, on occasions, to her Chinese blood. It was also a shorthand for those people out there somewhere who controlled the economy, an idea which could be used to explain this or that problem. It could also be a term of abuse. At school, Sal and her friends had teased a child whose parents where Chinese. First, they would yell '*olit intsit*' (Go home Chinese). Then they would laugh at the similarity between their word for Chinese and the English word for insect. But then again taunts like these were not reserved for the Chinese. Christine, who lived in a small ramshackle compound no more than two minutes walk from Inday's compound, had also been teased cruelly at school. She was obviously *mestiza*: her eyes bright green, her skin of the lightest tan, and her hair chestnut-brown. Her father had been an American soldier and, she had been told, of German blood. If everyone was now inured to her appearance, this was only because the callousness of childhood had left its mark so deep within her that she had about her a warmth which emanates only from those who have been taught to think nothing of themselves yet still know nothing of bitterness. So, too, the northern Tagalog, central Visayan and southern Visayan, each to the other, were a figure of fun. Ask a haughty Tagalog to look at the birds and they will look for ants on the ground! When the southerner says 'go there' he means 'come here'! Just listen to the coarse language and crude humour of the *provinceana*! Those who used such vague prejudices to include and exclude, and to pressurise others to behave and think as they wished, had come to be seen in some circles as obvious, unconvincing and ineffective; while broader common interests in, say, business, profession, charity and political ideology, or a shared connection with, say, a school or college, were regarded as kernels of a more valuable kind. Clubs such as the Davao City Chamber of Commerce, Rotary, Lions, JCs, Kiwanis and Masons now thrived with memberships which read like a 'who's who' of merchants, politicians and bureaucrats, both Chinese and Filipino; while the 'ethnic' Filipino associations, the Chinese associations, and the smaller, less numerous Japanese associations had all weakened. The Filipino-Chinese Chamber of Commerce, though it still administered the Filipino-Chinese Fire Brigade, settled disputes among its members, and circulated among them news about social events, laws and some cause or other in the Philippines or in China, was seen by many as quaint at best, and, at worst, as introspective and parochial, a font of gossip about who was doing well in business and who was in difficulty. The still more 'traditional' Chinese family associations have fared even worse in recent years. Daubed with Chinese characters, occasionally guarded by high walls, and always with a locked metal grill for their front door, these exhausted shells did indeed seem mysterious and imposing: an obvious subject for speculation and rumour. But if there was secrecy it was because of embarrassment with their own stagnation and lethargy. For the most part, activists comprised a few old men (loyally shadowed by their tolerant sons) gossiping about each other. The minor issues, which spawned the intrigue and the slander, the criticism and the bitterness, and the envy and the dogma, which now consumed their thoughts and their energies, were retained only as convenient nuclei around which emotions collected, magnifying these old men's petty concerns and pedantry into matters of great import. The 'unsociable' merchants either felt no pressure to legitimise their activities or to demonstrate altruism by joining these organisations or, if they did, they regarded that pressure as moralistic, judgmental, unjustified and self-righteous. To those who were more forgiving, 'ethnicity' and 'Chineseness' were anachronistic and restrictive fabrications which served mainly as a useful opposite against which the 'cosmopolitan' might be created.

The Ong association had more life about it than many. Its president also belonged to a Taoist group that preached an odd mixture of mysticism, palm-reading, fortune-telling, the supernatural, faith-healing, and vegetarianism. The Davao branch met once a month on the third floor of the president's home in a room that had once held his family's ancestral shrine. The new altar – a collection of heavy rosewood furniture- was given to him by the sect's Taiwanese members. They often visited Davao, and they had offered him various business opportunities. He was grateful, but had limited his ambitions for yet more money. Like many successful merchants who joined associations, he was looking for something different in his life, some new stimulus or sense of worth, and he seemed to have found it. His selection, first as a member of the group and then as its leader in Davao, had come at a time when he and his wife and children were being moved out of a house rented from the Villa Abrille. He had been led to understand by his father – who had founded of the Ong association in Davao, and who was a blood-brother of the head of the Villa Abrille family – that he would be left the house in which he had lived for so many years. When the head of the Villa Abrille family died, however, his son and heir would only give them the option of buying a nearby lot. The purchase of this land and the construction of a house required a substantial loan and entailed great risk. The Taiwanese businessman-cum-visionary who had recruited him into the Taoist group advised him to take his chances, and this he did. The house, which also served as a loading bay and warehouse, reduced his overheads, and, not much longer after that, the market in cosmetics (his particular trade) boomed. Destiny, he knew, had been with him, and it was time to repay her. But though his leadership of the family association was fired by these beliefs, the association had little work to do. It offered a handful of scholarships to those with the right surname. Some members had also been known to hold out a hand to others in the 'family' whose business had fallen on hard times. Aiding a fellow merchant, however, was something to be kept quite separate from the affairs of the association. If the association as a body was to pay out any money, and if envy was to be avoided, it had first to be decided whether the merchant's troubles were brought about by incompetence, poor judgment, or bad luck – distinctions which depended largely upon another's point of view. Help was rarely applied for, and none had ever been given. Most of the association's members were, in any case, financially secure. And because its ground floor was rented to a Chinese merchant who sold highly decorative nara-wood furniture to the few who could afford it in Manila, India and the United States, the building in which the association was housed paid for itself. Meetings that were supposed to be held once a month rarely took place and even then the association's officers would have to cajole as many people as possible to attend or else the turn-out was certain to be rather thin. Meetings with other branches of the association in Manila, Cebu, Baculod and Iloilo used to be held twice a year – once in Manila and again in each of the provinces in rotation. These events, too, were tiresome and expensive, and so their frequency was cut by half. The election of officers attracted still less interest: telephones were left off the hook, and people were difficult to find. No-one, it seemed, wanted to take on responsibilities. The solution was to rotate the office of the president among the eldest members, who then discharged their duties in a resigned but generally good-natured manner, and to promote officers automatically through the hierarchy. The secretary who was supposed to man the association's office had now become too old and stayed at home. Since everyone else was too busy, the building was usually left empty.

It is true that associations in their most inchoate form were still being formed. Faced with unfamiliar and uncertain existence, much as their parents and grandparents had been when they migrated to other parts of the Philippines, the Filipinos overseas have created associations which exist only as chains of relationships woven around place of origin – region, language, province, city, barangay, and even kinship. In Hong Kong, the officers of United Dabawenyos (whose members were drawn from Davao City) were dominated by the president's wife, two of his cousins, his uncle and his brother-in-law. In this association, place of origin, the welfare of members, the support of worthy causes in Davao, and the promotion of Dabawaynean culture were used explicitly to foster unity within the association; and to this end, too, the symbolic importance of commensality was emphasised by the association's celebration of *Araw ng Dabaw* (Davao's Founder Day). Committees were set up, dance and dress competitions were organised, and associations representing other parts of the Philippines were invited to take part. The money raised in this way for the association's main beneficiaries in Davao – Caritas, Davao Street Children, and a selection of tribal missions – was then channeled through the officers' friends and families in the Philippines.

Yet even overseas, the move away from 'place' and 'ethnicity' was evident. United Dabawayneans was just one of twenty-seven associations which formed an alliance at whose centre lay Unifil – a group of just five people. Through them the alliance was linked into two other organisation – both NGOs – the Mission for Filipino Migrant Workers, and the Asia-Pacific Migrant Workers' Association. The former was concerned primarily with migrant affairs in Hong Kong; the latter's interests lay in the Pacific, the Middle East and Europe. The Asia-Pacific Migrant Workers' Association had set up Unifil and similar organisations in Japan (*Kapisana ng mga Migranteng Pilipino*), Jordan (*Kapisanan ng mga Migranteng sa Jordan*), Bahrain, Canada, Malaysia, the Netherlands and other European states. The leaders of these organisations in Hong Kong were clearly experienced. The president of Unifil, a university graduate, had worked as a social worker for the government for seven years before resigning in frustration at what she saw as corruption and inefficiency, and turned to work for General Assembly Binding Women for Reforms, Integrity, Liberty and Action. During her time with the Assembly she became friendly with a senator who chaired a senate committee on women and migration; she had also campaigned on behalf of another senator for whom the president of the Asia-Pacific Migrant Workers' Association had also worked. The president of the association had a similar background. After graduating from university with a degree in community development she managed a number of NGOs and workers' organisations in

Manila. She had then left for Hong Kong with the intention of earning money and seeking out NGOs and other associations in which to serve. And they needed that experience. Holding the alliance in Hong Kong together was no easy thing to do. The migrants often found the association an unattractive forum for gossip, rumour, criticism and intrigue. This was especially true if they knew each others' families and wider social networks in the Philippines. A member's background in town or city, educational level, professional status, fluency in Tagalog and English, and dress sense, and the status of her family or spouse in the Philippines, could also generate, or be seized upon to justify, personal disputes, rivalry and envy. An ability to manipulate these symbols – and thus to move across divisions – were important qualities for the officers and, most especially, for the leader of any particular association. But such petty prejudice, magnified by place and ethnicity, could make it impossible to harness the money and support of other associations, Filipino businesses, the Consulate, and others sympathetic to their cause. As the organisation became larger and more complex, there was, necessarily, a conscious attempt to overcome or at least to control and direct 'ethnicity' by trying to broaden outlooks. This Unifil did by directing the alliance in support of various issues and campaigns which highlighted the treatment of particular workers in Hong Kong or elsewhere and were therefore thought to be a useful way of 'raising the consciousness' of the associations' members. The General Assembly of the alliance was described as the highest body responsible for making policies. Immediately beneath the assembly was a Council made up of representatives from each association in the alliance. The Council worked out the details of policies handed down by the assembly, made further suggestions, and transmitted the decisions and suggestions to each member association. The executive committee comprised the chairperson, the vice-chairperson of external affairs, and the vice-chairperson for internal affairs. It was an elected committee, though its members were usually also members of Unifil. They sat on the alliance's standing committees, and each member of the executive was also assigned a group of associations with which they would meet in rotation. Each association could pursue its own concerns and interests (such as bible study, beauty contests and welfare projects). Each had to take part in activities organised by the alliance. Each was also required to establish committees which corresponded with the standing committees (including Education, International Networking, Welfare, Socio-economic) set up by the alliance. And each had to field a representative for each of those standing committees. Not all the associations had the necessary experience to put together the relevant committees. In these instances, Unifil would run education seminars and even provide 'para-legal' training.

Regionalism, language and kinship, then, gave way to other kernels: shades of political opinion; organisational competence; the ability to move among different groups and draw them together; commitment to particular views and objectives; simple dress; and among the leadership of Unifil, an extreme diminution of their education and professional status in order that their crafted ordinariness and altruism could be displayed with an even greater flourish. Yet, while their vision had breadth, and the interests with which they were concerned had a broader appeal, they were still making politics, and these new kernels could also be used to divide. The Philippine Domestic Workers' Union was formed initially as a splinter group of the United Migrant Workers Overseas – an association which, at the time of the fracture, had been dominated by the chairman, his wife (who was also treasurer of the Ilocos Norte Federation), and two of his cousins (who were both officers in other associations affiliated to the federation). The chairman, who had worked as a campaign organiser for a congressman in Ilocos, had set up numerous associations in Hong Kong with the undeclared aim of raising money and generating publicity for that same congressman's election campaigns among his constituents abroad. Through them, it was hoped, more support could be garnered at home. The majority of the officers broke away to form a second splinter group, alleging that the clique had used the flat rented by the association for gambling and drinking, that they had failed to keep proper financial records, and that they had procrastinated over the registration of the association as a union. This second splinter group – the new Philippine Domestic Workers' Union – was registered under Hong Kong's trade union ordinance, and given a rather different mission. A flat was rented to give shelter to those of its members who found their contracts suddenly terminated; and connexions were established with British lawyers willing to give their advice and services free of charge, and with a number of other organisations including the Salvation Army and the Asian Domestic Workers' Union. The latter union was itself a splinter group of Unifil: in its lobbying of the Hong Kong government, a faction within Unifil evolved around a determination to emphasise pay increases rather than improvements to safeguards over conditions of stay – a strategy regarded by the mainstream within Unifil as an indication of that faction's 'half-baked' commitment.

Another problem faced by the 'prime-movers' of Unifil was the difficulty of 'raising the consciousness' of women who were, from the activist's point of view, lackadaisical, interested mainly in holding beauty pageants and popularity contests. Whereas 'the others' (the uncommitted) were concerned only with maintaining good relationships within the group by giving and taking, the activist would do and say what was necessary regardless of the offence it might generate. Improving one's own life and the lives of others, they believed, was an inherently political act which requires great personal sacrifice. And then there were Unifil's opponents – Filipinos who were hostile to the aims of the activists. Those, such as the Philippine *Tonight Show* and certain Filipino journalists who had labelled Unifil, the Philippine Domestic Worker's Union and the Filipino NGOs as 'communists' and 'frauds', were denounced by the committed as 'mouthpieces' of the Philippine Consulate. These opponents constituted the Filipino elite. They were identified not by language, place of origin, or wealth, but primarily (from the activist's point of view) by the callousness which they showed for the poor. The help which they did extend was restricted to cosmetic social events designed to legitimise the status quo. Even the Bayanihan Trust was regarded as no more than an outlet for the elites' sentimentality and superficial concern: the Trust, it was alleged, would not involve itself in matters of substance. It supported beauty contests only in order to further its members' own business interests; and it charged domestic helpers for venues which the Trust obtained free of charge.

These accusations, it has to be said, were not entirely fair. The Trust had been set up with a donation of fifty thousand Hong Kong dollars from the Philippine Association of Hong Kong. Participation in the Trust makes good commercial sense, and, whether intended or not, did help to legitimise commercial success. From the standpoint of those members of the self-conscious elite, the Trust would help to improve the image of Filipinos; and for those who were looking simply for a new stimulus in their lives, or who had a genuine concern for the circumstances of others, the Trust gave room for expression. For these same reasons, the Philippine Association of Hong Kong had been involved in numerous events, such as a Keep Hong Kong Clean campaign, in conjunction with the Philippine Consulate and the Urban Council, and two hundred domestic helpers. And although the Philippine Association of Hong Kong would not support or represent domestic helpers, some of its members, even those professionals who went to great pains to distinguish themselves from the domestic helpers, did go out of their way to provide legal and moral support to individual cases brought to their attention.

But neither were Unifil's suspicions entirely unjustified. The association was a social club; it provided a framework with which to measure social success and prestige; and it was, for some, a refuge for the ego. Consequently, the antitypes created in the minds of some of its members were a little more stark: the Hong Kong Chinese merchants do not take the Filipino businessmen seriously; the Filipino-Chinese (a hard-working race) are intent on protecting their dominance of the Philippine economy by spreading rumours that foreign merchants in the Philippines will be kidnapped, murdered and robbed; and while Filipino professionals may have sympathised with the circumstances of the Filipina domestic helpers, they had little in common with each other – a social division carefully emphasised by dress, behaviour, life-style, and an insistence on using English with those Filipinos who were not comfortable with the language. As one officer of the association put it: 'I have yet to see one of our members marry an ex-amah'.

The kernels of college and university, such as De La Salle, Ateneo, the University of the Philippines, Browns, Harvard, and the London Business School, around which relationships could be established, were also used to create an image of 'the cosmopolitan', and, by so doing, to create the image of an exclusive group. A number of the association's members were also members of the Philippine Business Council. The majority of its twenty-five members were Filipinos, though a few high-profile Chinese entrepreneurs with business interests in the Philippines, including Wu and Kwok, were also included in the Council. Nearly all the association's Filipino members were from Manila (though not all were born and brought up there), and many had attended the same college or university, particularly De La Salle, Ateneo and the University of the Philippines. These merchants were careful to distinguish themselves by their dress, mannerisms and language as part of the 'cosmopolitan' set. It was a group also defined by its antitypes – the corrupt, mercantile, unprofessional businessman who will try to establish mercantile relationships with politicians; the cold, ruthless, exclusive Chinese; and the Filipino migrants who soil the name of Filipinos. These images were to some extent indicative of the association's raison d'être – to promote trade and investment in the Philippines. The association was originally set up with the support of the Department of Trade and Industry (DTI), in Manila, and it was with high-ranking technocrats in the DTI and the Central Bank that the Council's members would do their best to establish and foster relationships. Politicians were not regarded as particularly 'serious people'.

In the association, whether at home or overseas, each person saw protection and security, companionship and comfort, pleasure and distraction, ambition and material advantage, altruism and compassion, exclusivity and one-upmanship; but rarely would they see in it more than fragments of their wider communities. No matter how formal it appeared to be, no matter how thickly laced with rules and procedures and legislation, the association would work only for those with influence, or would soon be rendered arthritic and moribund, or torn apart; or it would quickly wither as the kernels around which it had been formed lost their relevance. Its outward appearance was only a delicate facade that rested upon those manifold communities. And what was true of this rude political life, was also true of the formal polity.

The captain and the congressman

Those whose networks were already extensive, perhaps because they had been born into a political dynasty or a family prominent in some other regard, or whose work had brought them into the company of those with influence, would find sliding into place, almost by chance, relationships which could be used to propel them into political office. A desire to give vent to political ambition, however, and an ability to turn relationships to that end, would ultimately determine whether or not they would make use of those opportunities. David's position as a surgeon, as a director of the largest and most effective hospital in a small but growing market town, his charitable works, his business dealings, and the fact that he could count among his *barkadas* politicians and wealthy merchants, had, in the mind of the incumbent governor, made David an ideal candidate to run as vice-governor. And David was ambitious. His mother-in-law had served as a barangay captain; and his brother-in-law had run, unsuccessfully, as councillor on more than one occasion. He would not merely follow their efforts: he would better them. But Dee had objected, and so had Maria. Both had seen his ambitions as a distraction from his profession, and, perhaps, as a distraction from each of them. He had therefore decided, reluctantly, not to run. The governor was re-elected. David was irked: he could now have been vice-governor, and in a few years who knows what else he could have achieved? But he was not, and his future had been denied him.

Inday, too, had been asked on more than one occasion to run for barangay captain. Her strength of will and personality; her reputation for being vivacious, generous, perceptive, and altruistic; her children's reputations; and her tireless work for the GKK (*Gagmay Kristiyanong Katilingban* – A Little Christian Community) and Mother Ignacia; and the favours and advice she dispensed in the everyday course of their lives: all this made her an obvious and popular candidate. It was she who had persuaded Trejano to donate a small parcel of land on which Nazareth's small chapel now stood. It was she who gave over her house for weeks at a time to Sister Mayon and her legions of hare-lips. It was she who chivvied incumbent barangay captains and congressmen to lay proper roads, improve water supplies and dig new drainage channels. But she spent much time travelling between Davao, Cebu and Manila, keeping her affairs and her family in order; and both she and Dee felt uneasy about a step which in their eyes would bring only cosmetic benefit to herself, and great uncertainty, even physical danger, to her family. She was content, therefore, to free herself of any overtly political ambitions that she might have, and to wield her influence when she needed through those who seemed, curiously, to enjoy the burdens of office.

Gloria, the incumbent barangay captain, was like Inday in many respects. They were not true Dabaweynos, but they were counted among the original settlers in the barangay. They had both arrived in Davao in the 1950s when the city had been three small settlements gathered around markets and a dock, each separated from the other by groves of coconuts and acacias, a time when a trip to market or a walk in town would also mean a day and an evening spent cementing relationships and establishing new ones. Both had recently celebrated their golden wedding anniversary; both had built around themselves reputable families; their children were professionals and of good character; both were active in associations; both had a strong faith; both were involved in charity worlds; and both women, and their families, were known to be down-to-earth, unpretentious and able to mix as easily as with the poor and ignorant as with the educated, powerful and rich, and to do so without a hint of prejudice. But Gloria did have one advantage. Her brother-in-law was a city councillor; her husband had been the captain for thirteen years until he stepped down in 1987; and she had worked as his treasurer for much of that time.

Her accession to the post, however, was not planned nor was it immediate. It was more a question of latent ambition, circumstance and luck. She had been retained as treasurer by her husband's successor, and she remained at her post while he, after having received death threats from the NPA, chose discretion as the better part of valour and fled to Manila. She remained at her post even after the new captain, who proved not so wise as his predecessor, was shot and killed by the NPA. And she remained at her post whilst the captaincy was left vacant. In 1998, the Secretary of the Department of the Interior and Local Government (and a former mayor of Davao) summoned Gloria to Manila and, as allowed for under the Local Government Code, appointed her barangay captain. She was victorious in the subsequent round of elections, and in those same elections her son won a seat on the council in her barangay. She then set about appointing purok leaders. They, in their turn, appointed block leaders.

Simon was re-appointed as the leader of the purok Nazareth. He was not an original settler, but he had lived in Nazareth for more than twenty years. His daughter had been the very first graduate from the very first Nazarene school. At that time he had been the parent's president of Grade 6, and had invited Gloria's husband, then the barangay captain, to that very first graduation ceremony. That had been the start of their relationship. Simon was also very active in the GKK and the Gospel Business Filipino International, and he was the national coordinator of the Mambos Tribe. And he had proved himself during those troubled times when the NPA and every kind of criminal had brought death and fear to Nazareth. The men he now appointed as block leaders had been at his side risking their own lives when he had led the Alsa Masa, and had found himself, or so everyone now agreed, placed third on the NPA's death list. They were men who also lived in the less desirable parts of Nazareth and knew well, or were linked through kinship, to the very men and women who made those parts of Nazareth less desirable. The ubiquitous Jaime, Simon's right-hand man, wandered the tangled paths and ally ways of Nazareth and beyond, cigarette smouldering, moving from house to house, from barely formed *nippa* hut to *sari-sari* stall, quiet and watchful. He, in particular, was connected one way or another to even the worst brigands. Simon and his men owed their office and the respect they commanded only to their ability to handle and direct their relationships, to their social prestige, to their willingness to take on that office. For it was through the skeins of their relationships that others around them could be drawn into the personal orb of the captain. But in these leaders' smoking and drinking, cultivated mannerisms, tone and timbre of voice, swagger, off-hand gestures, conversation of guns and women, politics and past deeds, there was also much pose and bravado; and much puffery in their formal office. The greater prestige and influence lay with men like Jojo and Henry and with the women like Inday. Their reach was much greater, and consequently they had no wish, or did not feel the need, to act as large fish in this small pond. There was no clear match between the formal organisational arrangements and true influence. The authority of formal office may have augmented the personal somewhat, but it was no substitute for the *quid pro quo* of the everyday.

The barangay captain, then, was a key political ally, to be cultivated and secured. Link into the barangay captain and one would tap into a lattice of social networks which underlay formal institutional arrangements and offices, and inveigled nearly every voter. The captain, her purok leaders and notables such as Inday would therefore find themselves being flattered and wooed by political representatives (local and national) and their supporters from business and other walks of life whose aim was to impress, to persuade, to demonstrate their sincerity, to sell their wares. The captain would observe, judge their character, determine where their ambitions lay and how reliable and malleable they might be. Always the captain said she would support them. But once her mind was made up she would attempt to convince her constituency that only the candidate which she was supporting was the best. Indeed, if her candidate was the incumbent and had helped her in her work and in her election, then she could and would guarantee them – 'one hundred per cent' – the votes they needed. Her sway over the Federation of Barangay Captains (of which she was president) was less certain. The federation was intended only to provide a more coherent link between the barangays and mayor, and to circulate information and advice on how government worked, or so it was said; yet she would do her best to convince the federation to support her choice. In practice, her candidates were always victorious and in return she could expect to get what she wanted. Whether made explicit or left unsaid, this *quid pro quo* was clearly understood.

If this give and take of the personal was to be truly effective and long-lasting it had to have some emotional layering. Since the time her husband had held the captaincy, the congressman had become a regular house-guest, and he was an obvious choice as sponsor at their golden wedding anniversary.

He was an obvious choice, too, as a sponsor at David and Maria's wedding: David was the son of Inday, a stalwart in his district; Maria was the daughter of Audrey, a former barangay captain; and both Inday and Audrey, in common with Gloria, were women with the status and networks of influence he had need of. And as a sponsor, there was an informality, an affability, a closeness in the relationship which gave expression to genuine affection, or around which genuine affection could form. With the personal strengthened in this way, with the *quid pro quo* understood, one did not need to deal with each other directly in day-to-day matters. The name attached to a request became enough to command attention and elicit action. Both knew the other would do their best even if the request should in the end prove impossible to grant. But despite the give and take and emotional layering of these relationships, neither side was under any illusions that their relationship was in its nature anything other than supremely practical.

The captain looked to put senators and congressmen in 'the bank'; and if the congressman failed to deliver, then he could not expect her support in the future. The congressman would therefore spend much time upon the barangay, finding out what the captain wanted to see pass through congress, what her barangay needed, how she could be supported and strengthened, ensuring that funds reached her, and that in other ways the captain could meet her part of the bargain with her supporters. He also had to make sure that he was available not only to the barangay captain but to those she, or other notables such as Inday, referred to him. As he dispensed favours to even the lowliest voter, so he favoured her, reinforced her status, and thus strengthened his own position. Even when congress was in session he would set aside three days a week to deal with such matters, and so achieve a balance between his legislative and other interests in Manila and the constant need to secure the base upon which any possibility of furthering his career rested.

But it was precisely because of the barangay's importance that the congressman would want more than one string to his bow. Before an election a tactical assessment was made: who in the barangay were his supporters, who were his enemies, and who were those who seemed to be uncommitted? Waverers had to be won over, supporters buttressed, and enemies isolated. The more extensive his networks, the greater his influence; the greater his influence, the more opulent his largesse, and the more varied and imaginative were the ways in which he could starve his enemies of funds and favours. Push too hard on the congressman, demand too much, imply that support is uncertain, and the captain might find herself among his enemies, his generosity re-routed to others who, though they had no formal office, had the influence and ambition which would make it easy for them to wear the mantle of formal authority. The barangay captain, though she was of prime importance to the congressman, was just one of several people with ambition and influence; she was just a part of the congressman's still wider, more influential network of relationships; and her barangay, like any other barangay, was just one constituency in which the congressional representative had to establish good relationships. It was also for these reasons that the captain would never appear to reject any candidate who asked for her support: should they win, she would in any case have no choice but to switch her allegiances.

Close collaboration with those who hold sway in the city government was particularly important to the congressman if policies were to appear reasonably coherent and, more importantly, if his base was to be strengthened. The congressman was expected to fight for the city's interests in Manila, to lay his hands on such funds as were available and to ensure that allotments made their way to Davao. In return, the city would make sure that the congressman was able to deliver to his constituencies in the barangays. Kinship was an important kernel around which congressmen, senators and elected local officials[3] across the Philippines established such alliances. Kinship with a person or, better still, with a succession of people who had held some kind of public office at some time since the opening decades of the twentieth century was not uncommon: more than two-thirds of the House of Representatives and the Senate towards the end of the Ramos administration could make claim to some kind of dynastic heritage no matter how intermittent that line might have been. Attached to this kernel were whole sets of relationships established by one's parents or grandparents which – very much like the *barkada* and the twists of *compadre* to be found in Nazareth – could be re-worked, expanded and handed on yet again to the next generation. But it must be remembered that nationally more than four-fifths of elected local government officials, more than half of congressional representatives, and more than three-quarters of senators and senate officials had no kinship ties with other serving elected officials (national or local). Moreover, the general direction of those links which did exist was clearly vertical: more than four-fifths of all immediate kinship links (grandparents, parents, children, brothers and sisters) and a little under two-thirds of all intermediate kinship ties (cousins, uncles, nephews, nieces, aunts and in-laws) existed among people who represented constituencies, or who held public offices, within the same province or, more often than not, within the same municipality, city or congressional district. And most of these ties (more than 80 per cent) existed between individuals who held directly elected political offices.[4] In this vertical insularity there was much weakness; and much weakness, too, was there in a dependence upon the family. Whilst the individuals who were related to each other were more usually members of the same political party, kinship ties also reached across party divides. This might have indicated ideological and policy differences. Or it might have indicated (no less than a tendency for kinship ties to exist more usually among members of the same party) that family patrimonialism, rather than ideology or policy, mattered in the end: parties were essentially tactical material cut to suit the ambitions of the family and the individual. It might have also indicated that the family could be 'turned' into a political institution, and that family tensions and divisions were in essence political cleavages: the family in the Philippines, very much like the lineage noted in other societies,[5] was as much a political institution as a social one. Of equal, and often far greater importance than kinship ties, then, were the skeins of wider social networks built around some other kernel and the occasional strains of intimidation[6] which curled around the vertical axis and reached within and across areal administrative divisions (provincial, city, congressional district, city, municipal and barangay). From the vertical axis, then, only part sheathed by kinship, emanated broader, more expansive clusters of networks, as those politicians who made it into the House of Representatives or the Senate or the ministries and bureaucracies of central government looked to their own interests and to those of their families and their supporters, as well as to those of their home provinces, cities and municipalities. But perhaps the surest way to secure that base, and to protect one's back while dealing in Manila, was to have emerged out of the city.

The bishop

Juan was a tall man, his movements languorous, and his manner diffident. Yet often in his large, soft eyes the sheen of flint could be glimpsed. He began his adult life studying in a seminary in Cebu. He then entered the priesthood. But his ideas and ideals were too radical for a Church that he found too conservative. He left the Church for the National Democratic Front and the New People's Army. In the NPA he was responsible for imbuing its members with political ideals, and later for operations and strategy. He was captured in South Cotabato, and imprisoned in Davao. The fiscal prosecutor at that time saw in Juan a valuable political ally, and during Juan's three years in prison the two men came to know each other well. With the fall of Marcos and accession of Aquino, Juan was released and became the fiscal prosecutor's political consultant during his rise to vice-mayor, mayor and finally congressman. At the same time, the congressman's protégé, his former vice-mayor, became the city's mayor. The city government was now of the congressman's making, its key appointments were his men. He and the city were 'as one'. And those around him who handled his affairs in the city while he was in Manila he trusted implicitly. Together, Juan and the congressman developed what proved to be a valuable and distinctive mix of policies for social welfare, crime and disorder – a blend, quite literally, of milk and blood. They gave milk to poor mothers and, it was commonly said, sanctioned the ex-judicial killing of persistent criminals. Whether true or not, these were policies which fitted Juan's experience well, and proved effective in that they were popular. Juan also brought with him connections with the Church, among them a priest he had known since his early days in Cebu, who became the Bishop of Davao. This was a fortunate relationship for the congressman. The Church wielded considerable influence through its congregations, schools, colleges, and its work with NGOs, and it was held in high regard, far more so than any collection of politicians and bureaucrats; and for that reason it had a direct voice on various political bodies. Through Juan, the congressman would attempt to harness the Church to his cause.

The Church, however, was many things. Like the ballet school or piano class, the aerobics club and gym, the plazas, the roller-skating rinks and bowling alleys, the Church was, in part, no more than a diversion. It provided an excuse and opportunity to gather and to talk, to continue the endless cementation of relationships, to enjoy the camaraderie, to gossip, and to avoid the appearance of retreat, introspection and selfishness. For many, attendance was also an expression of their superstitions. Concern lay not with the nature of their faith, nor with the development of a philosophy for life, nor with questions of absolute right and wrong: the poor came to ask for something better; the well-to-do hoped to delay that time when they believed their good fortune would have to be paid for. Attendance at the Mass, Novena anniversary offerings and thanksgiving was also driven by faith, though whether that faith was genuine or born out of a rationalisation which had now become second nature, no-one knew or seemed to care. Thus did 'faith' mask the manipulation of the self and others, and take on the greater power. Once a course of action was chosen, sentiments, girded with religious dictums, were used to justify and legitimate that action: those who gave and sacrificed would, when the time was well-judged, quickly and sharply draw attention to their own selflessness and generosity, which had to be respected and repaid. Among the men and women of the Church, the image of faith danced more wearily with self-doubt, fear of the outside world, creamy sanctimony, self-righteous zeal, and ambition. There was in so many of those who played these charades, a sadness, a tired disappointment, a strange empty resentment. Having denied themselves what their desires and emotions demanded of them, they were left dry or fetid; and for this sacrifice, which was their achievement, they won recognition not for themselves, but for the cloth they wore.

Yet from these immortelles and rotting lilies would sometimes grow compassion, tolerance, selflessness and self-confidence of a kind which is found rarely, and then only among those who have released themselves from the weight of ego and sentimentality. And in these bravest of weeds was perhaps an earthly reflection of the Church's seemingly most esoteric teachings: that all are equal before a God who exists in each man; that no man, nor his

God, needs an intermediary to interpret or judge; that to his own conscience each is bound; that upon each man's conscience rest values and institutions; and that in these values and institutions no exculpation is to be found. In the working of the Church, too, weak reflections of these beliefs could be seen. The selection of the bishops was so confidential that even the candidates themselves did not know that they were being considered. The Pope's representative in Manila asked priests and laymen for their opinions; judgments were made about the candidate's moral integrity, his pastoral achievements, his ability to handle people, and, perhaps most importantly, his state of health: once 'married' to a diocese, there he would stay in all likelihood for the rest of his days.

There was much that was theatrical in all this: the appointee had to 'emerge' as if by the will of God. Ambition, back-biting and gossip there was, and there were always lickspittles who would try to ingratiate themselves with those whom they believed had influence, and occasionally they would succeed. But it is probably true to say that unctuousness was seen as unattractive, particularly by those who believed that their own rise in the Church was due not to privilege of favour, but to their own merits and God's will. And whilst a controlled ambition was understood, it would be looked at askance if it were thought to be too strong. Such a driving emotion would be poorly thought of in itself. It was also unsettling for others, and it was likely give rise to envy. Worse still, a man consumed by a sense of unfulfilled promise, who was not content and had not achieved a certain peace of mind, would not be able to give free reign to such qualities of balance, judgment and integrity as he possessed, qualities so important in a man who would probably remain in the position he had been given until he died, and in which he could exercise great autonomy. Except for the Pope, no-one (not even a cardinal) stood above a bishop. And, though it was expected that all would adhere to a particular line once it had been agreed formally by two-thirds of all bishops, and provided that he did not question the faith or speak out against canon law, he was free to speak his mind, to argue and to criticise without fear of losing his post. There were some 120 bishops in the Philippines, of which some 95–100 were active. They met formally twice a year, and smaller groups (such as a diocesan see) would meet more frequently than that. The scope for disagreement was therefore large. When Estrada made clear his intention to allow foreigners complete ownership of businesses and lands of many different kinds, and to extend the tenure of politicians, acts which would have required changes to the constitution, obvious accusations were made against him. Whatever the charms of his economic arguments, it was alleged that he wanted to repay those merchants whose support he had received during the elections (merchants with connexions overseas), and to extend his own time in office. There were few within the

Church who did not agree with this interpretation of Estrada's intentions. But Cardinal Sin and a number of bishops, it was said, had not merely allied themselves to Estrada's political and business opponents: they had them write their speeches. These 'speech-writers' may have included Aquino and others with whom the Church had worked to remove Marcos. But their motive was to promote their own political interests and to protect their own merchant empires. Once again, the poor, and justice, were but decoration for the wealthy and ambitious. The relationship between Estrada's opponents and the Church paralleled neither the relationship which had existed at one time between the Pope's representative in Manila, certain bishops in the Philippines and Marcos, nor Marcos' success in bribing Church officers, nor Imelda Marcos's request to the Pope to silence the cardinal. But whatever the rights and wrongs of Estrada's actions, Sin now appeared to the Bishop of Davao and others to be too close to vested interests of the liberal elite. Once a stand had been taken on a moral issue, one should not move regardless of whether or not it coincided with the beliefs and interests of politician, merchant, NGO or union. One had to talk with merchant, politician and rebel, do one's best to understand their position and views, and to their actions and decisions introduce a moral dimension. But appear to provide for one or other group a moral legitimacy, let alone work for them, and the Church would find weakening its ability to balance the various interest groups from the extreme right within the military, to the extreme and violent left, and all shades of politician, merchant and landowner in between.

In its very human imperfections, and in its disputes over the nature of its relationships with those outside it, the Church represented one of the few touchstones of the expedient absolute, and one of the few stands against the tyranny of no-truth and the pure absolute. In this respect, there was much of the secular about the Church. The nature of this influence made the Church difficult to handle, and perhaps impossible for the politician to harness. The bishop was happy to talk to politicians. He sat on the National Peace Forum and was member of the Anti-drug and the Peace and Order Councils. He was happy to invite the congressman and the city mayor to breakfast once a month, so that he might try to understand their concerns and thinking, and they his. He was also sure that whilst they had need of him, he had no need of them. There might have been a coincidence of agreement on some issues; but they knew that he would be careful not to be too close to them or even let that appear to be so. And if he should appear aloof from merchant or politician, so be it. He had negotiated with communist revolutionaries in Mindanao and the Netherlands; and he had been threatened, bullied and harassed by the military during the Marcos years. Accusations by the Davao City Chamber of Commerce and by politicians that he was arrogant were of little consequence. Those who had bribed their way into office, or who saw in their office only a means of making money, or who had for whatever reason nothing to take the place of an acquisitive drive, would see nothing advantageous in the bishop, and he would write them off as hopeless. The more sophisticated politician, of which there were now more, would see some advantage only in the coincidence of agreement, and their sense of how it was the bishop saw the world and how he might act in particular circumstances. Those politicians who saw their profession as a high and noble one – as indeed the bishop and others in the Church believed it should be – would understand the bishop's attitude, and would see in their relationships with him a distinction between the 'personal' and the 'absolute'. Each would wonder of the other how much pose was in the sincere, and how much sincere in the pose.

The bureaucrat

The relationships most charged with the tension between the personal and the absolute, however, were those formed between politician and bureaucrat, and among the bureaucrats themselves. Within the bureaucracy there were many who were determined to maintain their own integrity and to insulate the civil service from political influence. And there were politicians who shared this determination. Yet there were also many politicians and civil servants who saw the bureaucracy as little more than material to be shaped to their own advantage. Those who manipulated, and those whose attitude to relationships and institutions leant more towards the absolute, could not pretend the other did not exist. Both had to be politic and both had to strike the right pose. Each politician and bureaucrat was thus faced with the difficulties of finding within themselves a comfortable balance between thought and deed, obligation and being owed, altruism and ambition, appearance and substance, and of disentangling a mix of these qualities in other people.

The lower echelons[7] of the civil service were better insulated from the machinations of politicians; and it was unlikely that at these levels the bureaucrats were of immediate interest to the politician. There were, to begin with, many safeguards to appointments and promotions, and these were overseen by a constitutional body – the Civil Service Commission. For levels 1 and 2 of the civil service, posts had to be advertised publicly in the newspapers and in government offices. Candidates were chosen for interview and examination by the personnel selection board. The composition of the board was usually determined by the head or director of the agency in which the appointment was to be made, but the chairman of the board was commonly the assistant director. The criteria for the selection and final appointment included educational qualifications, training, experience, and the successful completion of the government exam. The exam, which was administered by the Civil Service Commission, was intended to assess IQ, mathematics, logical reasoning, and writing. The exam was more difficult for entry at level 2 (candidates had to hold a college degree) than at level 1 (candidates for entry at this level needed only seventy-two college units).

Movement up through the lower echelons (up to the level of a directorship), and security of tenure, were supposed to depend largely on performance, though length of service was also taken into account and, in the view of some directors, this was often the most important criterion. The performance of each civil servant was measured twice a year (once each semester) by their immediate superior, and the criteria for measurement were agreed upon between the superior and their subordinate in the form of a work contract. Meeting these agreed targets would earn a 'satisfactory' assessment; a worker who was 25 or 50 per cent above target would be judged as 'very satisfactory' or 'outstanding'. Those who were rated 'outstanding' during two consecutive semesters would earn themselves a double increment in salary; those who were twice rated 'very satisfactory' would be awarded a single increment; and those who received a 'satisfactory' rating for three years consecutively would be given a single increment. Two consecutive 'unsatisfactory' ratings, or one single 'poor' rating, were sufficient grounds for dismissal from the service. Civil servants who believed that they had been assessed or treated unfairly could raise their concerns, first, with their immediate superiors, and then, if they believed that they still had not received satisfaction, with the departmental head. Appeals could also be made to the commission which had the final say on such matters.

The criteria for the appointment and promotion of candidates to executive level positions (grade 25 and above) were rather less clear. Strictly speaking, whilst candidates need not have the qualifications required for lower-level appointments, eligibility required successful completion of the Career Executive Service Board (CESB) – a series of lengthy tests designed to assess mental aptitude and managerial ability. In practice, however, of those appointed, most were not eligible. Few candidates had attempted or passed through the CESB – a state of affairs which reflected the common view that experience had greater weight than yet another qualification, a view shared by the Supreme Court which had, in effect, ruled that too great an emphasis on qualifications would not be of benefit to the service and competent government. The Commission's attempt to make a Master of Arts a prerequisite for an appointment to a directorship was also seen by the Court to limit unnecessarily the discretion of the president to make political appointments. Responsibility for the administration of the CESB had also been moved from the Civil Service Commission to the Office of the President; and the requirement to publicise vacant posts had made it difficult to exclude candidates with political support at an earlier stage. In short, whilst the Civil Service Commission had attempted to bring within its compass the appointment and promotion to all ranks of the service, the executive level remained political appointees. A change in president would mean a change in undersecretary, assistant secretary and commissioners; and this would often be followed by a change, and rotation, of regional directors among the provinces. An instruction to move, though it could be seen as grooming for promotion, was more commonly understood as a punishment against which even those who held the CESB were not protected.

Those with ambitions for a directorship or more, or who wished to avoid their transfer, had to seek political support. This meant striking up a relationship either with the person (a high-ranking bureaucrat) who had influence over such decisions, or with someone – such as a senator or a congressman – who already had a sound relationship with that person. Establishing these networks would require working through more than one or two intermediaries, beginning, perhaps, with a classmate or someone with whom there was daily contact as part of the everyday work of the department. Or it may be that such relationships appeared quite by chance. Before he was made the director of a national line agency, one official was lucky enough to find himself, many years after his marriage, linked through his wife's kinship ties with a congressman. Such connections were often essential: a 'phone call, or a letter, or a quiet word from a high-ranking civil servant or congressman could be enough to avoid transfer, or to secure an appointment or promotion over better-qualified candidates.

This manoeuvering was quite deliberate and calculating, and it was practised by even the most qualified, able and honest civil servants; it was better that they should profit from such relationships if any semblance of a true meritocracy was to be achieved eventually. This, at least, was what they argued, perhaps with some justification. There was also the feeling that such connections were vital if one was to overcome what was perceived to be the centre's prejudiced view of the provinces. It was also suggested that meritocratic puritanism was neither feasible nor desirable. Even within a meritocracy more than just merit would be required; someone with whom one could work, who had a certain imaginative spontaneity and unconventionality, might be of greater value than those who were only technically competent and whose abilities, if they could be measured, were necessarily limited and rather artificial. There was also the advantage, for those already with influence, that their protégés would be more reliable and malleable. The strength of this *quid pro quo* between the appointee and his supporter glimmered in the rules governing the pre-election period: new appointments were not allowed during this time in the hope that not too many new shards of obligations between bureaucrat and politician would interfere with the election.

It would be fair to say, and this was, I think, recognised by the Civil Service Commission, that an ability to manage social relationships to one's own advantage was often more important than technical merit. Nevertheless, the picture was more mixed than I have implied so far. There were marked variations within and among departments of the government. These variations reflected differences in functions, personalities, ambitions and the balance between career and non-career servants in any particular department. Political influence over local government was particularly strong. Local government had the freedom to decide upon the composition and balance of its bureaucracy subject to certain minimum standards and guidelines set by the Civil Service Commission for national government agencies; and its appointments were confirmed by the Commission. In practice, however, the mayor appointed, and frequently had direct knowledge of, the heads of all departments; and he had a decisive influence even upon those key positions which were overseen by national line agencies. The city treasurer for instance, was selected by the secretary of the Department of Finance from a list of three names given to him by the mayor; and the mayor could refuse to accept all but the candidate he preferred. Even the city's chief of police, though appointed by the Department of the Interior and Local Government, was in fact selected from a list of possible candidates by the mayor. As chairman of the selection board, the mayor or his representatives (commonly the city administrator) could also influence decisively the appointments made at lower grades. The job which Inday secured for Louisa's father through the congressman was a case in point. At the national level, too, there were highly political departments whose bureaucrats were political appointees, though a political appointee was not necessarily a synonym for strong political influence. Political support did not necessarily mean that appointments were made for political reasons. Much depended upon the post, and upon the nature of those who were making the appointment and of those who were appointed. The head of the civil service was appointed by the president. His choice had to be ratified by the Commission on Appointments which comprised congressmen and senators elected by proportional representation from the various parties in Congress. The term of appointment was fixed at seven years for the chairman of the civil service, and at five and three years for his two commissioners. There were, then, certain checks on candidates' appointments and on their own ambitions to seek further tenure. Under recent chairmen it was also in effect taboo within the Civil Service Commission for any of its employees at any level to seek political support for a post or promotion. This pride in independence was common to many agencies. The director of the National Economic Development Agency (NEDA (Region XI) was not merely a political appointment, but a presidential one; and the president was also chair of NEDA (Manila). Political influence over appointments at lower levels was not unknown within this agency, but those whose appointments or promotions were determined in this way would be looked upon unfavourably by their colleagues, and there was generally within the agency an attempt to resist such manoeuvering. The same was also true of the Social Security System and the Bureau of the Treasury where political appointees were likely to receive a cold shoulder and have their lives made difficult unless and until they could prove themselves competent at their work.

A belief in the value of being insulated from political influence, then, was widely held, and often supported by religious faith, a certain territoriality, and a sense of honour in one's own achievements. Often with only a state education to start them off in life, many directors of regional departments had risen through the ranks from the most lowly of positions (clerks and barangay workers) due largely, they felt, to their own hard work, their own merit, and The Lord's help. They neither liked the idea of being superseded by light-weight courtiers, nor would they easily tolerate interference by such people. There was also much common sense in their rectitude. Promotions above the level of director would require them to live and work in Manila where the chances of political survival were not good. They would also, in most cases, have had to keep two homes – one in Davao and another, far more expensive one, in the capital. It would be a struggle, they knew, to put together new communities and in doing so overcome the prejudice of those who, even if not born and brought up in the north, were proud of their own position, and their survival, at the centre of power. Those who were approaching retirement and were hoping to end their days with a better pension might have looked to Manila; but many directors – most I think – were reasonably content to limit their ambitions to their directorship. They had to remain politic if they were to avoid disgrace or transfer; and, for the same reason, they had to avoid even the appearance of being too close to one or other politician whose fall might quickly be followed by their own demise. There was, then, a built-in insulation, but one that was personal and circumstantial rather than institutional.

Hierarchies and networks

The influence which existed at the upper levels of the hierarchy was also felt, if only indirectly, at its lower reaches. This had less to do with the authority of the hierarchy than with the nature of relationships among bureaucrats. These relationships were, as we saw in Nazareth, founded upon reciprocity, layered with emotions, shaped around kernels such as classmate, place of origin and kinship. And as they were played out in Nazareth and translated there into formal political life, so they were replayed and re-translated by the bureaucrats. Most civil servants, even in national-line agencies, were from Davao; and most of those who were not, came from neighbouring provinces in Region XI. They shared a common language, and they, and their children, had attended the same schools and colleges. Rotation within departments, or among regions, was not common at the lower ends of the hierarchy; and very commonly division chiefs and assistant directors and directors, rather like the purok leaders and barangay captains, had risen from the ranks. These executive-level bureaucrats, again like the purok and barangay officials, were commonly made the sponsors or godparents of their subordinates and their subordinates' children. To accept such fictive kinship ties, to become the *compadre* of one's subordinates, and to make such an offer to another, could be presented either as nothing more than an everyday courtesy or as a declaration that one knew the right kind of people. When a Gaisano brother was made Bert's *ninong*, it certainly did not indicate that Bert moved in the same circles as the Gaisanos. But offering and accepting such ties was taken to imply something else. There was in the relationship an ulterior purpose which, though it existed more as a possibility than as a definite and specific plan, represented more than just a ritual claim on each other. In the bureaucracy there was the hope in the subordinate that whilst his relationship with his superior might not necessarily secure promotion or elicit favourable treatment, it would help make sure that his length of service or good performance would, at some point, receive its just rewards, and that his faults and weakness, and even his occasional indiscretions, would be overlooked. Across the ranks, too, support, progress and protection lay partly in forming around oneself relationships strengthened by those very kernels – such as *barkada*, *compadre*, *ninong* – that we saw being used in Nazareth, and by all those emotions associated with give and take or favours and obligations.

The director, then, had considerable influence, an influence which owed much to his informal relationships with his subordinates and from whose ranks he was likely to have emerged. To the director, the subordinate would go with his problems from work or home; it was the director who would dig into his own pocket for money to help his subordinate through some crisis in the family; it was the director who, as their *compadre*, might find himself under an obligation to give money and presents to his godchildren. In these relationships the director could form an intimate knowledge of his subordinates' strength and weakness; and his subordinates, too, would learn something about his nature, about how openly they could express their true thoughts and feelings, and about what they might or might not do in particular circumstances. The atmosphere created was, at least on the surface, congenial, relaxed, even lackadaisical; a gentle hub-bub of chatter about girlfriends, boyfriends, husbands, wives and children, would float above the grating fans and rattling air-conditioners; people would go about their with graceful, swaying movements; around midday they would drift out to a nearby *caranderia*, or congregate in the office where they opened their lunch boxes, and perhaps set up a dart board or some other diversion; and they might, in the evening and weekends every now and then, go bowling together and attend parties.

Link into the civil servant, and the politician linked into strands of relationships (and obligations) which ran up and down the bureaucracy. He also found himself within a complex of networks which crossed departments and other agencies. The most important kernels in these relationships were: those of classmate, most commonly at Ateneo de Davao, the University of Mindanao, Ateneo de Manila, or the University of the Philippines; beliefs of a religious, moral, social or political quality; or a shared profession, such as law, accountancy or engineering. As we saw in Nazareth and as we saw overseas, these networks were also fashioned into formal organisations. Some of these comprised civil servants only or largely: the membership of ARENA (the Association of Regional National-Line Agencies), for instance, was exclusive to the heads and assistant heads of national-line agencies, while Davao Lady Lawyers also included a few lawyers in private practice. The civil servants' networks also reached into larger organisations with a much broader appeal. Here they had the opportunity to establish relationships with other civil servants and, as was more usually the case, with politicians, businessmen and other professionals. These organisations included: alumni associations; professional associations representing, say, civil engineers, chartered accountants and lawyers; religious associations, such as the Brotherhood of Christian Businessmen, the Catholic Women's League, Lie-in the Spirit, and United Methodists; military organisations, such as the Guardian Brotherhood; and those associations with humanistic, social and welfare interests such as Knights of Rizal, Knights of Columbus, the JCs, Lions Club, the Rotary Club, and the Masons. The Masons in particular provided the nexus for a wide range of officials at all levels and from all kinds of government agencies including the Commission on Audit, the Ombudsman (Manila Office), the Department of the Interior and Local Government, the Department of Public Works and Highways, the Bureau of Internal Revenue, the National Economic Development Authority, the Provincial Assessor's Office, the Provincial Auditor's Office, the Social Security System, the Department of Justice, and the City Veterinarian's Office. There, too, politicians (the mayor and vice-mayor) were to be found. But the Masons were dominated, as we noted earlier, by leading merchants – Filipino, Chinese and *mestizo*.

Kinship seemed to be a kernel of less importance. The need for qualifications and for probity (or at least for the appearance of probity); a desire to avoid the envy and suspicions which the presence of a relative unerringly created; and the regulations drawn up against nepotism: all were good reasons why those with a relative in one department would be persuaded either to look for some other line of work, or to enter a different branch of the civil service. And indeed, in both local and national agencies, the kinship links which did exist were more prevalent across departments than within them. Again, however, attitudes varied. In local government, up to 15 per cent of bureaucrats of all grades, and about a tenth of bureaucrats of the higher grades,[8] were related to each other.[9] Of all these relationships, about a third were to be found within, rather than across, departments. By contrast, such ties were rare within national-line agencies, though within the Bureau of Internal Revenue there was an unwritten custom that upon his retirement an official's son or daughter, provided they had the required minimum qualifications, could then take the place of their parent. Directors with three decades of service behind them would not find it strange to have had two generations of the same family serve alongside, or under, them. On the other hand, whilst kinship links among national agencies were few and far between, those which existed did so at the highest levels connecting the Ombudsman, the Commission on Audit, the Department of Trade and Industry, Land Transportation, the Department of Agrarian Reform, the Civil Service Commission, the Commission on Elections, the Department of Public Works and Highways, and, until late 1998, the Clerk of Courts, the Office of the President and the Board of Investments. Kinship ties also existed between various national-line agencies, such as the Bureau of Internal Revenue, and certain local government departments, such as the City Business Bureau.

Whether or not they found expression in associations, and whatever kernel they were formed around, networks which ran across departments (most especially at the upper echelons) lubricated dealings that might otherwise be taut, abrasive and cold. Expanding one's own community, knowing other people in other parts of the service, using pre-existing kernels or establishing new relationships allowed the bureaucrats to gather and disseminate more reliable information and advice with greater speed and efficacy. Official requests in writing would still have to be made, but these now followed rather than preceded the help given during a 'phone call, or informal meeting, or by fax. Such relationships also provided a better sense of how things were done in another agency and of how best to approach that particular agency with a request; they might even allow senior staff to keep an eye on their subordinates, as in the case of the director of the Bureau of Internal Revenue, whose membership of a business association gave her an unparalleled view of her subordinates' performance. These relationships also allowed problems to be dealt with more effectively. The tensions which were very likely to arise if, say, reports and budgets were submitted late by local government to the Department of Budget and Management were more likely to be avoided if those involved knew each other's personality and style of work, and if each understood the pressures that the other was under. So important were these relationships that without them departments would simply be unable to function properly. Although poorly funded, the Commission on Elections

– a constitutional commission charged with administering elections – had the authority to deputise other agencies. The status of its staff as the servants of this constitutional body was usually enough to elicit the information and compliance needed from other agencies, but only just. Broadening one's community so that it encompassed, most especially, the directors and assistant directors of these other departments made the administration of elections so much easier and more certain. Lie outside such communities, and life was made very difficult. For many civil servants in this and every other department, seeking out contacts and nurturing their networks was therefore an essential part of their work. This was especially true for those who come from other parts of the Philippines. A ranking civil servant from Luzon, who had the added disadvantage of not being able to speak Cebuano, found that his work in the Social Security System (SSS) was suffering precisely because his webs of relationships were not yet well formed. Before a merchant registered his business with the City Business Bureau he first had to receive clearance from the SSS with whom he was required to register his employees and begin making payments to their accounts. Yet many businesses were being allowed to register with the City Business Bureau even though they had not registered their workers with, or received clearance from, the Social Security System. And the City Business Bureau seemed entirely unconcerned about this state of affairs. Part of the solution, as he saw it, was for him to join ARENA and other associations, and, when his children moved down to Davao, send them to one of the best schools, probably Ateneo. By gradually expanding his community in these and other ways he would be more likely to discover the reasons why procedures were not working as they should. Then, perhaps, he could begin doing something about it. Merely to issue edicts to, and demand explanations from, people who were neither of his department, nor even of the national bureaucracy, and whose language he did not speak, would have only made him still less effective. If he could achieve a coincidence of community, institutions and rank, then tasks and routines would be carried out with an effortless and seemingly easy spontaneity. Without that coincidence, or if there was only hostility and suspicion, little would happen.

Professionalism and the corruption of corruption

Among civil servants there was at once a heavy reliance on the manipulation of relationships and emotions, and something more than a self-interested *quid pro quo*. To say that the service was fetid with introspection, mottled with patronage and self-abasing criticism, and starved of new thinking is certainly misleading. There was in many departments, more especially of the national agencies, a strong belief in 'professionalism'. By this I mean that there was a clear and conscious understanding of the need to distance personal relationships from the conduct of official affairs. With that distancing, and with the belief that relationships cultivated for their own sake possessed an ethical dimension, often seemed to come a better understanding of one's own nature and of the strengths and weaknesses of other people. In that, many directors, most especially those with a strong religious bent, felt there was much fulfilment. Even those of their subordinates, who would try to manipulate their relationships and the bureaucracy for their own benefit, could themselves be manipulated such that they worked for the institution or at least not against it. The hope in a subordinate that it would be to his advantage to make of his superior a *compadre* was clearly and unambiguously understood by his superior; but the subordinate was left to sow that expectation, that unspoken possibility, in his own heart where it became of great value to his superior. The subordinate was more open to suggestion and guidance, and he was brought closer to his mentor for whom pleasure now lay not so much in what he could gain, but in shaping others as he thought best.

Now that relationships had been distanced, and now that understandings were no longer smothered by image and by a concern for what could be gained or lost or owed, energies and attentions were focused more keenly upon the work at hand. With that shift in attitude came changes in practices and atmosphere. The need for each person to envelop themselves within their own community, and for that taut, watchful trust which did little to mitigate the desire for monitoring and policing, became less strong. At the highest echelons of the department, between the director and his assistant, a breezy informality emerged. Discussions were more lively and less defensive; ideas were broached and disagreements aired; and, as each began to understand the other, there was no need to enunciate, explain, justify or rationalise every thought, nor every line of reasoning. Rank was still observed. The subordinate understood that it was the head who must in the end make the decision and with whom responsibility for that decision lay, and to whom he must give his support. But the head must also had to check his own motivations, actions and decisions and allow his subordinate the freedom to develop the self-confidence which he would need if he was to succeed to his superior and if the quality of the department was to be maintained. At the lower ends of hierarchy, too, though rank, procedures and responsibilities were recognised, there was a degree of latitude, a sense that each was not under constant scrutiny: merit, if it was to have value, had to be given rein, and mistakes (upon which bickering cliques always feed) viewed by a broader mind. Tensions which seemed to introduce a necessary edge were left to do their work, while those thought to be inimical to the department were quickly defused. To these ends the director often took into his confidence a subordinate through whom he might gain another perspective of the relationships among his workers; and he would move staff around, though in this practice changes in the balance of tasks demanded by annual routines or the cascade of memorandums, and a wish to avoid sheer boredom and territoriality, were also on his mind. The apparent congeniality and cloying friendliness of the amateurish gave way to the alluring quietness of a serene, glassy calm, broken occasionally by a fast-moving, but highly polished hustle. This was particularly true of certain national-line agencies concerned with welfare, such as the Social Security System, and with finance, such as the Treasury and the Central Bank.

Curiously, perhaps, this air of professionalism also surrounded those agencies which were highly politicised. They were led by political appointees who were usually merchants and ran their new office as they were accustomed to run their own businesses. Their staff, though civil servants, were contractual and not so well protected by the Civil Service Commission. And their responsibilities and aims were clear: obey their political instructions and serve as a conduit through which money and influence could flow between the president and his allies in the city. In this we are reminded that just as the personal could itself be manipulated to serve the professional, so the professional could be turned to the advantage of those whose attitudes were those of the personal. But turning the ideals of the absolute in support of political machinations was a dangerous game. It not only left exposed the inherent instability of relationships and emotions, but removed a sense of redress. Where there was no attempt to realise such ideals as friendship, loyalty, trust, altruism and their associated emotions as virtues in their own right, and where feelings of envy, jealousy, rivalry and deceit were used similarly, there was, in consequence, no satisfying or effective sanction against perfidy and manipulation. The absence of such moral absolutes implied acceptance of envy, suspicion, jealousy, bitterness, resentment and other base emotions – all instruments of the politic individual. Manipulation was felt to be nothing more than a fact of life and, indeed, such relationships were the only channel though which sanction and retribution may be dispensed. Where these were not enough to take the flow of bile, and there was felt to be no righteousness in the abuse suffered and no publicly recognised immorality in the other's deceit, and where there was no strong personality or some external discipline present, then emotions might suddenly turn upon their puppeteer. In the confined atmosphere of bureaucratic departments, and among people who had often known each other for years, it was always likely that conflicts of personalities would find justification and focus in disputes over issues at work. If it was discovered that the professional had been sequestered by the personal and now formed part of its image-making, then petty matters were easily magnified into intense personal hatreds, to be followed quickly with accusations, legal action, counter-action, abuse and even objects being hurled across the department.

There was also the danger that as professionalism lost its credibility, the maintenance of probity would become still more difficult. Already the day-to-day relationships which bureaucrats and politicians strung among themselves fitted less well with the angular institutions and procedural shells in which they worked than with their social-cum-political world. Where professionalism had been degraded, the bureaucrat could fall into corrupt ways between one breath and the next. When help was received on a small matter, an obligation was left hanging. It appeared to be a little clumsy to ask for a favour in return immediately. But the weight of the favour gathered with time, and if left too long would begin to smell. So when the need arose, the obligation would be called upon. As part of her work, Sal was asked to organise a number of seminars which required liaison with local government officers. In the course of a casual conversation with one of these officers, Sal mentioned that her father had worked for the Bureau of Internal Revenue. The officer, Sophie, mentioned that her husband ran a business and was having difficulty providing the necessary receipts for his tax assessment: did Sal know of anyone in the Bureau who might be able to advise him? Sal gave her the name of Alma's remaining daughter – Diding. The next day Sophie approached Diding and mentioned their mutual friend, Sal. Diding gave Sophie the advice she asked for and, on behalf of Sophie and her husband, intervened through her colleagues in the Bureau. About a week later Sophie mentioned to Sal that Diding had been most helpful, and that Diding had this very day asked her for a small loan. Sal replied that she had, on the insistence of Inday, already refused her the money: she was always asking for loans and did not always pay them back when she should. But she also said that Diding was otherwise reliable. This seemed good enough for Sophie, and she thanked Sal. Sophie was now predisposed to help Sal with the arrangements for the seminars as best she could. Diding, too, thanked Sal for introducing her to Sophie, an introduction which had turned out to be so useful. All were now happy, all had benefited from the most casual conversations, which had lasted only a few moments and were quickly subsumed by the more important affairs of their everyday lives. The practice was corrupt but that was an idea which seemed to belong in a very different, far-away world. The bank officials who waived tiresome documentary requirements and extended loans at special rates to high-ranking civil servants with whom the bank dealt in the course of its daily work were being quite natural in their behaviour: it would have been discourteous not to offer, cold not to accept. Bringing pressure to bear upon a colleague in the office to find in favour of one party in a dispute over, say, the ownership of a private company, would only confirm or heighten the bureaucrat's status and his community's expectations of him.

The exchanges were manipulative and layered with emotions and sentiments; therein lay their power. When a tax assessor found a discrepancy in a merchant's accounts, and that merchant said he could not pay all that was due, the tax assessor would merely point to the discrepancy and give his advice. His manner was cheerful. He would touch the merchant's arm, and they would talk of the economy and politics, family and children, and other matters. The tax assessor would not ask for money or gifts. He had no need: an obligation now existed, and the offer he knew would come – a little something for your kind help. He would refuse it kindly. The merchant would insist, and the tax man would yield. But if he must accept, he would say, then perhaps he could offer something in return: a reduction on the amount of tax to be paid? And let him overlook this or that discrepancy. There was nothing amiss here: just two friends helping each other out, neither wanting to take advantage of the other. The tax assessor and the tax payer were now each part of the other's community. The tax assessor was seen as a good man, a fair man, not greedy, materialistic, or showy.

Those officials who demanded, threatened, or took were less likely to fare so well. Eventually they would be noticed. Someone would be upset and the whistle blown. When the court ordered a company to pay damages and costs to another company in settlement of a trade dispute, the money was placed, as was the custom, into the hands of the sheriff for delivery to the victorious party. The merchant, however, found that the amount being made over to him by the sheriff was short. The merchant refused to accept the money. The sheriff replied that this was all that he had received. (This at least is what the sheriff later claimed in court, though certainly the amount he delivered was less than the settlement fixed by the court and less than the company originally found in breach of contract had paid to him.) The sheriff walked out and held on to the money well beyond the period that he was entitled to by law. So the merchant filed a case with the ombudsman; and the merchant's lawyer was the brother of the ombudsman in Manila. The sheriff then agreed to pay the sum he had originally proffered to the merchant. But the amount was still short. Affidavits passed to and fro, and hearings followed. The sheriff claimed that the money he had taken was necessary to the execution of his duty: he had been asked to deliver money to a businessmen who lived outside the city proper in an area where guerrillas and bandits were known to be active. There was a risk to himself and to his bodyguards who had to be paid and fed. The court did not accept his defence and he was found guilty of malversation. The lesson was clear. If there was no *quid pro quo*, if there was no relationship, and if one was not part of the other's community, then the danger was all the greater.

The shift from the proper to the improper, though judgment and finesse were needed, occurred easily, naturally, effortlessly. No wonder that corruption was said to be extremely common. So common that it was often described, and thought of, as inevitable, as a 'cultural' feature of 'the Filipino'.

Certainly the attitude of the personal, combined with low pay, the compromises made on merit, the low esteem with which the bureaucracy was already held (and with which the bureaucrats often held themselves) conspired together to weaken the reasons why one should avoid falling into improper ways. To rail against those officials who gave succour to their own communities, and perhaps make a little something for themselves, appeared like the action of a tiresome and sanctimonious image-maker who, for his own personal gain, wielded self-righteousness and a feigned abhorrence as his sword and shield. But it was also true that all were well aware of what was, and what was not, permissible; and there were only a few who did not understand that unless distanced and redirected, the relationships of their social world would prejudice, distort and weaken bureaucracy and government. Those who left the obligations of their borderless communities uppermost in their minds did so only because they chose to do so.

In such a world, where corruption was layered with emotions and made to feel secure, where its practice was regarded more as a political act than a criminal one, where its discovery was seen only as a political weakness to be exploited, and where corruption had itself been corrupted, greater things were made possible. It was not uncommon for bureaucrats in one part of the bureaucracy to begin an investigation only to find that they had stepped into a circle of relationships which eventually linked back into their own department. The Special Investigation Bureau of the Bureau of Internal Revenue, if it was to pursue a politician's businesses, would have to tread carefully. The collection of evidence had to be meticulous, and if they were called off by their superiors this would not have been unusual. Smuggling, too, could grow into large, semi-authorised operations. When the Economic Intelligence and Investigation Bureau, part of the Department of Finance, was asked to exact some measure of control over the black market in gold, it quickly found that its job was being made impossible by other parts of the bureaucracy. The Central Bank's rates for gold were too low, its buying stations were few and far between, and black market gold was being transported under guard by the army in its helicopters to Manila for illegal shipment to Singapore and Hong Kong. Push investigations too far into this half-hidden, semi-official world and it would be taken as a political action, certain to attract swift, political retribution.

Under these circumstances the work of the ombudsman was made particularly difficult. The ombudsmans' powers were certainly broad, and greater than those of other agencies. His officials did not need an affidavit to proceed with a preliminary investigation; they could even act upon anonymous accusations, and use their own judgment as to what was or was not mischievous. They were permitted even to put aside the bank secrecy laws and to examine the accounts of those against whom complaints of ill-gotten wealth had been filed. They could demand of any agency that they submit all pertinent documents. And whilst the Regional Office could not investigate Congress or the Supreme Court, it could initiate proceedings for such investigations. But there was resistance. They had to work through the Economic Intelligence and Investigation Bureau, the national Bureau of Investigation and other agencies in which they did not have complete trust. The ombudsman had also been weakened by neglect. There were only twenty-seven legal investigators and sixty-three support staff for the whole of Mindanao, even though here the Office of Ombudsman's plantillas were full. Collecting evidence was therefore a slow matter and delays and backlogs (of some two thousand dockets) had led to a decline in trust, in morale, and in the number of complaints filed. And the more hostile the president, the more likely it would be that the ombudsman would suffer budgetary restrictions.

Monitoring and policing

Link into the bureaucracy, as did the politician, and one linked into communities which extended vertically and horizontally within the bureaucracy and beyond it. These communities could work well if, as we have said, they coincided with the institutions' boundaries, purpose and activities. But they also created tension, suspicion and conflict; and they raised questions of probity. The very fact that there were so many other communities to which one did not belong was a reason for doubt. Every community and every part of the bureaucracy were enjoined to watch each other ever more closely, and all were laced with still more rules and regulations and procedures. Then did the need for establishing and extending one's own community cry out ever more loudly. Then did the need for still more policing and monitoring become ever more plain. Had there been none of the freedom and openness which a belief in the absolute brought, the bureaucracy would soon have rotted away while its institutional shells, its statements of policies, objectives and missions, and its rules and procedures would have been picked over by the image-makers and its remainders used only as gilding.

There were nearly twenty departments which, at first sight, constituted the core of government. Each department was made of bureaux, boards, centres, commissions and offices. In any one department, these sub-divisions numbered as many as twenty. In addition to these agencies there were, in all, almost one hundred government-owned or controlled corporations. Some of these were attached to particular departments; others, such as the Central Bank, were free-standing organisations with administrative and fiscal autonomy.

Most of these departments and their composite bodies were charged with the general day-to-day executive functions of government. They educated and trained, regulated and adjudicated, collected and disseminated, conducted research and formulated plans and policies. But of these departments only two – Education[10] and the Department of Public Works and Highways – were big spenders with budgets some five to ten times that of the other departments. Most of the Department of Education's budget was consumed by the running costs of schools. The Department of Public Works and Highways spent much of its money on infrastructure projects. The third, and largest, tranche of expenditure was the Internal Revenue Allotment to local government (provinces, cities, municipalities and barangays) throughout the Philippines. These departments, and local governments, were constantly monitored by, and were dependent upon, another layer of departments: Finance, Budget and Management, and Interior and Local Government. These three departments had much smaller budgets but they were of greater import.

The Bureau of the Treasury (Department of Finance) monitored the disbursements and collections through authorised banks (which included the Land Bank and the Development Bank). The amounts disbursed by the banks to each agency of national government in the Davao was reported daily by those banks to their head offices in Manila who then informed the Treasury in Manila, and to the regional office of the Treasury in Davao which also informed the Treasury in Manila. The Treasury in Manila then reconciled both sets of reports. The Treasury, however, ministered only the flow of money. Authorisation for the release of funds was controlled by the Department of Budget and Management. Authorisation was passed by this department to the Treasury, and a notice of cash allotment was then passed to the agency that was to receive the money. The authorisation to make such disbursements had been devolved piecemeal from the centre to the regional offices, and by the end of the 1990s the regional offices in Davao had authority to release funds even to the big spending departments of Education, Health, and Public Works and Highways. Daily reports to Manila on these releases were made by the regional office of Budget and Management; and all expenditure by national-line agencies appeared on the accounts of the Treasury.

Allotments which had not been spent within a specified time were supposed to be returned to the Treasury. This did not mean a cut in funding in the following year. Money for general maintenance, operating expenses and capital outlays had a two-year life-span, and could be carried on from one year to the next. During that period, however, money which had not been used in one month would be deducted from the following month's release; only if all of the funds released in that second month were used would the unused amount from the first month then be released. From the agency's point of view this forced it to spend money unnecessarily and prematurely; but the officials at Budget and Management saw this as a way of ensuring that money was used as budgeted; and since a large proportion of the sums released were barely enough to cover basic operating expenses and maintenance, the presence of any unused funds, or so Budget and Management argued, indicated inefficiency.

For obvious reasons, the politician found the Department of Budget and Management attractive. He might not have been able to extract more than had been set in the budget for a department to carry out a favoured project, but he could influence the timing of releases and make sure that all the funds were indeed released. The Department of Budget and Management was also responsible the release and monitoring of the Internal Revenue Allotment to local government, and this made it still more attractive. The allotments were released into the bank accounts of local governments every month in the case of provinces, cities and municipalities, and every quarter in the case of barangays. Although a formula based on land area and population was used to calculate proportions, the amount which each division eventually received was determined ultimately by what central government believed the country could afford. Funds were paid directly to each division of local government so that each was independent of the other at least as far as this grant was concerned. In the case of the city, the money was received by the city treasurer who then informed the city budget officer and the mayor. The budget officer, paralleling the Department of Budget and Management, then issued an allotment advice to those agencies who were to receive funds. The amounts released and purposes for which the money was to be used were set out in the city's annual budget. The budget was prepared by the City Budget Office and in it, and in accordance with Mr Micawber's advice, estimated expenditure was not permitted to exceed estimated income. Cities and those provinces classed as highly urban had to have their budgets ratified first by their Sangguniang Panglugsod and their mayor or governor, and then by national government. The budgets of other local government divisions had to be approved only by their provincial government. The budget became effective in January when he first tranche of funds was released. The Department of Budget and Management had no say over what the local governments did with the money (within legitimate and sensible limits), though built into the provisions of local budgets and the Internal Revenue Allotment was the requirement that a fifth of the grant had to be spent on 'development' projects which had to form part of 'integrated and long-term local development plans'. These plans were reviewed by the Department of the Interior and Local Government whose mandate was to strengthen the efficacy of local government.

Both the Treasury and the Department of Budget and Management, then, kept an eye on allotments and monthly expenditures. The Treasury also monitored revenue collections raised through the Bureau of Internal Revenue – another bureau under the Department of Finance. The monitoring of revenue followed a route similar to that for disbursements. Taxes were paid not to the Bureau of Internal Revenue but directly into Treasury accounts held in authorised banks. The money was transmitted by these branches to their head offices in Manila. Each day the branches in Davao reported on the amount of tax deposited with them to their head offices in Manila and to the Treasury in Davao. The banks' head offices and the Treasury in Davao also made daily reports on these tax deposits to the Treasury in Manila. And the Treasury in Manila would reconcile both sets of reports. In those parts of the country where there were no banks through which taxes could be paid, the Bureau of Internal Revenue arranged for its authorised collection agents to receive and forward deposits. Whether taxes were paid to the banks or to collections agents, the amount deposited and the kind of tax paid was also checked by the Bureau of Internal Revenue against its assessments. These records were also examined by the Treasury. The Bureau of Internal Revenue also conducted selective audits of different lines of businesses. Businesses were selected for auditing either at random, or if they were reporting incomes, profits or sales less than those being reported by other similar businesses of a similar size. The list of businesses chosen for auditing had to be confirmed by a Letter of Authority from the Bureau of Internal Revenue in Manila.

Various committees and commissions (around sixty or so) provided a second monitorial layer, though these organs were less concerned with government income and expenditure. Some of these were charged with formulating policies, others with regulating, say, gambling and oil prices; others supported particular initiatives such as the privatisation of government corporations or the recovery of ill-gotten wealth. Many, such as the Presidential Commission for the Urban Poor, monitored those other agencies which were responsible for the implementation of specific favoured policies. Others, such as the Presidential Management Staff, monitored the progress of a much broader range of national policies. But it was the Office of the President which monitored the general direction and progress of government agencies. The Office comprised a variety of missions, committees and councils. Its extensions – the regional offices – were led by presidential assistants who were appointed personally by the president and had technical authority over all other branches of the executive within their region. The Office monitored whatever the assistant thought relevant to the president's interests; and it worked to coordinate and focus or, in the view of some, to undercut and circumvent the bureaucracy, most especially its upper echelons in Manila. The bureaucrats there, at the centre, were often thought by staff in the regions to be uncertain about which provinces were to be found in which part of the Philippines, patronising in their treatment of anyone who was not from

Manila, and ignorant of what the regions wanted. Through the Office, the president's allies in the region had a direct line to him, and he had a more reliable means of ensuring that central and regional bureaucracies worked his will in support of his allies and so his own political base.

An organisation of particular interest under the Office in Davao was the Mindanao Economic Development Council (MEDCO). The Council was housed in suitably plush offices and staffed by non-career, contract civil servants. It was usually led by Davao's presidential assistant (who was most often a merchant), though in more recent years another close ally of the president had been appointed as its head. He was also a merchant, chair of the Mindanao Business Council, and a former chairman of the Davao City Chamber of Commerce. The Council comprised: the chair; twelve congressmen (two from each region of Mindanao); the chairmen and co-chairmen of each region's development council (both of whom were political appointees, and both usually merchants); and other private sector representatives. Its declared purpose was to coordinate planning and policy formulation across the regions of Mindanao. It became the formal umbrella organisation for the regional development councils, and it also served as the Philippines' Secretariat for East Asian Growth Area which included Brunei, Indonesia and Malaysia. The Council's four key strategies were physical integration, international trade, peace and development, and poverty alleviation. By coordinating the efforts of national government agencies – most especially those of the Departments of Public Works and Highways, Transport and Communications, Agrarian Reform, and Trade and Industry (which was also the signatory authority for the Philippines in the East Asian Growth Area) – the Council was intent on easing the movement of goods and people within Mindanao, and between these islands, the rest of the Philippines and nearby countries. The Council emphasised physical integration and international trade, though it was envisioned that this emphasis would gradually be redirected towards poverty alleviation as the economy improved. The initiative for the various programmes and projects which formed the details of its general strategies originated in Manila (these were the president's 'flagship' projects), and in the regions. Projects suggested by the regions had to be filtered and endorsed by the Council and the regional development councils before they could be 'placed' with the Department of Budget and Management, which was also responsible for budgeting directly the bulk of national-line agencies' operating and maintenance expenses. The regional development councils also received and scrutinised the wider development plans, investment programmes, regional frameworks, and 'special' plans suggested by local and central governments. All this material was supposed to be crafted into a coherent strategy which itself was supposed to be incorporated within MEDCO's still broader strategies for Mindanao. The regional development council also ratified or rejected the regional national-line agencies' budgets for capital outlays. If ratified, such funding for these agencies was not then guaranteed, but without the regional development councils' endorsement it was certain that no subventions would be forthcoming.

Another organ involved in this complex of plans and projects was the National Economic Development Authority. Although its chair in Manila was the president and the secretaries of selected agencies also sat on its board, NEDA was mandated to work independently of the government. Its advice to its own board, and to other national-line and local government agencies, was said to be technical and impartial and, as we noted earlier, its civil servants were rather proud of their independence from political influence. In common with the Department of the Interior and Local Government, NEDA's civil servants monitored and scrutinised the policies implemented and planned by the various development councils of the regions, provinces, cities, municipalities and barangays. Indeed, whilst MEDCO might have seen itself as the umbrella organisation for the regional development councils, these councils formally lay under NEDA. In Davao the regional director of the Authority and his assistant director were, respectively, vice-chair and secretary of the regional development council, which comprised the regional directors of those departments (fifteen in all) represented on the NEDA board in Manila, and, for good measure, a number of other agencies including Education, Tourism, and Social Welfare. Also sitting on the regional development council were: the provincial governors, the city mayors, the presidents of the league of mayors in each province, the mayors of capital towns and provinces; and private sector representatives (merchants and non-governmental organisations) who made up a third of the total membership. Given its membership and the pressures its members were under from so many different quarters, it was inevitable that the meetings of the regional development council should have been heated. Analyses were done, reports made, and statements issued; and all of this was drawn on, rejected or ignored as the bargaining proceeded. More money for one project in the constituency of one politician for this year would have to be balanced the next year by a project in another constituency. And much depended upon personality. The politician with a reputation for securing votes and funding would be more able to manoeuvre arguments and views his way; so, too, did the influence of the regional directors of national-line agencies, and their ability to secure funding for their own departments, depend less upon the status of their department than upon their own character and their own reputation as an *éminence grise*. Even the director of a large department could be outdone by the director of a smaller, less prestigious agency.

MEDCO, then, sat alongside a quagmire of monitoring, policing, suspicion and bickering interests – political, bureaucratic, civic and business. From this, the Council moulded its legitimacy. As the umbrella organisation for the regional development councils it was clearly part of what was evidently a set of democratic institutions and procedures with their own checks and balances. The Council provided the coordination and direction for economic development which those institutions did not seem to have. Its emphasis upon physical infrastructure, trade links and foreign investment were supported by well-rehearsed economic arguments. Its involvement with merchants, too, made for a better appreciation of economic circumstances than would otherwise have been the case. And these business interests were balanced by the presence of politicians and, in the regional development councils, by civic organisations. All this was image. MEDCO's true purpose was to by-pass the very mire of interests, procedures and agencies from which it derived its legitimacy. Merchants, politicians and the heads of the regional development councils, rather than jump into that mire with bureaucrat and every other interest group, preferred instead to enter the much smaller forum of the Council. Here they were insulated: from the competing designs of politicians and bureaucrats in Manila who exercised their influence through civil servants in the regional offices; from the regional bureaucrats' own more parochial interests; and from the concerns of civic organisations. Here, in the Council, they could present, discuss and pursue their own ambitions with greater clarity. Here, with their direct line to the president, and with the authority of the Office of the President behind them, politician and merchants had a better chance of asserting their will over the bureaucrat. The Council would not throw its weight about, though its representatives did approach other government agencies with the expectation that they would do as they were told whatever influence they thought they had, and whatever authority they thought they derived from their central office, from NEDA, or from the regional development council. If the Council's representatives did not receive the cooperation they expected it would be suggested quietly to the recalcitrant bureaucrat that his obstinacy might not be appreciated by his superiors. What the bureaucrat did then depended upon his assessment of the relative strength of his communities and of theirs. As for the elaborate plans and reports and analyses, they were but tinsel used to decorate and legitimise political decisions and interests.

In these ways, through the Council, or independently through their communities in Manila and Davao, would politician and merchant work. They would work first to have the regional development councils, the Department of Budget and Management, and other agencies (including, if possible, NEDA) support and rubber stamp their proposals. Then they would work to secure funding from whatever source they could. There were, in addition, funds earmarked in the budget for every congressman and senator, theirs to dispose of as they wish. The combined sum of this 'pork' was greater than the budget of many central government departments. This 'pork' would commonly be pushed towards projects of concrete, brick and iron. Whatever the use or irrelevance of these favoured projects to the economy and ordinary lives, and however connected or unconnected they might have been to wider plans and strategies, the project was the most visible demonstration of the politicians efficacy, the most obvious sign that he was delivering. It also strengthened his alliance with merchants. The project was usually tended out to private businesses through the Department of Public Works and Highways, which had its own large budget set well above the tiny running costs to which most other agencies were confined. 'Pork' and other money channeled towards this department soon ended up in either the pockets of the merchant or the politicians' and bureaucrats' bank accounts. Contractors regularly built into their costs payments to the Commission on Audit, bureaucrats at the Department of Public Works and Highways, and to the politicians who secured the funding and mentioned the right name to the right people. These additional costs often made the construction business rather unattractive to the smaller operators with their already small profits. Not surprisingly the contractual civil servants in the Council found it necessary for the sake of appearance to monitor closely and chivvy the Department of Public Works and Highways: targets had to be met while their political masters pursued their own more immediate interests. During the last half of the 1990s most projects (about two-thirds) funded nationally and undertaken by the Department of Public Works and Highways in Davao were handled by eight firms owned by five families. More than a third of these projects were awarded to just one family. Much the same could be said of projects funded locally: just under a half were awarded to nine companies. Seven of these also monopolised nationally funded projects. A very similar picture emerges if we trace the destination of foreign investments. More than 40 per cent of companies with projects approved by the Board of Investments (whose director was the brother of the presidential assistant) were either among the top 2,000 firms in the Philippines or among the top companies in Davao, or were owned by merchants whose other business interests ranked among the top 2,000. These same firms were also responsible for more than 70 per cent of all investments in Davao approved by the Board of Investments, and for a little under 60 per cent of all such investments across Region XI. These same firms accounted for more than half of all companies attracting foreign investment and registered with the Board of Investments, and for about three-quarters of all foreign investment. Among those companies which attracted the largest share of foreign investment were those owned by merchants who had been elected to, or whose relatives served in, the House of Representatives. There was, it would seem, a small political–merchant elite attracting foreign capital, and taking advantage of the tax concessions which followed in its wake.

Inevitably, however, MEDCO also found itself at odds with those agencies that it was supposed to coordinate. Whereas MEDCO saw advantage in the flow of labour overseas and in these migrants' remittances, and had pushed for the removal of barriers to the movement of labour and for the deregulation of recruitment agencies (something which the workers themselves did not object to), the Office of Overseas Workers Administration (which fell under the Department of Labour and Employment) had become more and more worried by what it saw as a drift towards an uncontrolled market. The Office extended insurance cover to migrants; it offered a small number of loans and advice to those migrants and their families who might wish to set up small businesses in the Philippines; and it awarded a few scholarships to help migrants' families in Davao to train for a better jobs at home. Most of the Office's time, however, was spent helping migrants who had run into trouble overseas. The migrants would usually contact their families in Davao; and it was their families who would contact the Office. The Office would then work through its representatives overseas and through its contacts with the migrants' own associations, which, as we saw earlier, often had political objectives and an international reach. It was not just that the work of the Office would be made more difficult by deregulation. Far worse was that there appeared to be an attempt by other agencies, including the Office's own Department of Labour and Employment, to contain its power. There were also mutterings about the size of the Office and about its budget swollen with the fees of overseas workers. The Office was forced to route all its communications through the Department of Labour and Employment in Manila and through the labour attaché in the Philippines' embassies and consulates. MEDCO's concern, and that of the Department of Foreign Affairs and other agencies, was that the Office's narrow obsession with welfare and its contacts with left-wing associations at home and overseas would conflict with broader diplomatic and economic interests.

Centralisation by default

There was, then, much pose in the declared missions of institutions, in their regulations and procedures, and in their plans and projects. The same may be said of the devolution of power to local government. Decentralisation was both a democratic imperative in the wake of People Power and, to some extent, a pragmatic necessity. The 'assistance' offered by national-line agencies to local governments was one of the masks of supervision. But there were still more effective ways of clawing back power to the centre. Centralisation was better achieved by default than it was by design.

The total sum of the internal revenue allotment from which each local government received most of its funding was fixed as a proportion of the Bureau of Internal Revenue's receipts in years prior to the current fiscal year.

The final amount, however, could be reduced if it would otherwise push central government into an unmanageable deficit. Around one-fifth of this amount was divvied out among all provinces; another fifth went to the cities, and another to the barangays; and the largest share, a little under a third, was given to the municipalities. The amount then received by any particular city, municipality, province or barangay was determined mostly by land area and size of population. Local governments also received a proportion of tax receipts from businesses engaged in mining, forestry, oil and gas within their territorial jurisdiction. They also had the authority to raise their own taxes on individuals (professional and community taxes) and on businesses. The rates of taxation, however, were prescribed by the central authorities, and varied with categories of goods and services, and with type of activity (such as wholesale and retail). In general, these rates were set at a higher level in the cities than in provinces, municipalities and barangays. The range of categories and activities on which each local government division might impose tax was also prescribed by the centre, and was different in each division. A city, since it was independent of a province, could impose all of the taxes that a province and a municipality would normally have imposed. This complexity arose partly from an attempt to ensure that within this nested hierarchy individuals and businesses were not overburdened with local tax: no person or business should have been taxed for the same thing by the various divisions of local government. It was also for this reason that local taxes accrued only to the local authorities in which a company's head office or main books of accounts were sited. Branches, sales offices and warehouses which accepted orders and issued receipts also had to pay tax to the local authority within whose jurisdiction they operated. Plantations, experimental farms and factories, though, had to divide the tax they paid between the local government in which they worked and the authority in which their principle office was sited.

All of this, combined with the weight of national taxation, and the requirement that businesses also had to contribute to their employees' social insurance funds, created ample room, and much incentive, for businesses either to limit their operations or to play with definitions, to misrepresent, and to evade. There were other problems, too, with the organisation and administration of tax, both local and national. We mentioned earlier the power of the ombudsman to examine the bank accounts of individuals accused of ill-gotten wealth. Yet, with the exception of that particular crime, and with very few other exceptions, it was extremely difficult to discover what went in and out of the bank accounts of businesses and individuals. The secrecy laws made it illegal for banks to disclose the details of an individual's or company's account to any person or agency of government, central or local. Tax assessments had to be calculated, therefore, from gross sales. And the sales were recorded by the businesses themselves.

The first difficulty, then, which the city government had to face if it was to collect the taxes due to it was to determine which businesses within their administrative jurisdiction were liable to pay tax. Businesses were obliged to register for a licence with the City Business Bureau, and it was these records which formed the basis of taxation. Yet the Bureau had to rely for all intents and purposes upon the willingness of firms to register, and to do so accurately. Corporations were also required to register with the Securities and Exchange Commission (SEC), and they could, if they wanted, also register with the Department of Trade and Industry (DTI). However, they did not need to do so with the SEC and DTI offices in Davao; and such records were in any event regularly passed on to Manila. Sole proprietorships also had to register with the DTI, but again they did not need to do so in Davao; and again these records were passed on regularly to Manila. Checking the Business Bureau's records of registration against those against held by the Securities and Exchange Commission and the Department of Trade and Industry would have required pulling and matching records from offices in Manila and many other parts of the Philippines. The results would have been expensive, time consuming and almost certainly unreliable. There was, in practice, no way of establishing who was operating in Davao and who was liable to pay tax there, short of walking the streets and conducting a physical census. And that is precisely what was done every five years or so. The difference in numbers between the forty thousand or so businesses recorded in long-hand in numerous volumes at the time of the previous census and the nineteen thousand or so businesses registered in the late 1990s was telling. Some of those 'missing' businesses had ceased trading and chosen not to inform the Business Bureau. There was, after all, no reason for them to do so: if they went out of business before the end of tax assessment period they would still have had to pay a tax for the whole year calculated from extrapolated gross receipts. Other businesses had moved out of Davao. Many others had simply failed to renew their licences. Others which had started up for the first time in Davao, or had moved into Davao from other parts of the Philippines, had not yet registered. And many of those which had registered had done so inaccurately, perhaps as sole proprietorships (which attracted a slightly lower rate of taxation than did corporations); or the category and activity of their business had been misrepresented, again because of differences in tax rates. Such delinquency was practised even by the largest, brightest, most profitable companies: they were already registered in Cebu or Makati and saw no reason why they should pay local taxes yet again to yet another local authority. The Bureau of Internal Revenue faced many of the same problems in its attempts to monitor the payment of national taxes. Like the Business Bureau, it found it difficult to identify which companies were operating in Davao and liable to pay tax within their jurisdiction. Businesses only needed to subject themselves to the scrutiny of the Revenue office in whose jurisdiction their principle office or main books of accounts were held. That the Bureau's regions for revenue collection did not always coincide with the administrative regions of the Philippines complicated matters still further. The Bureau of Internal Revenue, too, depended upon a door-to-door census and an occasional amnesty to establish a baseline for numbers of businesses and business earnings.

The regional offices of the Bureau of Internal Revenue, and the City Business Bureau, had much to do if they were to sort out the chaff from the wheat. And this even before they could begin to make their assessments. For reasons already set out, tax could only be assessed on the basis of sales within the jurisdiction of the City Business Bureau and the Bureau of Internal Revenue, and had to be declared by the company itself. Businesses were therefore required to issue official receipts. Such receipts had to include a coded authority from the Bureau of Internal Revenue to show that the Bureau had authorised the printing of the receipt. Receipts also had to be numbered serially, and they had to display the business's identification number. This number had to be registered with the Bureau of Internal Revenue. Businesses were also required to keep proper books of accounts. Monitoring proper book-keeping and correct issuance of receipts for sales and purchases, however, was extremely difficult. Revenue district officers could recommend which businesses were selected for audit but, as we have already noted, approval had to be sought in Manila before the regional director could authorise the auditors to go to work. And whilst the Bureau had the authority to carry out the surveillance of businesses, the surveillance had to be overt and conducted over thirty days. Officers had to ensure that proper receipts were indeed issued for every transaction during that period. The sales and purchases for that period were then compared with the previous thirty days recorded by the company. If the level of sales for that latter period were more that 30 per cent below that recorded by the Bureau's officials during the surveillance period, then it was concluded that the business had been under-reporting its sales. The Bureau could then recommend closure for ten days, after which time the company's books could be examined. Again authorisation for closure and examination first had to be granted by the Bureau's office in Manila. If a business refused to submit itself to an examination, the Bureau could then turn to the courts to compel it to present its books. And, indeed, the Bureau's legal division spent much of its time countering such refusals. Meanwhile, the merchants had plenty of time to alter or to create anew their accounts, and to marshal their communities to their defence. The problems of the Bureau did not stop here, however. As we have said, the Bureau had to be meticulous in the way it gathered evidence to prove evasion, particularly if the merchant was also a politician. But the courts, or so it seemed to the Bureau and other agencies such as the Economic Intelligence and Investigation Bureau, were generally partial and were more likely to find in favour of the merchants, whoever they were. Then there was the fact that the number of people in the Bureau dedicated to the investigation and pursuit of businesses was very small – no more than five in the regional office. During the last half of the 1990s the Bureau's special investigation section brought to court only four cases of tax fraud and evasion. Two of these were referred to the Bureau's Manila office. Two were still winding their way through the Regional Trial Courts.

If assessment and investigation was difficult for the Bureau, it was impossible for the city government. The Business Bureau had an *ad hoc* team which was supposed to identify and pursue delinquent businesses. Local government also had the power to examine books, and it had recourse to administrative and judicial remedies including the seizure of property (including bank accounts), subject to the ruling of the courts. But examining the books of larger companies in Manila, and gathering evidence of sufficient quality, required accountants more skilled and resilient than local government could afford.

The effect of selectively observing the very procedural, legislative and legal complexity with which the image of devolution and democratic accountability had been created was to help to concentrate businesses and tax revenues in the National Capital Region. As we shall see in the next chapter, the majority of the largest and most powerful businesses were based here; and it was here that vast bulk of internal revenue collections (around four-fifths) were generated. Bureaucrats and politicians at the centre were happy to keep revenues close to them, and out of the unsure hands of local governments and the Bureau's provincial civil servants in the rest of the country. And merchants, as they struck agreements at the centre of power with the national offices of the Bureau of Internal Revenue and with national politicians, were happy to ignore the wishes of local governments in the provinces. The convolutions and weakness of tax administration had another effect. They made it easy to conceal, and difficult to uncover, what it was that businesses were doing. This worked against the interests of a national government as an institution, but in favour of those people who comprised it.

Surviving the personal

Government and bureaucracy was made of communities which extended within and across the branches and divisions of the executive, legislature and judiciary. The 'absolute' was perhaps stronger among politicians and bureaucrats than it is sometimes thought, but for the most part the 'personal' dominated. Among these battling communities, suspicion nurtured a desire for monitoring and policing; defensiveness strengthened; image-making, already a natural and important part of everyday life in places like Nazareth, was made inseparable from survival and ambition; even corruption was corrupted by such image-making; and the ideals of the absolute, too, seemed more and more like a feint. Thus were bureaucrat and politician thrown back upon their networks of relationships, and faith in government and civil service allowed to dwindle. Suspicion fed again, and the tangled mass of networks hove once more.

Even of the judiciary there were doubts. The judiciary, it was true, commanded far greater respect than politician or bureaucrat: like the Church, it was a symbol, imperfect though it was, of the absolute. The judiciary was certainly better insulated from executive and legislature. The decisions of the lower courts were reviewed by the Court of Appeals and by the Supreme Court (the court of last resort), whose justices were appointed by the president from a list of names selected by the Judicial and Bar Council. These justices were appointed for a fixed term without reappointment; and they had the power to remove judges in the lower courts. And whilst there were necessary restrictions on the judiciary's power to interfere with the reasonable decisions of government agencies, there also existed between the judiciary and the bureaucracy, more inquiring, more searching, tendrils. Disputes over an election result, for instance, were lodged either directly, or on appeal from the lower courts, with the Commission on Elections in Manila. The Commission's regional offices had the authority to investigate allegations and to issue subpoenas for the production of documents, though first they had to secure permission from their head office in Manila. It was also the head office which assigned cases to its officers in the regions. Appeals against the Commission's findings could be made to the Court of Appeals and, in the last resort, to the Supreme Court. Another such tendril was the Tanodbayan or, in other words, the Office of the Ombudsman. The ombudsman was selected by the president from a list provided by the Judiciary and Bar Council. He and his regional assistants investigated allegations of improper behaviour among bureaucrats and politicians. They also had their own court, the Sandiganbayan, which had prime jurisdiction to try and render judgments against politicians and bureaucrats at grade twenty-seven and above who, it was alleged, had violated the Anti-Graft and Corrupt Practices Act. They could also hear appeals against judgments made in the Regional Trial Courts in cases involving lower-ranking officials. All their decisions could be reviewed by the Supreme Court.

Yet the lower courts (the Metropolitan Trial Courts in Manila, the Municipal Trial Courts in cities and municipalities outside the capital, and the Municipal Circuit Trial Courts, which served more than one municipality), and the second-level courts (The Regional Trial Courts) could still be influenced by the politician. Nor was the judiciary free from the vices of neglect, connivance, self-interest, or as a *cri de coeur* against the political establishment, extreme leniency. And even if people were now more aware of their rights and privileges and believed that these could be defended and exercised through the courts, justice was slow and delays were lengthening: litigation had become more common, the budget remained small, the number of courts had stayed the same, the courts' rules of procedure were complex, and cooperation between the judiciary and other agencies (such as the Department of Justice, which handles state prosecution and state defence) was poor. Worse still, the reputation of the judiciary for impartiality, and the ideals of the absolute, could also be turned to the service of the personal. Laws and procedures defending secrecy in financial affairs were rigorously observed, but government agencies crucial to the administration of the state's financial affairs were left weak, such that circumstances and judgments inevitably swung in favour of the merchant, the politician with business interests, and the centre.

It was with an easy cynicism that those responsible for scrutinising the probity of government were portrayed by the venal as charlatans clothed with righteousness, and constantly accused by them of wrong-doing. The righteous then became so defensive in their behaviour, and their concern with their image became so acute, that they began to look both paranoiac and guilty. After a high-raking official at the Commission on Elections dismissed a case brought by a losing candidate against a victorious one, a complaint of bias and collusion was then made against that official and lodged with the ombudsman. The matter was then referred by the ombudsman to Commission on Election in Manila. The official knew that his reputation was an honourable one, and he knew, through his membership of ARENA, through his day-to-day work in the Commission, and though his kinship links with other departments, that this reputation was well known to all. He knew, therefore, that at the very least those who sat in judgment of him would not be prejudiced against him. The allegations were duly investigated and then dismissed. But the affair was worrying, and even though he was cleared, accusations would leave a smell. Had not his friends in the service, some would say, merely closed ranks? It would have been much better to avoid accusations in the first place. Every request made of him for advice and information, and every reply he gave would have to be documented; every 'i' had to be dotted, and every 't' had to be crossed. As a chairman of the Board of Canvassers, that same official was bound by duty to proclaim the victory of the city mayor, and by courtesy not to refuse an invitation to the new mayor's victory celebrations. But though he did not say 'no', he did not say 'yes' either; and the celebrations went on without him. Had he attended the party, he believed, the losing candidate would have declared the election rigged. Defensive behaviour such as this had even cost him his ride to work. Every morning the regional prosecutor (in the

Department of Justice) had given him a lift in his car until the day that prosecutor declared his intention to resign his post and run for councillor. From that moment on he would use a jeepney. Officials in the Office of the Ombudsman had to play the game. It was not uncommon for an investigating officer to find that a civil servant who was in some way connected to, or the subject of, the case they were working on was a fellow alumni or classmate, or known to a colleague in the Office. In this event the officer concerned had to make sure that she did not leave herself open to allegations of collusion: she would not even attend the same parties or other social gatherings as the official who was under investigation. It was all a question of her own political survival.

As they looked at all this, those who were not politicians or bureaucrats could easily be forgiven if they felt that they had no choice but to rely on their own communities. And if they should have had dealings with politician and bureaucrat, then why should they not have done their best to turn these public servants to their own personal advantage? Unfair though it is to tar all with the same brush, these seething communities, driven by the noble and the base, the pose and the sincere, appeared from the outside to have no purpose other than to perpetuate themselves. If one was not part of them, they seemed unapproachable, self-interested, and partial, while the bureaucracy's institutions, yawing and rolling with the swell and uncertain currents of these communities, looked precarious, fragile and flimsy. Policies and plans were produced for decoration; and running costs, though difficult to estimate, were high. At best, such costs probably amounted to more than a quarter of the budget. When combined with expenditure on local government, the armed forces, the police and debt repayments, that figure rose to more than half of the budget. Add in the salaries of teachers, and maintenance of schools, and that figure rose again to around two-thirds of the budget. The remaining money was fought over all the more fiercely by congressmen and senators – all hoped to keep their constituencies happy and themselves in office.

3 Making relationships pay

Introduction

The social and political, as we have seen, were not merely blurred: the one lay within the other. Institutions did not merely arise from networks of relationships; they were, in a very real and practical sense, a nexus of such relationships. And what was true of the society and polity was also true of the economy. Around whatever kernel that was best suited or convenient, relationships were formed or manoeuvered into place; and upon these an operation capable of turning a profit was set up. Most people in the Philippines who worked (more than half) were either self-employed or worked unpaid in their family's businesses; and of the remainder, most received a wage from a non-profit association, charity or religious organisation of some kind, or from their own family, or from businesses that were usually organised around kinship. As in political and bureaucratic life, the translation of relationships into economic organisations was shaped by the personal and the absolute. But so much more central to the everyday life of so many people were economic matters, that the manner in which relationships were made to pay was bound to have the most profound implications for the character of the Philippines' society and polity.

Family business

From the gloom behind the bars and nets of the *sari-sari* stalls in Nazareth, disembodied faces peered out. A dozen or so of these cells had been knocked together in recent years with money sent back from sons and daughters, fathers and mothers, and uncles, aunts and cousins working overseas. The goods – cigarettes, beer, rum, sweets, cans of fish and corned beef, mosquito coils, sweet bread rolls, lighters and oil, and whatever else took the owners' fancies – were most commonly bought retail or wholesale from supermarkets, and then resold in their stalls at a slightly higher price. All the stores' owners offered credit: how could they refuse it to their families, friends, and neighbours? Most debtors would pay their debts eventually, though at the end of each month it was usual that more credit than hard currency had been earned, and buying in new supplies was made difficult. The store made a little something every now and then, but for many owners it became a diversion in which their tattered dreams rattled around. The 'Chinese' store was more successful, partly because it was an offshoot of a larger empire, and partly because its owners were able to keep their relationships within Nazareth on a strictly business footing and yet remain accommodating. This they did by giving credit and heavy discounts or crates of beer and bottles of rum to Inday, Dee and other notables. It was less a question of being an outsider than of melding their own community into those which they found around them in Nazareth, and of doing so on their own terms. But this was much easier done if one came from the outside; and this Henry appreciated. The competition and rivalry with which he had felt himself surrounded had persuaded him to farm his own land away from Davao. When in the army he had been assigned to a municipality in Zamboanga where the Abu Sayaf, other Muslim groups, and the New People's Army had been active, and bloody feuds between families were common. Officers could not expect to be effective with only their own regular troops to command. As in Nazareth, the guerrilla and informer could be husband, father, friend, neighbour, petty criminal, thug and idealist. They were like a gas. Only when they changed their nature, when they hardened temporarily into an organised band, could they be sought out, attacked and killed. The only way to counter them was to build relationships with those who were themselves already, or could make themselves, part of the webs to which guerrillas and warring families belonged. They became his militia, his friends; they provided him with intelligence and security; they followed those of whom they were suspicious from one house or meeting place to the next, and would try to find out what was said and what was being planned. Meanwhile, Henry kept his regulars disciplined and in good order; and he plied his hosts with favours. He set up a nursery in the town, near to the municipal hall, and stocked it with seedlings and cuttings which he took from his parent's farm in Binugao. Durian, mango, and jubelina he brought in their thousands, and gave to his hosts. And from the municipality he took farmers in their twos and threes back to the farm in Binugao where he taught them what he had learnt in college, and from experience, about cultivating such crops. The reputation he soon established for himself was that of generous man, fair and just. When people looked at the trees which had been raised in the nursery and now lined the streets, and when they looked at the new crops being grown by the farmers, they would think well of him. And all this was what he had intended. He saw here an opportunity to set up his own farm, his own business, his own life, free of what he felt to be a lifetime of subordination, slights and mean comparison.

With one member of his militia, who subsequently became the town's mayor, he was fortunate, or sagacious, enough to form a strong friendship. He was the sponsor at Henry's wedding, as Henry was at his son's wedding. It was as mayor that he pointed Henry in the right direction when he decided to buy land there. The mayor and the other leading lights eyed carefully those who came into the municipality intending to buy land there. Opportunists would be dissuaded by fair and foul means, and those who they felt had higher motives would be encouraged. With money loaned to him by the army (and repaid little by little through his salary), Henry gradually bought forty hectares of land split into four unequal parcels in two barangays. To build his house he needed only to buy its materials. Such was his reputation, and such had been his generosity, that men gave their labour free of charge. Even now, after he had left the army, the mayor would arrange for his land to be watched and protected and tended while he was away on his visits to Davao.

These were not always happy visits. He longed for the good times, for his childhood, to be a part of his family as it had been. Yet he also wanted independence and recognition. His emotions bubbled and gave energy to old frustrations. The Binugao affair chafed him most especially. It was good land. It had given him thousands of fine, strong plants for Zamboanga. He had tried to register the farm as a corporation. But David, seeing this as a move by Henry to position himself for a claim on their parents' estate, had opposed it. Henry had thought David's suspicions and opposition foolish. If they would only follow his vision and work with him, much could be achieved: they only had to look at Johnny to see that.

Johnny and his wife had come to Davao at about the same time as Henry's parents had arrived. Johnny had been a teacher, but had not enjoyed the work. The Bureau of Internal Revenue was the only other opening to him available at the time. It was known then, as it is now, both within and outside the civil service, as one of the best departments to make some money; and knowledge of the Bureau's workings was useful to his wife's furniture business which, though more of a hobby than a vehicle for ambition, turned a small profit. They saved, and with their savings they bought land. For them, as for Inday and Dee, it was a form of security; it was a good investment; and it gave Johnny in particular an opportunity for exercise. The city expanded, land prices rose, and he sold his plot to a religious institution at some gain to himself. With this he bought a much larger plot further from the city. There he would go each day after leaving the office, and, as the sky turned purple, he would sow whatever occurred to him in an earth of deepening vermilion. His wife too occasionally pottered about with a trowel in hand. It was she who had the idea to grow orchids. This she did, for pleasure at first, and then for pocket money. It was their daughter-in-law (through Giddeon, their eldest son) who suggested that they should try cloning their flowers. Before reading medicine she had studied agricultural science. With her knowledge and with the help of Giddeon (who had been steered into medicine by his mother) they could now manufacture orchids of identical quality and in large numbers. This would turn their occasional business into something quite different. Johnny and his wife borrowed from the banks and bought irrigation equipment, netting and incubators, and they made their own jars and shakers. They took their new employees from the surrounding farms: once drawn into Johnny's community, they would be less likely to pilfer from him and more likely to act as a buffer against those who would. And he and his wife began to add to their business, transforming the nursery into what was also a pleasant retreat with conference and seminar rooms, a restaurant and cafeteria.

They enjoyed running and profiting from their business. Only when they could no longer manage it would they hand it on as a corporation to their children. Until then their children and their spouses, though they had helped in their different ways, would be kept quite separate from the business. Giddeon and his wife had their own practice; and aside from the technical advice they gave they did not have much to do with the nursery directly. Through a flower shop opened by their eldest daughter's husband in Manila, and through another shop established separately by their youngest daughter in Davao, they sold a small part of their orchid crops. But the nursery did not rely on the shops for its market, and the shops did not rely on the nursery for their supplies; and there was no cross-subsidy. If money was needed it was lent formally under contracts and at interest. Nor could their children's enterprises benefit from various tax exemptions to which they would have been entitled had they been a part of Johnny's business and therefore classed as an agricultural venture. Nor could they benefit from the half-closed eye with which the Bureau looked at one of their own, retired though he now was. Johnny distanced his children's businesses in this way to encourage independence, and to cut away the responsibilities and worries that he and his wife might otherwise face in their advancing years. While they were alive and still sensible, he would not allow disputes over business to intrude into family life. It was also partly for this reason, and partly in order to reduce the tax which he might otherwise have had to pay, that he would buy and sell only in cash, and would never extend credit to his friends. He had over the years known too many businesses which had failed because of emotional turmoil within the family. One only had to look at Lucy, with whom Johnny and Dee and their families had become such good friends. When Lucy and Inday had first met they discovered they were from the same town in Cebu; vague, and never-specified, kinship ties were then concocted to help explain their close friendship and Indays' empathy with Lucy and her struggle to keep afloat the restaurant where she and Dee and her children would so often eat free of charge.

Lucy was very close to her mother who in recent years had begun to drift into senility. Her mother had started with a small, open-air stall that offered half-a-dozen kinds of food. Lucy had worked with her before and after classes throughout her school and college days. Over the years the business flowered slowly into a restaurant, with its own branch, and a livestock division which bought and sold live pigs and cattle in Davao, Cebu and Manila. The practices and techniques which her mother had used as the businesses grew, Lucy adopted and continued. Profits were kept small but the turnover was high. Most importantly they worked hard at their reputation for cleanliness, good food and good service – a reputation which spread by word of mouth through their customers, through Lucy's networks and those of her mother, her brothers and her sister. In this way they established a sound and ever-growing core of patrons who returned again and again. Of particular value were the bureaucrats. If they liked the food and the atmosphere they would return most days, and sometimes in the evenings and during the weekends too. And if they were throwing a party at home they would be certain to ask Lucy to cook the lechon and other dishes. In return she lavished them with discounts and credit (anything from ten or twenty days to eighteen months) and even a free meal every now and then. She would sometimes extend the same courtesy to her other customers, though if she did not know them well or if she thought that they had come to expect a discount and were taking advantage of her, then she would first raise the price before offering to reduce it, and she would be hesitant to offer them credit. Her refusals were made with humour and affected exasperation: she did not want to offend but she could not ask her friends to keep her in poverty.

Her own children she dissuaded from entering the family business. Her eldest son was, with a kind of inevitability, encouraged to read medicine; the others studied agri-business and marketing. She, too, wanted her children to be independent, though lent her eldest son money to set up his clinic; and she was saving to give her other children the same advantage once they had qualified in their chosen professions. There was also a desire on her part to broaden the family's base: resting her future and that of her children upon the vicissitudes of the catering business was not in her view a wise strategy, and would not provide them with the status that she wished for them. Above all, perhaps, was the concern that her relationships with her children, and their relationships with each other, might be tainted – much as her relationships with her brothers had been – by arguments over the business. As Lucy's mother aged, she let the livestock division fall into the hands of Lucy's brothers, and gave Lucy authority over the core of the business – the restaurants. The two parts of the company remained under one business licence (registered in Lucy's name) but were run independently. To her brothers the arrangements seemed unjust. As if to add insult to injury Lucy would not favour their supplies of live pigs over those of their competitors: she would only buy what she thought to be the best meat at the best prices. And whilst she had, to begin with, lent them money, she had not received the return she had expected and was reticent to lend them any more. The livestock trade may well suffer from the difficulty of late payments, she had said, but the catering trade was also risky. She would not add to her risks at a time when she had, for the first time, borrowed a large sum of money to set up a new branch that was only just beginning to break even. All this, too, caused bad feeling. Then her brothers had acted clumsily.

Lucy had been careful to renew her business licence and pay her taxes. After 30 years she had learnt that rather than play them for fools, it was always better to establish good relationships with officers of the Bureau of Internal Revenue who, in any case, with their strong *corps d' esprit* and deep pockets, made good customers. And she and her mother had indeed built up a sound understanding with them. They would take into account the vagaries of her trade, the loans she now carried, and the news that she had until recently been subsidising her brothers. They appreciated that she was only trying to make a living in an uncertain world; and she knew that they needed to bring in a reasonably convincing stream of revenue. They would negotiate with her in a calm, friendly, informal manner, and reach a settlement in which she would be allowed to under-declare her sales, and stagger her tax payments. Her brothers, however, had under-declared their sales, and had tried to hide it from a Bureau officials who lay outside her community. When the official examined the port authority's records of shipments, and found that the volume of trade was far greater than her brothers had made out, the lie was discovered. As holder of the business licence under which her brothers operated, it was Lucy who was liable to pay their back tax and penalties. There was also the possibility that it might seem as if she had gone behind the back of those officials with whom she normally dealt. So she paid for her brothers' cack-handedness and explained to her friends in the Bureau what had happened. She then turned on her brothers: she had lent them money and received nothing in return; now she had paid their taxes and their fines; and she had had to patch up relationships which she and her mother had worked hard at over many years. She instructed them to apply for their own permits, and she made arrangements to turn her side of the company into a corporation. She would hold 50 per cent of the shares. Of the other half, her sister was given the majority and the remainder were divided equally among her brothers, who were thus left with a small stake in a business from which they were effectively insulated and would find difficult to tear at after their mother's death. In return for this reprieve (Lucy had toyed with the idea of giving them nothing) they could expect no help in their own business affairs.

There was much bitterness now, and much sorrow. Lucy had seen her mother struggle all her life to give her family something, and she had struggled with her. Lucy was now repaying that debt and affection and carrying on her mother's work; and with a light humour she and her children and her new bouncy grandchildren had accepted the inconveniences which her mother's failing mind and body caused them. Her brothers, she thought, had been remarkably selfish in their actions and had threatened to undo all that had been done. By distancing her own children from the business and by encouraging their independence, she hoped to spare their future from the heartaches of her past. She had not ruled out a successor. If there was to be one it would be her eldest daughter. But her daughter was interested in other things at the moment and Lucy would not press her into a business which guaranteed nothing.

This was not a crude response by a small-time trader with a shaky education. Insulating the business from one's own relatives, and in other ways distancing relationships within the organisation, was a solution to the problem of instability arrived at by the larger and more illustrious of merchants. Noy was in a similar line of business as Lucy. He owned half-a-dozen or so restaurants and bakeries. He had been born into purple. His family were landed, and all were true Dabaweyneans, migrants who long before the second war had arrived in Davao and there had bought land from the indigenes or married into their families. From the sprawling verandah, positioned to welcome the cooling breeze which swept in from the sea, turning the leaves and long grass pale, his grandfather would view his estate, planted with abaca. Even at that time their way of life and their standing was being challenged, though they did not know it. Their estate had been worked by Japanese emigrants from Kyushu, Okinawa and western Honshu who had first come to the Philippines to help the Americans to construct roads. The Japanese were not merely good estate workers; they also proved themselves adept at managing large estates and acquiring land despite legislation introduced in 1919 to limit their growing wealth. More importantly, they came to dominate commerce and it was they, rather than the Chinese, who controlled retailing and industries such as hemp, fishing and lumber. After the war, with the decline of the abaca and the disappearance of the Japanese, commerce began to thrive more than ever as new merchants from the north moved in. It was not that Noy's grandfather had missed an opportunity; it was simply that he was not prepared to change. Neither he nor his family would borrow money or dirty their hands in business. And so, little by little, they sold off their land and property to keep themselves in comfort, and to pay for the education of their children and grandchildren who would be expected to secure the family's name in the professions. For Noy, law had been chosen. Although it required him to undertake menial tasks (as would any profession) it was more than a cut above trade. So it was with great disappointment and shame that he failed the bar exam. His choices were now limited. Take the exam again, knowing that even if he should pass he would be tainted with that failure always. Or try his hand at business. It was not what he wanted: the merchants, though in the ascendancy, were still immigrants who were merely buying up symbols of prestige and worth. Yet he had no option; and perhaps there was more value in the merchant than his material wealth. His wife, who he had met at high school, and her family were, after all, of this new breed from the north. He borrowed money from her relatives, and from the sale of a few remaining parcels of his land and property, he generated some cash of his own. With this they set up a small restaurant with a handful of employees. In his own stock, too, dated though it was, he saw much that would be of use in business. With his connexions, and sense of etiquette and taste, he could soon make their restaurants fashionable and prosperous. In the feudal relationship which had had at its core the landowners and estate workers sense of mutual responsibility, Noy also saw much that would be advantage. He and his company were deliberately paternalistic. He created in his employees the sense that their community, their networks of relationships, lay within the company and not outside it. After his workers had been with him for more than two years, he bought land and houses which he would sell on to them at no profit to himself and by installments without interest over as long a period as they wanted or could afford. He also provided them with grants for furniture. As the company expanded, or as workers left or died, and vacancies arose, his employees' children were given preference. This supplemented his employees' wages, and made it more likely that his new workers would be inculcated with the values and practices which he had endeavoured to instill in their parents. For the uneducated, and especially for the Bagobo to whom he traced his ancestry, he had a soft spot. They were, he believed, a simple people in whom his values and beliefs could be sown and nurtured with even greater ease. The company was to him, as it should be to his employees, a family. He did not count the hours he worked, and he did not expect them to measure the length of their days either. Loyalty mattered above all else. Just as he was responsible for them, they had a responsibility to him and to each other.

These relationships were undoubtedly manipulative and stylised. Noy achieved over his workers a moral supremacy, and established in them a sense of obligation, a sense of demiurgic paternalism, and he used the relationships which they had formed among themselves to control and monitor. But also there was in these relationships genuine affection on both sides, and with this came an easy informality. One of his weekly meetings with his key staff to discuss affairs and problems began slowly: they were suffering from a late night and seemed to have no energy to think or speak. On this he commented, adding that they probably needed something to eat. For this he would pay, and on to the table he threw a ragged and dirty bank note of twenty pesos – a derisory amount. They looked at the limp shred of paper on the gleaming table and, with heavy sarcasm and broad smiles, began to discuss what they should buy. The same joking informality with which he treated them, and they he, also marked his relationships with more junior staff. It was not unusual for a young woman to knock at his door and ask for a contribution to this or that charity, or for some or other function. Always, a feigned grumpy rebuke from him; always the childish pleading and a gentle stamp of the foot in reply; always the burst of laughter and the money produced. Of his lowliest employees, too, he had an intimate knowledge of their circumstances and troubles, such that during birthdays and other celebrations he could wander from one house to the next without invitation gifts in arms to find himself welcomed at one house after another with a warm respect.

There was also a strong sense of the absolute to which that affection, warmth, informality and respect owed something. He would not be the *ninong* of his workers: in that practice he saw favouritism, and favouritism he discouraged. Preference may have been given to his workers' children and to the Bagobo. It was his judgment of their qualities and abilities, however, that was paramount: break the rules and you will fire yourself. He gave voice to his belief that there was in human relationships an inherent worth. You should treat others only as you would have them treat you. Fairness, honesty, warmth and affection – these were good and proper qualities in their own right. These beliefs, sentiments and values he proselytised with religious zeal. Every Good Friday he held a retreat, in which he, his family and a selection of the great and the good from Davao, cooked for and served his employees, who were compelled to attend. Here he would entwine the spirit of his company with religious teachings and programmes for husbands and wives. Then they would pray together. His enthusiasm did not stop there. He organised similar gatherings which were neither compulsory for, nor restricted to, his employees, and in which he had embroiled the energetic Inday and the reluctant Dee. There was no artifice in these gatherings, no contradiction or hypocrisy, at least none of which I think he was aware. The webs of relationships which he used consciously to hold his company together and to give it direction were also shaped into a convenient pulpit from which he preached his belief in the absolute: relationships and the noble emotions were inherently right and just, and in their treatment as such much practical value also lay.

Nowhere did he practice what he preached more assiduously than within his own family. When old enough, his children were brought into the company to experience its working. But only he and his wife (who was its treasurer) and one son were involved in its day-to-day operations. His other children – though directors – had their own lives and professions. They were teachers or lawyers, and one owned a business overseas. And it was made quite explicit to all that their family relationships should be kept quite separate, emotionally and institutionally, from their work within the company and their interests in it. Once a decision had been made, even if should prove not to have been the best, everyone must rally in support of the company without qualms or bickering; and disputes over matters at work should never be taken into the home. There were to be offered no discounts or free meals in the restaurants or bakeries, and none were to offered to their own families or friends. Pay was strictly controlled, and whilst the company would provide medicines for family members, they would be given no cash no cash with which to buy those medicines. And any other businesses in which they might be involved were to be kept financially separate from the company. Distancing relationships in this way had an almost spiritual as well as practical quality. Their relationships with each other, and the warmth and affection which they felt for each other, were to be treated as important in their own right. This was a moral imperative. It would also help to keep the company on an even keel. If any reminder of the damage which family tensions posed to the company was needed, then they only had to look at Gregory, a relative of theirs who ran a popular and successful beach resort. He employed around two hundred workers, many of whom were the children or grandchildren of those labourers who had worked on the estates built up by his father and grandfather. Gregory bought up land and houses, just as Noy had done, and at no profit sold them to his workers by installments over two or more decades free of interest. He also spent much time cementing his relationships with his employees and their families. He was known to all them, and would often eat with them at their homes: he was treated by them 'as if a King', and they were his *bata-bata* (or, very loosely, 'runner'), willing to do him any kind of favour because it was an honour for them to be asked. And he would help them in all sorts of ways. He would use his influence if they or their kin have problems with the police; if their kin or close friends needed a job, he would do what he could to help them find one; he would even mediate in their arguments with their neighbours. Each week he would have to set aside several hours if the tide of petty disputes and problems in which his workers and their families had become embroiled was to be turned. But although he worked hard to create in his employees the sense that their community was the company, his relationships with his own family deteriorated. He owned the beach jointly with parents and his brothers and sisters, and they had demanded that he should turn his company into a family corporation. From his point of view this was nothing short of theft. Until he had made something of the beach his family had been disinterested in it. Their claims acknowledged his success and their failures. His brothers and sisters were envious; and neither his father and grandfather – both of whom had presided over the decline of the family's wealth and standing – had the skill, ruthlessness or willingness to take the risks necessary to run a successful business.

Noy had no intention of letting such bile spill into his company. He was also careful to distance the company's external relationships. These were no less crucial to its survival and success. Over the years he had set to busying himself in various associations. He became president of the Lions, director of the Rotarians, head of the Hotel and Restaurant Association, and national president of the Baker's Association. He was also a member the Davao City Chamber of Commerce, and of numerous religious associations by invitation of the bishop. He did not join these associations to meet customers, suppliers, bureaucrat or politicians. Such contacts could be made in the association, but this was a passing consideration. Far more important to him was that the association brought new dimensions and balance to his life, and gave him something beyond the routine of business and money-making. In his religious, charity and civic world (in to which he drew his employees) he felt that he was doing others some good; and as a representative of other merchants in his trade he also had a say on wider political and economic matters of the day. But it was the manner in which that influence was wielded that mattered in the end. One had to be acutely aware that in such organisations it was and easy to find oneself in relationships with the kind of people it was usually better to avoid. A merchant with money, and with standing in the association, had the advantage over the politician; and it would be more likely that the politician would want to seek out the merchant than vise versa. The merchant was useful not only for his money but for his business contacts, his influence over his trade, his workers, and his wider community. The politician who wanted to tap into notables such as Inday and Gloria would also want to tap into men with still broader communities. The merchant had to be careful. If his relationships were built around the give and take of money and favours, then he may become as obliged to the politician as the politician is obliged to him. The merchant would now be more vulnerable to the politician's fall from grace and to the politician's opponents. Noy therefore tried to establish relationships for their own sake, and to make this intention clear to bureaucrat and politician, even at the highest level.

It was as he lobbied politicians, asking them to break the monopoly over flour prices, that he met Shahani (the sister of Ramos) and Ramos himself, and struck up a friendship with them. He ran their campaigns in Davao, and when they visited the city they would stay at his house. He gave no money to support their campaigns, and was not asked for any. He helped because they seemed to believe with him in personal and institutional probity. He was therefore ideal to appoint as a director of the Philippine National Bank where he set policy, and assessed, granted or refused loans. On his appointment he was given strict instructions by Ramos in person not to allow politicians to influence his decisions. Shahani, too, asked him to judge applications on their merits regardless of whether others used her name, and, interestingly, regardless of whether she wrote in support of them. He did indeed receive informal applications and requests, though not from Shahani or Ramos, which he logged and ignored. He was even pursued to his house in Manila by representatives of this or that politician who asked no favours but wished to ply him with gifts, which he refused. And when he was taken to restaurants he would, without telling his hosts, leave his credit card with the cashier before the orders were made, with instructions that all charges should be made to his card. As among the bureaucrats, the extreme care he took to retain his purity looked so idealistic that it began to look more like image-making than substance. But he had to be so careful precisely because the absolute was so weak that even the most righteous behaviour could be presented in this unflattering light. By establishing relationships with Ramos and Shahani for their own sake, a certain steely clarity was introduced which did away for this uncomfortable, awkward obsession with the appearance of propriety. Such relationships not only distanced his work for the bank from his political friends, they were a symbol that both he and they were honest in their intentions, that each could rely upon the other. It was not a question of trust. Trust was merely to be expected of men and women who were professional and moral.

There was no doubt a certain amount of ambition in Noy's actions, and hubris in his altruism. But I do not believe he was driven self-aggrandisement, nor was it his intention to promote his business. His desire to distance his relationships was explicit, and he would act as he thought proper. He was of an age and mien that, for him, the mark which he, in quality of his being, would leave upon others mattered more than the acquisition of power and money. If by moving a little closer to the absolute he strengthened his reputation, and if this did his business well, then so be it. The fact that such benefits had been incidental would enhance his reputation still further. An association was simply a forum in which he could establish contacts with customers and suppliers if he wanted; and there he could, if he wished, find bureaucrats and politicians who might help avoid red tape. But these were small, mean, insignificant motivations. He could always find a civil servant: he knew the right people at the highest levels of national government; and his sister was a ranking officer in the local government. So broad was his community in the polity and among merchants, and such was his standing, that he had all the contacts he needed. Orders were made, credit agreed, and periods for repayment were fixed in a moment by word of mouth. And when he met a supplier in the street, or at some function, they could ask him with a smile when they might receive their cheque? Not yet? Will I get it? God

Willing! The easy, joking repartee was possible only because they knew he would not renege. With a broad community and sound reputation established outside the company, his authority within it was unquestionable.

The relationship between merchant and politician, then, could be far more complex than that of greed, bribery and privilege, and this was, I believe, the case more often than it is commonly thought. Less than 60 per cent of congressional representatives have interests in economic concerns of one kind or another. Of these representatives, around a half had declared ownership of, or investment in, land holdings (predominantly farmlands with an average value of a little over 2 million pesos) alone; less than 40 per cent had declared interests in both land holdings and business companies; and just under 20 per cent had interests in companies alone. As a proportion of all congressional representatives, only 7 per cent of representatives had declared investments, or held directorships, in companies (numbering 18 in all) which ranked among the top 2,000 companies; and just 2 per cent of all congressional representatives had interests, or held office, in companies among the 100 strongest companies nationally. The business interests of most senators, too, were in companies which did not rank among the top 2,000. One notable exception was Enrile, a minister in former administrations who accumulated considerable wealth during the Marcos years, and who, under Ramos, served as chairman of the Ways and Means Committee and of Government Corporations and Enterprises. His business interests extended through a number of companies that were directed primarily by his children.[1] Indeed, it may be that, on the whole, the very strongest companies may prefer to find entrée into government through a retired politician (a former secretary of foreign affairs, for example, has taken up directorships with the Equitable Card Network and Philippine Long-Distance Telephone) who knows well the machinations of politicians and civil servants, but is sufficiently removed from it all that no unwelcome and possibly harmful attention will be attracted. Or it may be that both company and politician will prefer their relationship to take the form of official appointments, setting their relationship, at least in appearance, upon a more professional, more predictable basis: politicians are appointed to directorships of private companies in which the government has a stake; and merchants are appointed to directorships of public companies. The San Miguel group, many of whose companies are among the top 10 or 50 companies in the Philippines, have as members of the board of directors a commissioner on the Presidential Commission on Good Government, a former under-secretary of foreign affairs (who is also on the Board of Governors of the Philippine Ambassadors' Association), and, until his death in 1998, secretary of the Department of Transport and Communications. This latter appointment was especially interesting in view of the strategic importance of distribution networks to the drinks industry. San Miguel's share of the market in this sector is substantial; and its share of the market of some products such as beer and hard liquor is well over 50 per cent. A number of San Miguel's directors also hold directorships of a number of public or formerly public companies including the Social Security System and the Government Social Insurance Scheme.

The estimates I have given are only indicative, and the extent and depth of the politicians' business interests was very likely to have been much greater than I have suggested. It may also be argued that the interests of many politically influential families in non-agricultural activities were not only growing, but – within the constraints of an élitist democracy and patron–client relationships – also represented a move away from the traditional social structure founded upon an agrarian economy. Certainly there were problems with the available records. Declared interests were generally incomplete: the names of businesses were not properly specified; and more often than not, declarations failed to show the value and precise nature of the politicians' interests. There was also a reluctance to make public what were supposed to be public declarations of assets and liabilities. Nor were the lists of officers and directors produced by companies, and the lists of owners and shareholders filed with the Department of Trade and Industry and the Securities and Exchange Commission, the City Business Bureau and the Bureau of Internal Revenue always entirely complete or accurate: owners and shareholders would operate through a third party or 'dummy'. In Davao, certainly, the connexions between, and the merging of, politician and merchant in Davao, were, in many instances, telling. The former mayor (pre-1998), and then congressional representative (1st district Davao), together with his former vice-mayor (who is now the mayor of Davao City) had major interests in one of the ten strongest companies in Davao City. This same congressman also had interests in a company that formed part of an extensive web of interests linked indirectly to the central web in Manila. His predecessor continued to offer what were described as 'services' through a business which he ran while he held political office. Another congressional representative (2nd district Davao), owned a law firm and a realty company. His daughter was married to the son of one of his two partners in the firm; and both his partners and his son-in-law were congressmen or former congressmen (in Isabela and Zambales). Neither company rated among the strongest 2,000 companies in the Philippines. But another congressman (1st district Compostella Valley, RXI) had extensive interests in one of the 50 strongest companies in Davao (Vitarich). This company was also one of the 50 strongest companies nationally and formed part of the central web in Manila. Yet another congressional representative (2nd district Davao del Norte), had close kinship ties with the merchant Florendo, who had extensive interests in a group of ranking corporations in Davao, two of which numbered among the strongest

2,000 companies in the Philippines. The office which he now held had previously been occupied by his relative Del Rosario, a former minister of the environment and natural resources, who now served as the governor of that same province, and held financial interests in the Florendo companies.

Nevertheless, the reasons why merchants and politicians were often reluctant to make known their interests in each other may also have been the reasons why they may have wished to 'distance' or professionalise their relationships in practice, and why the links which did exist between politicians and those businesses with the very strongest national presence tended to be more indirect than direct. To the merchant, politicians may be useful, even vital, at times; but the merchant cannot afford to be associated too closely with the rise and, as is the way in political life, the inevitable fall of the politician, more especially if the merchant is truly professional and if the politician is only a shallow courtier. In this regard, the relative decline of the once-dominant entrepreneur Florendo and the growing prominence of the Alcantaras in Davao during the Aquino and Ramos administrations, and then more recently under Estrada the strengthening of Cojuangco and Tan, apparently at the expense of the Sorianos and Ayalas, may be instructive lessons. Nor can those politicians who wish to establish for themselves weighty reputations leave themselves vulnerable to the charges of corruption (true or false) that are a part of the everyday cut and thrust of their profession. For both merchant and politician the distinction between the use and misuse of relationships is often so fine – no more than a word, or look, or conversation – that it is easy to leave oneself open to charges of misconduct when no impropriety has in fact occurred, or to find oneself too closely associated with another's political or business opponent. The patchiness of records tracing relationships between politicians and merchants which are, or appear to be, less extensive than might be expected, may have as much to do with the fear that some intrigue or charge of bias may be concocted around that relationship as it does with conspiracies to conceal, say, tax evasion or some other wrongdoing. This ever-present fear deepens around the time of an election when rumours fly, when journalists are especially busy in their attempts to uncover misdeeds, and when, more than usual, the observer is in danger of being fed, or of inadvertently drawing upon, misinformation that has been put about in the heat of political disputes which are often intensely personal. Both from the point of view of the high-profile merchant, and from the point of view of the politician, there is much sense in distancing their relationships either by placing them on an official footing or by feeding them through a retired politician or a smaller intermediary business.

In short, the tension and uncertainty in the relationships between merchant and politician may have stemmed, in part, from ethical concerns. Whether or not pure in intent, merchant, politician and bureaucrat had to make it appear that their conduct was proper, and would go to extraordinary lengths to create that appearance. These concerns may prove to be no more than a fashionable political tactic that will soon lose its value. Corruption, as was suggested earlier, has itself been corrupted; probity, too, can be part of the image-making which the personal induces. It would not be the first time during the last thirty years that the distancing of politicians from merchants and other shifts in nature of the relationships among politicians and merchants have been observed.[2] But it would seem unwise, then, to rule out the possibility that attitudes towards personal relationships in business, politics and everyday life are beginning to undergo just such a shift. As Tria Kerkvliet[3] has pointed out, it would be difficult to claim that the vision of all officials in all branches of the government and bureaucracy of the Philippines is limited by their personal ambitions. Even during the years 1961–86 there was a tendency for the Supreme Court to rule in favour of those people with less wealth and less influence from the poorer areas of the Philippines. By contrast, in the UK and the USA, judicatures were more likely to rule in favour of the establishment.[4] The return to democracy in the Philippines, the loss of patience with Estrada, the gradual professionalisation of the armed forces of the Philippines[5] and the civil service, the slow maturing of politicians,[6] and attempts by the Church to cultivate institutional and personal probity among politicians and members of the armed forces,[7] and the professionalisation of business practices, have been accompanied by, or have allowed more open expression of, a strengthening interest in kinds of debates – such as those surrounding the rule of law, individual and institutional probity, business ethics, moral codes, and contending ideologies[8] – commonly associated with the evolution of a market economy and mass representative democracy. These trends have perhaps stimulated, and have been stimulated by overseas Filipino migrants,[9] a comparatively broad and open education system, a lively media, and international trade; and by attempts to implement policies designed to favour smaller enterprises,[10] break up cartels, open up the economy to domestic and international competition, improve the tax system, reduce the exposure of banks to the property sector, reduce the volume of their non-performing loans, increase their minimum capitalisation,[11] and bring greater transparency, stability and predictability to the operation of financial institutions.

Professionalising the company, and creating the oligarchy

The shift in attitudes which occurred even within the smaller companies towards relationships seemed to strengthen in the larger, more polished organisations. This might, perhaps, have suggested the presence of a continuum born out of pragmatism. Those smaller enterprises whose merchants were less willing or able to distance and thereby translate their relationships into larger and more stable enterprises surrounded with broader opportunities for buying, selling and striking deals would soon find themselves and their companies outpaced by those merchants whose attitude was closer to the absolute. Transition along this imaginary continuum would have been marked by greater authoritarianism within the family company and the idealisation of trust and honour – qualities which brought stability, predictability and focus, and so enabled relationships to be 'turned' more effectively towards trade. Eventually, emotions such as affection, romantic love, trust, loyalty, friendship, altruism and kinship would have been transmuted into ideals thought of as definitively good in their own right, while jealousy, envy, resentment, perfidy, manipulation and bitterness would come to be seen as definitively 'bad'. Merchants would thus have come to rely more and more upon institutions, legislation and procedures while their dependency upon kinship and other limiting bases, such as ethnicity, would have become less sure.

In Davao, as across the Philippines, most companies (corporations, partnerships and single proprietorships) were based on the family. Those which appeared to form part of fairly complex networks (again framed around kinship) were clearly stronger than those organisations which operated either as part of much more restricted webs or as independent entities. The strongest companies which formed the primary core in Davao did not appear to form part of these more complex networks (Figure 3.1). But most of these companies (70 per cent or more) had a national or international scope, and most[12] were either branches, or the head office, of companies which ranked among the top[13] 2,000 companies in the Philippines. And seven of the strongest 10 companies in Davao, two-fifths of the strongest 53, and nearly a third of the strongest 124 companies were connected either directly or indirectly (through smaller companies which nevertheless rank among the top 2,000) with the Philippines' leading 100 companies, the majority of which were linked into a series of networks centred on Manila. The largest of these northern webs comprises nearly half of the Philippines' leading 100 corporations (Figure 3.2). Although kinship was still an important kernel around which these larger national companies and their networks gathered, it was less obvious and less complete in its dominance than among the smaller companies and webs in Davao.

Ethnicity, too, and most especially that well-worn *point d'appui* of 'being Chinese', seemed to wear thin as companies strengthened. Companies which formed the central, largest, and most powerful single web of corporations in Davao were predominately, though not exclusively, Chinese (as defined by names of the owners or major shareholders). And the proportion of 'Chinese' sole proprietorships expressed as a percentage of the total number of companies whose registered gross sales fell within P250,000 and P499,999, P500,000 and P999,999, and P1 million and P4.99 million, rose steadily from 11 per cent to 16 per cent and to 21 per cent respectively. But the proportion of 'Chinese' sole proprietorships then fell as sales increased: to 13 per cent (of all enterprises registering gross sales between P5 million and P9.9 million); and to less than 10 per cent (of all enterprises registering gross sales valued between P10 million and P49.9 million). Much the same could be said about partnerships and corporations.[14] Around a quarter of all partnerships and corporations registering gross sales between P250,000 and just under 50 million pesos were 'Chinese'. But more than 32 per cent could be described as 'cosmopolitan' – that is, their partners or shareholders comprised 'Chinese' and 'Filipinos', or 'Filipinos' and foreign nationals, or 'Filipinos', 'Chinese' and foreign nationals. If branches and subsidiaries of foreign multinationals – even though dominated in the Philippines by 'Filipino' (non-'Chinese') interests – could be described as 'cosmopolitans', then the proportion of cosmopolitans among the strongest 120 or so companies in Davao (each of whose sales exceed P50 million or, as is the case for the majority of companies, more than P100 million) rose to around 40 per cent. Among the strongest 100 companies in the Philippines, the proportion of 'cosmopolitans' rose to nearly 80 per cent, while the proportions of companies whose partners or major shareholders were exclusively 'Filipino' or 'Chinese' fell to 13 per cent and 5 per cent respectively.

But all this has about it the smell of the lamp. The substance of our relationships stays the same. It is only our attitude which shifts from the personal to the absolute, and the mind can always be changed, swiftly and easily. The strengthening and weakening of ethnicity is the most graphic expression of these casual, often momentary, shifts in attitude. Dried out by the personal, our many dimensions are left to form a sticky concentrate, a clot of surly difference. Diluted by the absolute, the clot dissolves, and our dimensions, and, thus, our sameness, become more apparent. Within the merchant, as within the Nazarene, this transmutation could occur in an instant; and the extent to which the Filipino or Chinese was seen to adhere to the personal or absolute itself became part of that ethnic caricature. The Chinese were – to many Chinese and Filipinos – clannish. They viewed emotions, circumstances and relationships objectively. They saw their relationships as being utilitarian. They saw politics as a business, not as the exercise of power for its own sake. They believed strongly to certain maxims: trust only those whom you know well; save for future investment; live within your means; negotiate hard but keep to your word; protect one another; perpetuate business through volume not through large profits. The Filipinos were, to many Chinese, outgoing, friendly and undisciplined. They were good singers and dancers and they enjoyed life, but they were unable to work hard or with a clear focus.

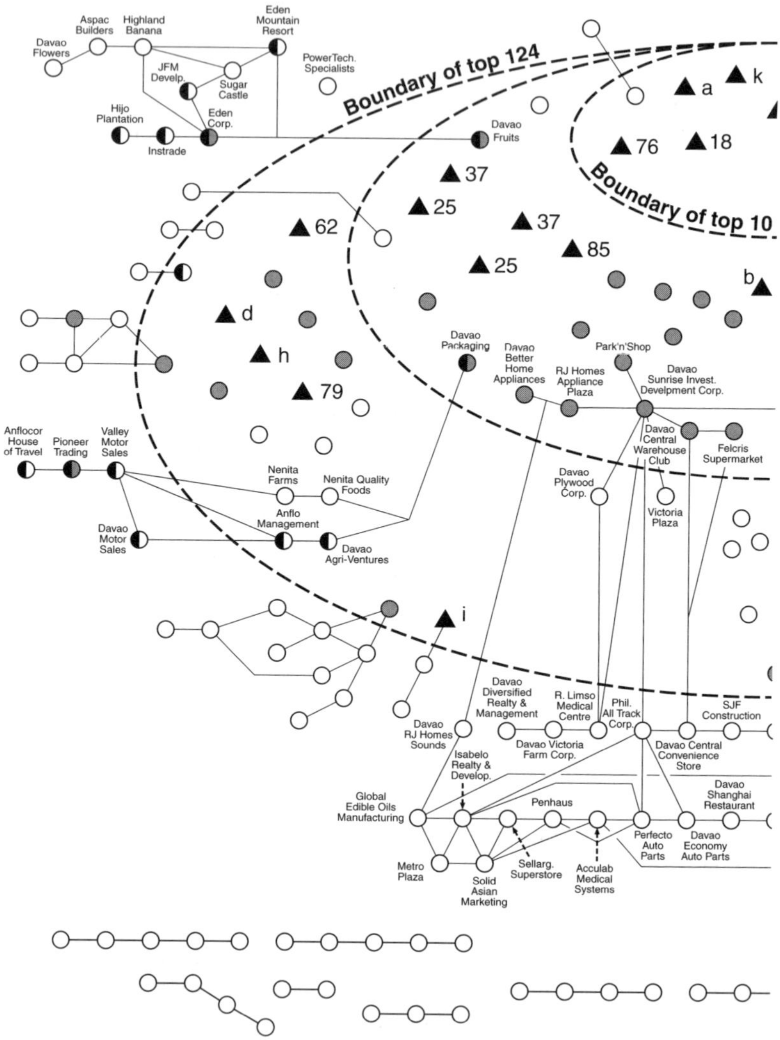

Figure 3.1 Merchants' interests in Davao

Key to Figure 3.1

—— interconnected ownership, directorship or major share holdings.

○ ranks among the strongest 300 companies in Davao.

● ranks among the strongest 2000 companies nationally. Predominantly branch companies but also includes some local companies.

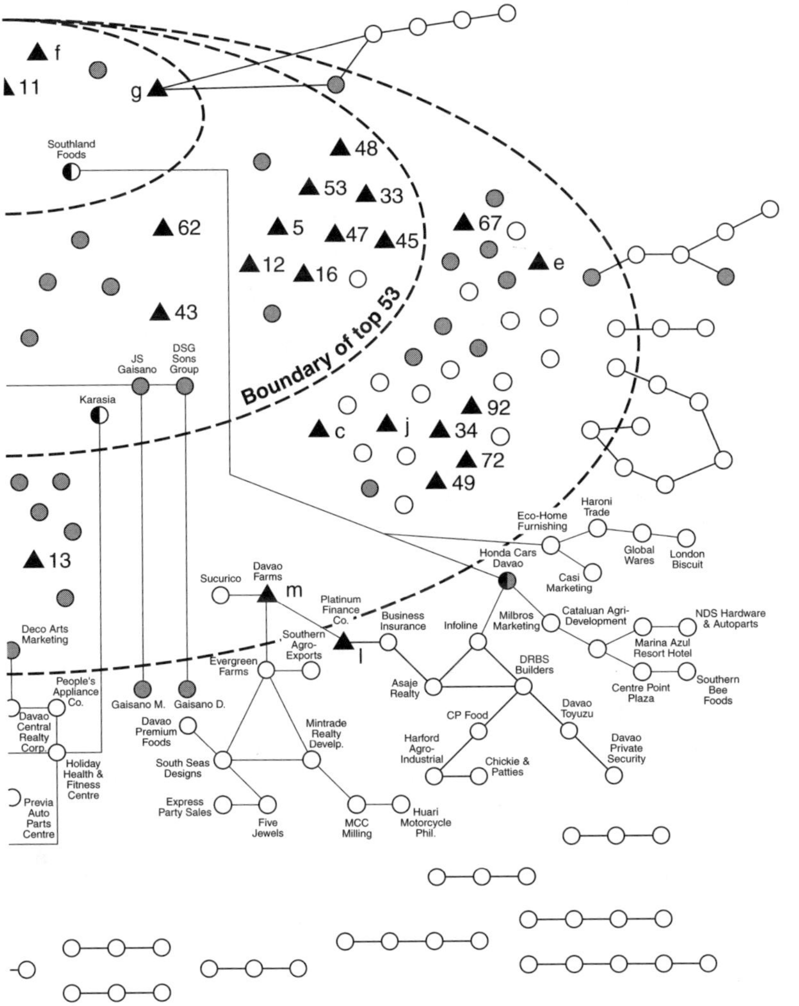

◐ ◐ owners, directors or major shareholders also hold political office.

▲2 also represented in Figure 2. Number refers to ranking among strongest 100 companies nationally. Letter indicates company lies outside strongest 100 companies nationally, but ranks among the strongest 2000 companies nationally.

(Note: details on named companies are shown in Figure 3a)

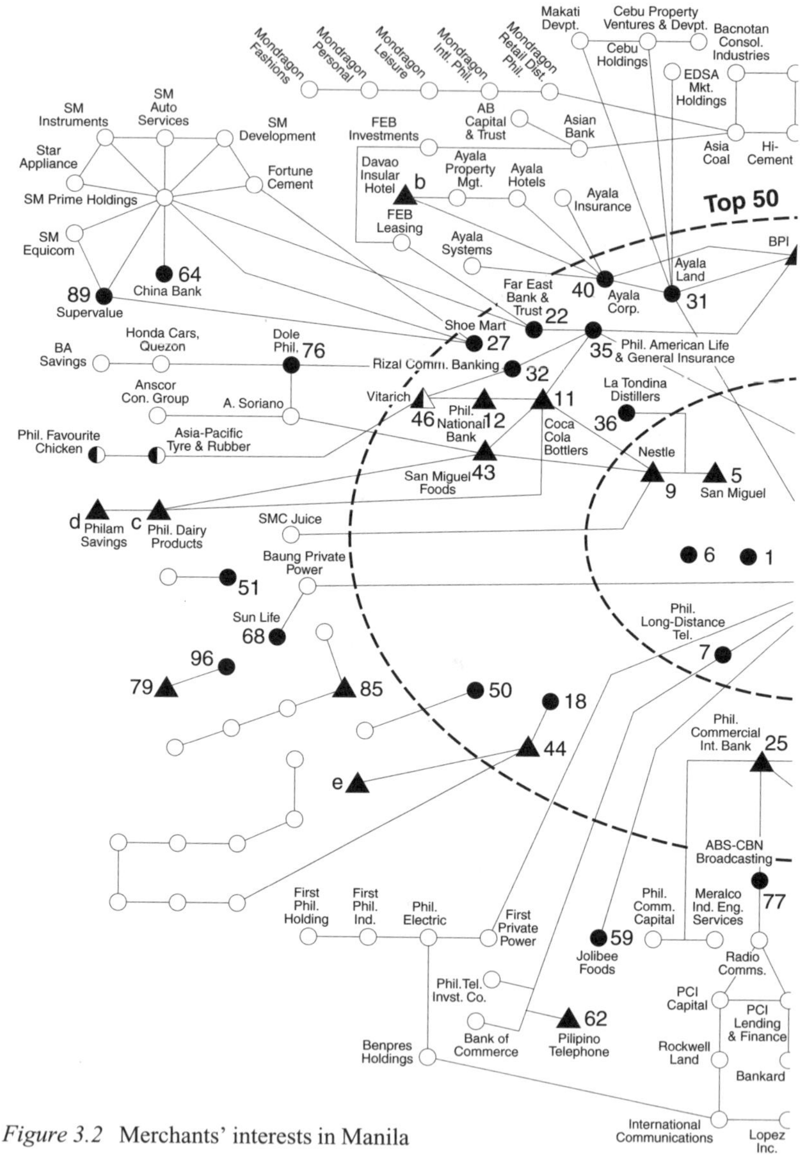

Figure 3.2 Merchants' interests in Manila

Key to Figure 3.2

—— interconnected ownership, directorship or major share holdings.

○ ● company ranks among the strongest 2000 companies in the Philippines.

● 3 number indicates ranking among the strongest 100 companies nationally.

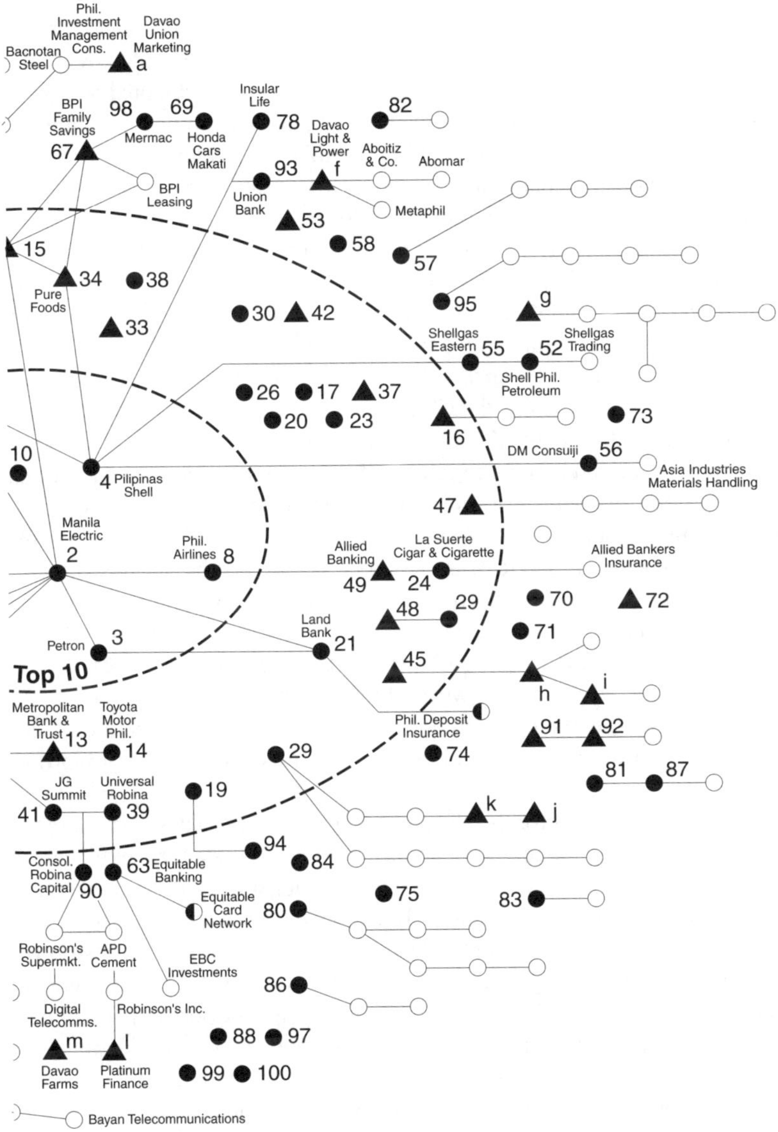

company also represented among the strongest 300 companies in Davao (Figure 1).

owner, director or major share holder also holds political office.

(Note: details on named companies are shown in Figure 3b).

They thought only of the present; in business they were interested only in quick and easy profit; and so they depended upon political connexions and raw influence. They were (paradoxically) too romantic and kind to treat relationships as a commercial instrument, easy to negotiate with, unable to keep to their agreements. The ethnic caricatures which the Filipino and 'Chinese' merchants created of themselves and each other for whatever purpose were different from the merchants and customers they dealt with every day, and of this they were aware. The merchant could therefore hold in his mind one or more caricatures entirely oblivious to, or uncaring of, any contradiction and paradox that they might pose. The successful Filipino merchant would lament the inability of 'Filipinos' to succeed in business; Chinese merchants who turned to Confucian explanations of their success saw no difference in the way Chinese and Filipinos ran their businesses; to be 'Chinese' was an extension of being 'Filipino', yet 'the Chinese' were inherently different because of their culture; a farmer would not trust 'the Chinese', yet he would associate with, trade with, and rely upon, close Chinese friends rather than another Filipino to buy his crops; a Filipino whose great-grandfather was Chinese would complain about the clannishness, secrecy and dishonesty of 'the Chinese', yet he was proud to bear a surname which is Chinese; 'the Chinese' were fundamentally different from 'the Filipinos', yet there was no point in trying to make a distinction between the two. When faced with envious criticism of his success a 'Chinese' merchant would retort that 'we Chinese, unlike Filipinos, rely upon our word of honour in the conduct of business'; and yet he would, in the same breath, acknowledge that Filipino merchants depended upon their honour and operated just as effectively by word of mouth.

For the merchants, as for the Nazarenes, ethnicity was a device with many aspects. It was a vehicle for anger and frustration. It was a lazy, explanatory shorthand. It was a kernel around which a relationship could be formed. In the same way that a Neuva Ejihan or Ilocano would use their place of origin and language as a common point from which to begin a relationship (or to consolidate one already established), so a 'Chinese' would use whichever nuclei of 'Chineseness' seemed appropriate to improve position and opportunity. And, as among the associations, and as among Nazarenes (though here less explicitly), ethnicity was also seen to be limiting and parochial. Then it was transmuted into an opposite, a negative kernel around which the cosmopolitan would cluster. By creating 'the Filipino', who was not competent at business, yet good at dancing and establishing relationships for their own sake, and by creating 'the Chinese', who was a cultural automaton skilled at a limited form of commerce which is peculiarly 'Chinese', 'the cosmopolitan' (whether they were Filipino or Chinese) conjured up an imaginary, unidimensional society from which they were distinct. Trust and reliability were emphasised. The merchant dealt on his reputation, and each day he proved himself reliable and honest be built upon his reputation a little more. Agreements had to be stuck to, supplies delivered on time, and payments made on or before the date due. A Chinese may, perhaps, have been more open with another Chinese; but if either had a poor reputation, then the other would not deal with him, or would be very careful in doing so. A Neuva Ejihan may have been willing to accommodate another Neuva Ejihan, but neither would trust the other merely because they were both from the same part of the Philippines. Fictive or genuine kinship ties with another of high standing could open doors, but would not ensure survival, let alone success. The son of a reputable Chinese businessman in the milling trade who began his own business with a strong network of contacts inherited from his father was soon found wanting. He was late with his deliveries, his cheques bounced, he fell behind with his repayments; and as his networks crumbled, so did his business. His credit lines were reduced and then suspended by a Chinese supplier who, at the same time, was happy to provide a reputable Filipino merchant with a credit line of hundreds of thousands of pesos. And all along, though given precedence over ethnicity, place of origin and kinship, trust and relationships were not treated as absolutes. If virtue and relationships could not be used to open up new opportunities for deals and profit, they would be neglected and allowed to whither, perhaps to be replaced once more by ethnicity.

Among the top firms in Davao (some of which are also ranked among the top 2,000 nationally), it is true, attitudes did seem to be moving with greater certainty towards the absolute. The owners of some companies excluded their own kin entirely if only to avoid giving the impression to the rest of their workers that their decisions were coloured by nepotism. Others kept their in-laws off the board, and well away from the management of the company. Outsiders were hired by many companies and given command at the highest levels. They would insulate family members from their other employees, and, more importantly, act as buffers among family members who, motivated by all kinds of emotions and thoughts, would not always clarify, or keep to their own, areas of responsibility. And in all companies the cult of the professional was propagated. Trust and relationships began to shine with their own inherent virtue as the former came to be seen as a quality expected of the ordinarily decent and competent, and as the latter were explicitly distanced. Sons and daughters were groomed: they were sent to the best schools and universities and were given experience of different jobs and at all levels from clerk upwards. They were to learn the common touch, while any introspective preoccupation with shyness or awkwardness in handling power was to be ironed out. Even their choice of wives and husbands were vetted: emotions were not to be manipulated at the company's expense. If they did not measure up, or would not pull their weight, they would be left to live out their lives as decorative and unhappy dilettantes. Employees, too, were made aware that certain standards of behaviour were expected from them: the company's clarity of purpose and its direction had to be maintained. Relationships which interfered with the smooth running of the company would not be tolerated. It was clearly understood, and made quite explicit, that the personal either had to be suspended or redirected. In one company (a 'Chinese' company as it happens) a clear line was observed between the director (who was also one of the owners of this family enterprise) and his employees He knew all his employees well: many were, as in Gregory's company, the sons and daughters of his father's workers; and with them he would eat and drink after work, or during the weekends, or on the occasional public holiday. Neither he nor they appeared to feel that 'He is their boss and they are his workers'. Yet all knew that they were *expected* to inform him of any problems at work or at home which affected their performance. The director believed that he was good to them, but he saw to it that he got something in return. Despite the long-standing relationships bequeathed from one generation to the next, employees who began to fail in their duties would be given three warnings and then removed. In other companies the owners' and managers' personal involvement in the affairs of their employees at work and at home, and the help they gave to their families, was institutionalised still more carefully. Emergency needs (within reason) and benefits of various kinds were provided through cooperatives governed by company policies. The logical extension of these professionalised communities was to be found on a plantation owned by a merchant-politician, and run by young, lively educated managers. Here an entire village was created replete with housing, hospitals schools, clinics and plating fields.

Yet the personal remained strong; and the concentrate of ethnicity could still be tasted. The selection of outsiders to manage a family company often followed lines of relationship set around a pre-existing kernel of one kind or another. Benny was the manager of the Davao branch of a company centred in Manila that processed and exported copra. As well as running operations in Davao, he oversaw the buying and processing of copra by his stations in Cotabato, General Santos and Padada. Although the company was owned by a Chinese family, less than 5 per cent of its managers were Chinese. The rest were Filipinos, and it was they who held key positions including those of auditor and heads of station in the outer provinces. Anyone who wanted to join the company, or was looking for promotion, would have to pass through examinations held in Manila. Competence and ability were among the most important qualities for those with ambition. Benny, however, had taken a somewhat different route. He and his wife were Chinese. The couple and their children spoke Chinese, though only his wife read the language. He was also linked to the owners through the marriage of his cousin. He was not particularly close with them. He met the owners infrequently, and ritually, once a year in Manila on the occasions of the company president's birthday. And he had had to work his way up from warehouseman over twenty-two years, proving his trustworthiness, reliability and loyalty again and again before reaching his present rank; of this he was proud. But kinship had opened the doors for him, and it was, he believed, the trust which the owners had in him which allowed him the freedom to do his work. The upper prices at which he could buy were fixed by the central office in Manila where a better view of price movements nationally and internationally was to be had. Otherwise he was his own man. Appointments in Mindanao were in his hands. His wife served as his secretary. She received no salary but was privy to his decisions. The Filipinos who held positions of authority and who ran the provincial stations had been appointed on his recommendation. He, after all, knew their qualities, and the values according to which his judgments were made were righteous, almost Calvinistic. To be sure, punctuality and competence mattered; sobriety, chastity, faithfulness, thrift and abstinence from gambling, though, mattered even more. Did their wives complain about their drinking in private? Did they drink too much in public? Were they womanisers and gamblers? Or did they drink in moderation, eschew gambling and fast women, and keep only to their wives? Were they good family men? Did their thrift manifest itself in the smallest nuances of behaviour? Would they turn off the air-conditioning when they left the office or when it was already cool enough for them to work? He was careful in his selection, for just as their success would reflect favourably upon him, so their failures would be his. To instill in all his workers the proper values, and to guarantee the success of his appointments, bible studies and prayers were made a regular part of company life.

Freedom, too, he was allowed in forming those external relationships so important to the company's success, and about which there was much of the absolute. Many of his suppliers were Chinese, but only prices and profits mattered. When buying or selling, merchants in his business would tout for the best deals in different parts of the country. And when a deal was struck there would be no reliance on trust. Contracts were drawn up, then faxed, and then sent by post just as fast as the post office would allow. It was not that each merchant could not expect the other the show common decency. It was simply that with so many deals being made so quickly, mistakes would be made, and misunderstandings would arise, unless agreements reached after much haggling were written down formally. He joined not the Chinese associations, but the more cosmopolitan organisations, including the Masons. As with Noy, he was careful to distance his relationships. Help was given and received, and friendships made for their own sake. Should he come under pressure to reciprocate in a way that made the relationship manipulative, he would claim that he was only a branch manager and could not make decisions for himself. But in the Masons he could meet bureaucrats from Customs and the Bureau of Internal Revenue, and politicians from local and national governments. If he had a problem with the supply of electricity he could ring the president of Davao Light and Power; if he needed to expedite shipments, or protect them from the red tape of greedy bureaucrats, he could always have a word with the politicians who were always willing to help a thriving company which earned dollars.

In other, still larger, companies, the personal in the selection of managers was more overt. A plaza owned by a Chinese family was organised into four divisions – supermarket, dcpartment store (food), mall, and the main department store. The departmental manager of the supermarket ran the original 'Park 'N Shop' in Buhangin before it was bought up by this family. The departmental manager of the department store (food), who had considerable professional experience of managing stores in Manila, was recruited through a family friend. The manager of the mall was a classmate of Richard, the president, at high school. The main department store was managed directly by the president. His assistant manager, a Filipino in his sixties and with long experience of managing stores in Manila and London, had been hired initially as a consultant. The president's operations manager within the department store was a graduate of La Salle, Manila, and a member of another prominent Chinese merchant family who also held shares in the plaza. Shadowing the management section was that of finance. This was also headed by the president. Finance did not merely countersign all cheques signed by management it also reviewed management's decisions. The vice-president of finance, Vicky, was married to another prominent Chinese merchant, and the daughter of a Chinese lumber merchant who was also a shareholder in the plaza, and a partner in another of Richard's companies. The departmental comptroller of the supermarket was Vicky's schoolmate; and the three Filipina comptrollers of the department store (food), the main department store, and the mall were all long-time friends of Richard, were all long-standing friends of Richard. Ties such as these made for strong, direct control; and, as in the copra business, they also allowed managers to operate with a fair degree of autonomy. Once decisions had been reached and plans had been formulated by the president and the board, managers could be left on their own. They had the authority to hire and fire employees of the rank of supervisor or below, and, for the most part, they were responsible for arranging supplies, though some goods from Hong Kong (where Richard and his family had property) and China were routed through his sister in Manila until her death.

As the personal became still more overt so the appetite for still tighter monitoring and policing sharpened. A flourishing enterprise which imported and sold construction materials, fixtures, wallpaper and carpets for homes and offices had soon established nine branches: three in Davao (including the main office) and one each in Tagum, General Santos, Zamboanga, Cagayan de Oro, Cebu and Manila. Most of these stores were run by professional and qualified Filipino managers. Some were hired through agencies, some through personal contacts, and some had become acquainted with the president, Tommy, through his previous dealings. Even so, he worried about control over his disparate company. So he placed his relatives in each branch. And every two months or so, Tommy or his internal auditor or his operations manager would tour all nine branches. His relatives were not supposed to interfere in the stores' operations: their job was to report on the general atmosphere in a branch and on any actions or decisions which they thought damaging. But tensions between the managers and their overseers were inevitable: the manager resented the interminable scrutiny, while the relative's carping zealousness grew with frustration at their own impotence. As a consequence, Tommy had to spend much time during his visits patching up rifts between his managers and their unwelcome shadows. There was much use in this, or so he thought. It kept his managers on their toes. But there was also danger. He had introduced emotions and friction which only made the cohesion of his company more difficult. He therefore centralised decisions in himself and found still other ways to keep an eye on his stores. Each branch manager's duties were defined and limited. A decision to grant credit or appoint or dismiss employees had to be referred to Tommy. He also made himself responsible for arranging the supply of goods. Most items were imported from Europe (mainly Italy, Germany, Austria, Greece, Spain and the United Kingdom), Brazil, America, Japan, Singapore, Malaysia and Taiwan. Branches were not allowed to hold stocks and were required to buy their goods through him. If the value of goods held in a branch was greater than money paid for those supplies, or if the money returned to head office after sales was less than the money paid for goods plus profit margins, or if they were unable to buy the same or a greater quantity of supplies, then he would assume something was wrong unless it could be shown that growth has been faster than projected, and had outstripped the collection of credit within the time limits agreed between head office and the branches' customers.

At the lower end of the larger companies, and most especially where the personal has been given more rein, monitoring becomes the obsession. A common problem is the coagulation of informal groups or cliques. If made to coincide with the company's boundaries and its ambitions, and if seeded, as in the bureaucracy, with a superior's mole and confidant, the group could be turned to the company's advantage, and on the whetstone of rivalry, a useful edge honed. But this was not done easily. By identifying its leaders, and by allowing its members to have a say in decisions, the group could be slotted into the company's organisational arrangements. In one large company, a supervisor of some 3,500 men tried to mould these informal groups into quality circles – bands of front-line workers who were expected to identify and then find solutions to problems in production. The experiment did not work because each man was concerned with being part of the group, and with its use either as a reservoir of emotional support and companionship, or as protection against uncertain and badly paid employment. Rather than appear to vie for greater prestige it was much easier to tow the line. If he were to appear to jostle for higher status within the group or to turn his back on it, then accusations of selfishness, ostracism and pressure to demonstrate unthinking loyalty would be thrown up in the defence of its unity. All this well served the group leader's crude philosophy of leadership.

There were other dangers too. Once given licence, groups would begin to scramble for influence. Workers now refused to cooperate, preferring instead to peddle false information and find other ways to ridicule each other. Or they would begin to link together, or perhaps inveigle their superiors, perhaps as their *ninong* or *compadre*, rendering the *padrino* manager's decisions questionable. That employees were co-workers or each other's *ninong* or *compadres* was in itself a kernel around which networks of relationships could be extended beyond the company. Their relationships within the company were also their relationships outside it. And as they broke across company's boundaries, these communities would throw up clouds of uncertainty, envy, jealousy and suspicion.

From the perspective of the owners and mangers, the greatest threat from these informal groupings was their potential to merge with or transform themselves into unions. At this point the group become overtly political and entrenched. Whims and demands, legitimate and fabricated, reasonable and unreasonable, sensible and ludicrous, become as one: vital economic issues and moral debates used to support relationships and relative status within the group and among different groups are merged. Inevitably, the company becomes snarled up with bickering, politicking rivalries and the struggle for prestige. If groups cannot be turned to advantage, or monitored and controlled, then they must be suppressed. As soon as the owner of one 'Chinese' company notices groups developing he will remind individuals of their loyalty to the company – objectives must be realised, and clarity of purpose must be maintained. An employee who continues to behave in a manner which runs counter to, or obscures, those objectives, will be removed. In the larger 'Filipino' company of the Alcantara, supervisors spent much of their time identifying and breaking up these informal groups; and, in their turn, *padrino* managers (or supervisors) were immediately dismissed. Rank-and-file employees were shifted around every six months as a matter of routine.

Oligarchy

The shift from the personal to the absolute, then, was not consequent upon or bound to the elaborate courtly dances of grand structures or magical forces which move gracefully, and predictably, within our minds to their staged conclusion. It was the sum of chance, of countless people whose attitudes emerged like bubbles, here or there for just a moment, or for just a moment longer. Only gradually as they expressed their views and acted upon them did they begin to alter the quality of their own lives and of those around them; only gradually did they alter the social world, and in the most dramatic ways. Nor was this an easy thing. The transition of inchoate companies into more formal, stable and effective organisations was, no less than in the bureaucracy, fraught with difficulties. It was not just a question of experience, taxation, government policies, international circumstances and luck, important though these were. The relationships (most especially among kin) so important to the company's internal cohesion, to its external connections through which information, markets, supplies and loans were secured, and to the extension of credit, also generated severe tensions. Disentangling jealousies, resentments and antagonisms from the operation of the company required considerable authoritarianism, though the authority of matriarch or patriarch was not always enough: professional managers unrelated to the owners had to be brought in while family members and in-laws were excluded; codes of behaviour, areas of responsibility, criteria for assessing performance, and chains of command had to be clarified, and decisions made less secretively; the business concerns of family members had to be separated, and loans between them cast in a legal framework; the external connections of the company had to be hardened with formal contracts; and, in all this, attitudes would have to shift from the personal with its reliance on kernels such as ethnicity and kinship, and a dependency upon trust and loyalty, towards the absolute, bringing with it greater stability, predictability, wider opportunities, and a broader range of experience and competence.

And yet, as we have seen, though relationships became rather less personal, less exclusive, and more extensive as they were distanced, the personal was not lost. Networks were not so much replaced with an atomistic pattern of enterprises whose internal and external relations were defined purely by impersonal and contractual obligations, as they were made far more complex. More companies were drawn in to form larger webs that were set in competition with each other. These economic oligarchies, then, were more professionalised and competitive; but they remained oligarchies. In Davao, the strongest 65 companies represented less that 0.4 per cent of the total number of enterprises in the city, and yet they were responsible for just under 40 per cent of all sales; the strongest 124 (or 0.6 per cent of companies) and 1,800 (or 9.5 per cent of companies) accounted for just under 50 per cent and 90 per cent of sales respectively.[15] The bottom 15,169 (or 79 per cent), were responsible for just 8 per cent of registered sales – a figure which may be an overestimate for is assumes that all companies who registered sales of less than 250,000 pesos, achieved sales of 249,999 pesos. Figures for the top 1,800 companies, on the other hand, were compiled from their actual registered sales.

The dominance of those companies which had the strongest national presence (as measured by the volume of their sales nationally) appears to have been even more striking. As a proportion of the total sales, assets and profits of the strongest 2000 corporations, the first 60 accounted for 41 per cent of sales, 46 per cent of assets and 43 per cent of profits; and the first 100 for more than 50 per cent of sales, assets and profits.[16] Figures for the aggregate national sales of all companies do not appear to have been compiled. Nevertheless, it is possible to give an indication of the top 100 companies' share.

If it is assumed that the proportions for Davao (where the strongest 0.436 per cent of companies are responsible for 42 per cent of sales) hold true nationally, then the strongest 100 companies in the Philippines would have accounted for around 21 per cent of sales. But if it is assumed that the average sales registered by each company in Davao held true nationally, then total sales of all enterprises throughout the Philippines would have amounted to less than half the total sales registered by the strongest 2,000 companies, and so to only slightly less than the total combined sales of the strongest 100 companies. This inconsistency might suggest that the disparity between the top 0.5 per cent of companies nationally and the remainder – especially the bottom 80 per cent – was even greater than the case of Davao suggests, with the top 0.4 per cent of companies nationally accounting for two-thirds of all sales, and the strongest 100 companies being responsible for 33 per cent of all sales.

Or it may suggest that the bottom 80 per cent of companies nationally were far stronger than was immediately apparent in Davao. There are good reasons to think that this may be so, and these have little to do with any doubts about the city's representativeness. To the contrary, Davao had one of the strongest economies in the Philippines outside the National Capital Region; and the characteristics of, and weaknesses in, the collection of revenue which may have skewed estimates of the relative strength of companies in Davao were probably replicated across the archipelago. We noted in the previous chapter that in Davao the number of organisations recorded in long-hand in fifty or so volumes by the Business Bureau (a local government department) at the time of the last census in the mid 1990s reached more than 40,000; by the end of the decade the number of companies renewing their business licences annually with the Business Bureau (as they are legally required to do) had fallen to around 20,000. These licences served as the basis for statistics and the collection of local and central government taxes (which are calculated for each company from their registered sales). A large proportion of companies simply went 'missing' from one year to the next, and even those companies which reapplied for a licence annually regularly under-reported their sales by about 40 per cent. This figure coincides with the World Bank's (1992) estimate that only about 50 per cent of income tax (which in the case of many small businesses is indistinguishable from business tax) was collected; and it is not at odds with Devarajan and Hossain's (1998) observation that there was a fair amount of room for increasing business tax collections: even the richest 10 per cent of the population paid less than two-tenths of 1 per cent of their income in business tax.

It is also possible that both explanations of the inconsistency between estimates of the strongest 100 companies' share of total national sales were, to some extent, true. Let us assume that the strongest 2,000 companies in the Philippines were responsible for 42 per cent of all sales, that the actual sales achieved by each of the weakest 79 per cent of companies in Davao was double their registered sales, and that this latter figure held true across the Philippines. Under these assumptions, the bottom 79 per cent of companies nationally would still have been responsible for less than 4 per cent of total sales, leaving a band of companies (representing about 20 per cent of all companies) between the bottom 79 per cent and the top 0.4 per cent responsible for slightly more than 40 per cent of total national sales. This middle band, when viewed in aggregate, may have been more powerful than the top 0.4 per cent of companies (which, it is assumed, generate 42 per cent of sales); but, as the case of Davao appeared to indicate, this band was in practice split into many smaller and competing networks which, though influential at regional, provincial and sub-provincial levels, were greatly overshadowed by – and, in many instances, are linked directly or indirectly into – the primary webs centred in Manila.

We might imagine, then, that there lay across the archipelago a thick blanket of small economically weak enterprises which would probably exhibit what has been described elsewhere as a cellular pattern. If the dominance of these primary webs in Davao was repeated throughout the Philippines, then we might also imagine that set atop this blanket were collections of enterprises organised into webs. The most significant of these webs, although very firmly centred in Manila, extended beyond the National Capital Region, fed into, stimulated and competed with smaller webs, most especially in Region IV (immediately around the NCR), Cebu and Northern and Southern Mindanao (Figure 3.3). The main settlements of the Philippines, then, were in a very real sense an expression of the expansion and interaction of complex social networks. The data from which this picture may be formed are limited and uncertain, but they do lend themselves to this interpretation.

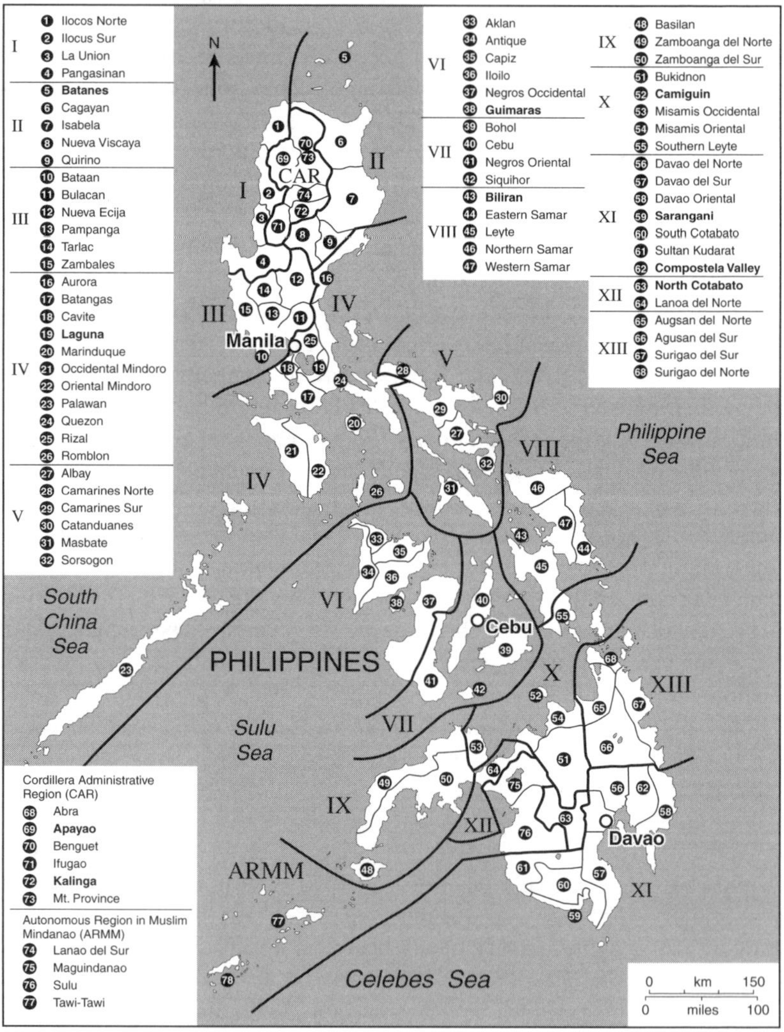

Figure 3.3 The regions and provinces of the Philippines

Outside the National Capital Region, the proportion of the total number of enterprises within each province engaged in a particular sector was very similar: around 23 per cent were engaged in manufacturing activities; 43 per cent in wholesaling and retailing; 28 per cent in community services; 3 per cent in financing and banking; less than 2 per cent in transport and communications; and less than 1 per cent in each of the four remaining sectors – agriculture, construction, mining (and quarrying), and utilities (electricity, gas and water).[17] Even when these variations were taken into account, the boundaries within which the sectoral pattern of every province outside the National Capital Region fell appeared to be fairly narrow.[18]

Data from the Island of Mindanao suggest that this sectoral pattern was, in general, reproduced within individuals cities (of which there are eighteen in Mindanao) and municipalities (which number more than four hundred). Here, in each city and municipality, the sectoral pattern ranged from: 15 to 22 per cent in manufacturing; 44 to 51 per cent in wholesaling and retailing; 24 to 33 per cent in community services; 1 to 6 per cent in financial and banking services; and less than 1 per cent in each of the remaining sectors. There was a noticeable concentration of companies operating in particular sectors in the cities which together held around 36 per cent of all manufacturing enterprises; 38 per cent of those engaged in wholesaling and retailing; and 47 per cent of those whose activities are classified as community services. But this concentration was not as striking as might perhaps be expected: 60 per cent of all enterprises in Mindanao, a little more than 60 per cent of manufacturing, wholesaling and retailing enterprises, and slightly under 60 per cent of those providing community services were scattered fairly evenly across more than four hundred municipalities, each of which was characterised by a sectoral pattern very similar to that exhibited by provinces across the Philippines.[19]

The replication at sub-provincial levels of national and provincial sectoral patterns may have held true across the Philippines: each province's share of the total number of enterprises engaged in particular sectors outside the National Capital Region appears to have been distributed reasonably evenly. Notwithstanding the occasional disparities within regions among their respective provinces' share of the total number of enterprises operating in a particular sector, no province had more than an 8 per cent share of the total number of enterprises in a particular sector outside Manila except for Negros Occidental (with 20 per cent of agricultural enterprises), Occidental Mindoro and Pangasinan (with 12 per cent and 10 per cent respectively of mining enterprises).

There were, then, variations in the sectoral patterns exhibited by each province, city and municipality; and there were disparities both in the share of the total number of enterprises operating in a particular sector outside Manila, and in the share of regional and provincial totals. But these variations seem to exist within fairly narrow bands, and, taken as a whole, there would seem to be little marked specialisation of activity across the archipelago.[20]

A second strand of evidence may be teased from the data on the distribution of enterprises of different sizes (as defined by the number of their employees). These show that the larger enterprises tended to be concentrated in the cities of a small number of provinces. These provinces are gathered around the National Capital Region, Cebu and Davao City. These larger enterprises were also slightly biased towards manufacturing.

Outside the National Capital Region, the vast majority (a little more than 80 per cent) of companies which operated within each province employed less than 5 workers; a further 12 per cent of companies employed between 5 and 9 workers; and another 6 per cent employed between 10 and 49 workers. Less than 2 per cent of all enterprises within each province outside Manila employed 50 or more workers.[21] Most of the top 2000 companies fell within this narrow band and they accounted for about a quarter of all enterprises of this size identified in the Philippines.[22] Again, while there were variations, these proportions were, in general, reproduced by every province, and, if the evidence from cities and municipalities in Mindanao held true throughout the Philippines, then at the sub-provincial level too. However, data from Region XI suggests that there was a marked concentration of larger enterprises in five (out of more than 80) settlements with municipal or city status. Together, these settlements – Digos and Koronadal (the municipalities), and Davao, General Santos and Tagum (three of the Region's four cities) – contained: around 50 per cent of the smallest enterprises (enterprises with between one and four employees); some 64 per cent of those enterprises employing between five and nine workers; and more than two-thirds of all companies employing more than ten workers. And nationally, whilst the largest provincial share of the total number of enterprises in any particular category of size operating outside Manila amounted to no more than 16 per cent, the largest share for every category (except the very smallest) was held by Cebu. Cebu was also one of only ten provinces (referred to as Gp 1 in Figure 3.4) whose share of the total number of enterprises in each category of size outside Manila was more than double the average share held by all other provinces, and whose share of the total number of companies in each category of size varied above the mean to a greater extent than did its share of the total number companies operating in particular sectors. Another eleven provinces (Gp 2) could be identified whose share of the total number of enterprises of all sizes was greater than, but less than twice, the average. Figure 3.4 also shows a further nine provinces (Gp 3) whose share of the total number of enterprises in each category of size (except the very smallest) was below the average, but whose share of the total number of enterprises (operating outside Manila) could, in at least one sector, be ranked among the ten largest; and another five provinces (Gp 4) whose share of the total number of enterprises in each category of size (except the very smallest) was below the average, but whose share of the total number of enterprises (operating outside Manila) could, in at least one sector, be ranked above the mean. The gap between the first ten provinces and the remainder became more evident when their share of the total number of enterprises in each category of size was set against their share of the total number of enterprises of all sizes. Only among this first group of ten provinces was their share of the total number of the smallest enterprises below that which would have been expected given their share of the total number of enterprises operating outside the National Capital Region; only among these ten provinces was their share of the total number of the larger enterprises greater than would have been expected; and only among these ten provinces did that share continue to rise progressively with the size of the companies.

Between these ten provinces and the remainder there were also noticeable variations in the sectoral patterns exhibited by companies employing ten or more workers. The average share of the total number of these larger enterprises operating outside Manila in manufacturing, community services and mining was very close to the average share of the total number of all enterprises of all sizes operating outside the National Capital Region in these three sectors (about 23, 28, and less than 1 per cent respectively); but it was some ten times higher in the agricultural and utilities sectors and 50 per cent lower in the retailing and wholesaling sector. Among the first group of ten provinces, however, more than 30 per cent of the larger enterprises were classed as manufacturers, and less than 24 per cent are engaged in community services. Among the second group of eleven provinces, the figures were 19 per cent (manufacturing) and 29 per cent (community services); and 15 per cent and 36 per cent among all the remaining provinces.

The third strand of evidence is derived from the fact that the first group of 10 provinces, and the second group of 11 provinces, each comprise part of those regions – regions IV, VII, III, VI, X and XI – with the strongest economic indicators outside Manila. Regions IV, VII, III, VI, X and XI were also, in that order, the largest contributors outside the National Capital Region to central government revenues.[23] Region XI's contribution to central government revenues was perhaps lower than would be expected (at under 20 per cent of the mean) given its relatively strong economic indicators and its share both of population and the larger companies. There were, as we noted earlier, questions surrounding the efficacy of tax collection in Region XI, but there is no reason to think that the Bureau of Internal Revenue was less effective here than elsewhere. The main reason for Region XI's poor showing would seem to be, as we noted in the previous chapter, that the jurisdiction over the taxation of any particular company lay with the district

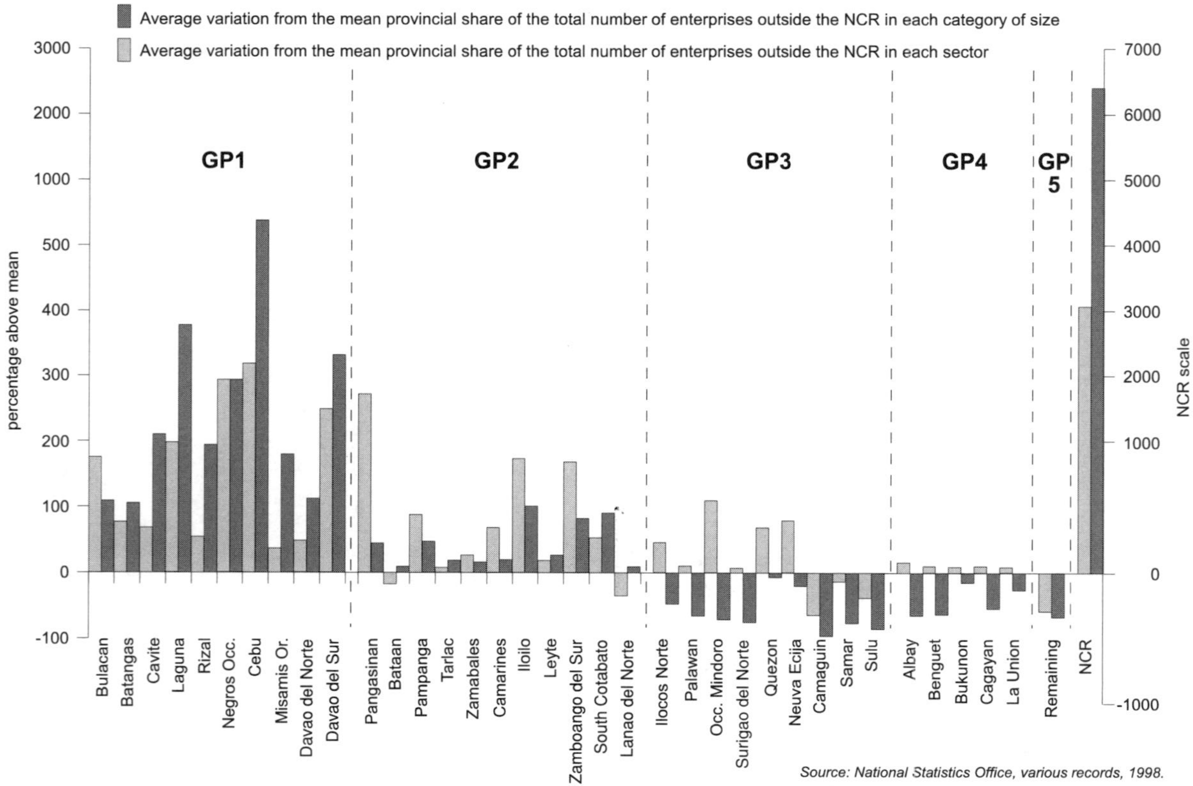

Source: National Statistics Office, various records, 1998.

Figure 3.4 The size and sectoral characteristics of enterprises in selected provinces outside the NCR

in which the corporation sites its principal office or held its main books of accounts. The relatively low contribution of Region XI to central government revenues, then, may simply have reflected the presence there of a larger number of enterprises from other parts of the Philippines.

The 'professional' oligarchies which radiated out from the National Capital Region were important politically for two reasons. Economic power obviously lay with them. If nation, province, city or municipality was to make money and progress materially, then they had to attract, or raise their own, merchants. Business was also the source of most revenue collections. Companies in the Philippines directly generated about 26 per cent of internal revenue collections. They also supplied revenue through excise taxes, taxes on individuals (companies with ten or more workers employ about 11 per cent of the work force), VAT, other percentage taxes (such as a tax on international carriers), and other miscellaneous taxes. These five categories of tax accounted for around 20, 19, 15, 6 and 6 per cent of internal revenue collections respectively. The competition which existed among provinces, cities and municipalities as they tried to encourage merchants to settle in their jurisdictions may have been intense but it was, for reasons considered in the previous chapter, very much stacked in favour of the National Capital Region, where most of the strongest 2,000 companies were sited. Makati and Quezon alone contributed more than 70 per cent of national internal revenue collections; the inclusion of Valencia and the city of Manila brought that figure up to 83 per cent.

More importantly, these oligarchies helped to scatter and strengthen the absolute throughout Philippine society. Even if we take a less charitable view of merchants and assume that their interests were no more altruistic than those of the politician or bureaucrat, the national economy had to be their arena, and its cohesion and stability was to their advantage. They took a view of circumstances, attitudes and outlooks that was more intimate and broader than many politicians might otherwise be exposed to within the cloistered battlegrounds of central and local government. The connexions between, and the merging of, politician and merchant transmitted to the politician in an immediate and vivid manner a pragmatic sense of the economy and an emotional concern in its wellbeing. Thus, while politicians may have shared little or no political vision, and perhaps saw others outside their self-selecting cliques as either marginal or as obstacles to their own ambitions, they did share a strong interest in the success of business: and whatever the motivation of merchant and politician may have been, this feeling of a national economy was fed back into a political life that was more parochial and factionalised, binding together those individuals who comprised the formal institutions of the polity and who might otherwise easily drift apart.

In this way, perhaps, merchants and their oligarchies might help bring about a more precise fit between their communities and those of the politicians. And this, perhaps, will make for a more effective coincidence of interests, activities and policies. Stability and progress in the long run, however, seem likely to follow only if the shift to the absolute gathers pace. Only then will those who are not politicians or bureaucrats strengthen their faith in the institutions of government, and see less need to establish their own communities and lay these aggressively across different walks of life. Only then will greater clarity be brought to the division between public and private, civil and political, economic and social, and the institutional and non-institutional. Only then will coordination and focus be sharpened, and tensions more easily defused.

* * *

What we may be witnessing, then, is a profound shift from the personal to the absolute. Its leaders may be the merchants and migrants: towards this possibility look the nature of the merchants' political significance, the extent of overseas migration, the exposure of merchant and migrant to a wide range of attitudes towards relationships and reciprocity, and the shift from the personal to the absolute demanded by the organisation of companies and the husbanding of the merchant's and migrant's hard-earned wealth. Beliefs, attitudes and practices transmitted through the networks of relationships established by these revolutionaries may be altering the context in which those same relationships are interpreted, such that the absolute comes to be seen, rightly or wrongly, as less officious, less cold, less manipulative, more idealistic and romantic, and more liberating. Politician and bureaucrat in the long run may have little choice but to adapt. Whoever the revolutionaries are, the re-shaping of institutions and practices which follow in the wake of this delicate sea change in attitudes is neither more nor less than an expression of the redirection of even the smallest and apparently least consequential actions, attitudes and behavioural nuances that make up everyday life.

4 Between two worlds

In the introduction of this book I wrote that an elaboration of the reasoning underlying the arguments and interpretations pursued in the first three chapters would be left until Chapter 4. This was so, I asserted, because it was not always helpful to view the true world, and what we read, through our academic constructs. By these academic 'constructs' I mean the assumption – fundamental to so much social science of both the modern or post-modern tradition – that there exist forces or structures which, though produced by individuals, now shape or even determine individual action. This assumption – sometimes made explicit and sometimes implied – is shared so completely by what might be broadly termed culturalists and the institutionalists, that the point at which culture ends and the institution begins is unclear. And so, while the culturalist sees a need to disaggregate institutions into their cultural elements, those who see in institutions generic, even universal, processes believe that it is to those institutions we must look to understand society, and that culture itself may be strongly influenced by the institution. It has been no difficult thing, then, for there to emerge the view that culture nestles within global structures, each mediated through the other, each subtly altered, but neither subsumed, by the other. The question is no longer whether, but the extent to which, culture, structure and institution exert an influence. The individual is now secondary or residual consideration, or, a mere fiction *in extremis*.

Such is the power of the belief in this assumption of social science that it has become customary, even obligatory, to state it in some or other form of words at the beginning of a book or scholarly paper, and around it frame all that is subsequently written. Try, without artifice, merely to understand what it is that we are, and such efforts are likely to be regarded, at best, as a self-indulgent and haphazard collection of amateurish muses. Each writer and, perhaps, a few of their readers may, by way of these cathartic exercises, realise some understanding themselves, and, in this limited way, improve the quality of their own lives. But no cumulative body of scholarship is established, no sense of progress is conveyed. It is all fundamentally second-rate.

In previous studies on China and the Overseas Chinese, I have looked critically and in some detail at how this assumption of the social sciences works; and, although this has not been my meaning, it has appeared to some readers as if I have rejected social science in its entirety. My argument is only that this 'apathetic fallacy' (as Toynbee (1949) once described it) is strong within our thinking. And it has taken on the pre-eminence it has precisely because it does not have to suffer the discipline of what seems to be an external order beyond the imagination of its practitioners. It is, in truth, little more than a way of legitimising preconception, belief and faith. To interpret in the light of theory and its retinue of etherealities, and to present that interpretation either as proof and justification of the theory, or as fact, gives the lie to prejudice. To say that it is second-rate not to assume the existence of such etherealities is to despise other views merely because they are not one's own, and to leave oneself without bridges. Despite the illusion of its grandeur, the assumption of this science confines us to a mean little place, to just one small part of what we are, to just one thought-experiment in a much bigger world.

My concern here, however, is not to repeat these criticisms. It seem to me that it is now more interesting to explore ways of thinking about our social world which are not founded upon this assumption of social science. And it is, at least in part, with this in mind that this book has been written. Such an inquiry, I believe, necessarily begins with an old, yet vital matter to which so many debates and problems must eventually return: the nature of, and the connexions between, the individual and the 'whole' (which I use to include community, culture and society). It is a debate which is often avoided merely on account of a reluctance to question the validity of our 'apathetic fallacy' as a starting point for interpretation; and in so doing we eschew an expansive, bright-lit landscape of ideas and possibilities. My intention in the following section is not to provide a comprehensive summary of this debate, but simply to indicate something of the range of ideas generated by it – ideas which lead us into, and may in turn gain something from, a more explicit consideration of the arguments underlying much of this present study on the Philippines.

The individual and the whole

The same *ménage à trois* of culture, institution and marginalised individual so prevalent in social science writing today has been common for the last fifty years at least. For many writers, society was the hierarchy within which individuals were positioned, and culture the standardised patterns of behaviour, socially acquired; to others, society was the totality of social relationships or, more specifically, the 'structure' or networks of relationships among and within systems of groups, and culture the content of those relationships.

And just as culture might influence the society, so might society influence the culture, though as to where the balance of power lay, every writer had their own view. But there was less uncertainty about the significance of the individual. For many, the individual was incidental and individual freedom an illusion, for once culture had come into existence the individual then became permanently subject to this irresistible force; for many more, culture and society were the context, the precedence, the ready-made solutions, the limitations on a possible range of actions and responses by which the individual was constrained but within which individuals might vary their actions. The individual might reflect the culture but not exactly so. Small variations in the behaviour and relationships of some individuals would bring about alterations by other individuals; alterations would build up; circumstances alter, making certain discoveries or new practices and changes inevitable; and so, through a kind of convection or conduction or drift, even the basic patterns of culture and society might change.

Even when the word 'culture' was hardly mentioned, and the attention was on society, a force of some kind was ever present. For Elias (1994) it was the unintended actions of individuals. Under the pressure of competition, social functions became more and more differentiated. As they did so, people became more interdependent and therefore had to attune their conduct more strictly; they had to behave correctly, though the sum of their actions and plans gave rise to changes and patterns in the web of social relationships that no individual had planned. Thus did the patterns blindly formed from social interaction blindly produce changes in human mentality that were imprinted upon individuals from early childhood. Thus arose an order more compelling and stronger than the will and reason of any individual.

But if Elias's writings indicates that there was, around the middle of the last century, more of an interest in society and the individual than in culture, then perhaps the work of Rank (1932, 1945) – who, while acknowledging the significance of context, gave more prominence to free will – was indicative of a shift away from an even stronger emphasis on the individual, that which had already been present for some time. Can we perhaps detect a diminution of culture as we look back through the twentieth century and into the nineteenth century when the word was used – to borrow Cohen's (1974) phrase – in its rag-bag, global form? Was there also perhaps a stronger concern with the balance between society (though still carrying the assumption from which culturalists would later fashion their arguments) and the individual, with the stress upon the individual?

Certainly writers of Elias's and Rank's generation had been born in a century by the middle of which a view of society comprising individuals had already been well established: each rational, each engaged in the pursuit of happiness and profit such that they would do no harm to each other, each bound by a social compact or contract which secured their inalienable rights and set out their responsibilities, and who together formed a civil society constrained by laws moral and judicial, explicit and implicit. This was an ideal – a concourse of individuals for whom self-imposed and self-created obligations lit the way to true liberty – which even then reached back nearly 200 years to Smith (d.1790), Locke (d.1704) and Hobbes (d.1679)

It was also an ideal that found an easy synergy with views about nature, science and man. The atomistic philosophy of Democritus and the Epicureans implicit in Locke's belief that apparent (or secondary) qualities such as colour and taste were no more than feelings produced in the mind by the action of real bodies upon the senses had been revived earlier during the seventeenth and sixteenth centuries. Both Gassendi (d.1655) and Cudworth (d.1688) had argued for atomism in its strictest sense; and whilst Hobbes, like Bacon (d.1626), had not thought those particles necessarily indivisible, he had already had gone further than Locke (who thought mind to be quite separate from matter) in arguing that it was possible to see in consciousness a kind of motion. But it was in Descartes' (d.1650) work that the individual and the mechanical and mathematical treatment of matter was most emphasised. The only thing I can be sure of, reasoned Descartes, is that I think. And since I have the thought of a perfect being who, in accordance with Anselm's (d.1109) ontological argument, must therefore exist, and who will not deceive me (though my demons may try to do so), I am therefore able to have a clear and distinct knowledge (mathematical in character) of matter and to see the world as it really is. Saved by Anselm from knowing only the thinking mind, Descartes had thus opened a path which led through the individual to a window on the universe.

If there was a synergy between conceptions of social world and the scientific conception of the natural world, then there was also a synergy between the individual and God. By the time Luther (d.1546) had begun to rail against the ordinances and penalties proscribed by the Church, a move within the Church towards the individual had long since been underway. What was the nature of God, the Son and Spirit? What was the nature of the part-human, part-deity Christ? What was human will? How much of the good that men did was due to themselves or to God? In dealing with such questions God had come to be seen as accessible to all men, in touch with each individual soul and, through Jesus, in direct material contact with the world.

In the development of this view, the Churchmen had, initially at least, looked to Greek writers for the intellectual authority to support their own faith. Plato had described a world of eternal natures or Ideas which found imperfect definition in a visible world created by God. The Stoics, though they did not adhere to the excesses of the Cynics' determination to live only the simplest life, sympathised with the spirit of that determination, and believed that each person should be prepared to bear the vicissitudes of life, for man as a species and as an individual had – by virtue of God's will and design – a special place in nature. The Churchmen also found much in the neo-platonists, chief among them Plotinus, who argued that if the individual was to claim access to God and to find for himself a unique and valued place with Him in the universe, then he must do so through a life of scholarly monasticism, alone, free of encumbrances and distractions. St Augustine's writings, strongly influenced by Plato and Plotinus, helped to keep alive something of Greek learning after the fall of Rome. Boethius, too, a minister of the barbarian chief Theodoric (d. 526), fearing that much was in imminent danger of being forgotten, translated from Greek into Latin many of the works of Plato, Aristotle, Euclid, Archimedes and Porphyrus (fourth century AD). Not all his translations survived, but those of works on elementary logic by Aristotle and Porphyrus (whose chief concern was the relationships between genus and species, the individual and the whole) constituted a most important part of the education of many subsequent writers, including Abelard (d.1142) and Bernard of Clairvaux (d.1153).

When, however, the works of Aristotle, besides those which dealt with elementary logic, and those of other Greek writers, were discovered or re-discovered in the twelth and thirteenth centuries, contradictions between Christian doctrine and Greek philosophy became still more apparent. Aristotle's views on the individual, for instance, were ambiguous. In the sublunary world where bodies were made from elements that were unstable and therefore perishable, the form (the kind) could achieve immortality only through the multiplication of individuals and, of each, nothing could be said which could not be said of another. Only in the higher levels of the universe, above the order of the moon, was each individual heavenly body imperishable and therefore without the need to produce several individuals of the same kind. The world, being, in order, above the moon, was eternal. But consciousness, reason, and the soul, had their origins in the body of the individual who, being of the sublunary order and *of* the form, was therefore mortal. The philosophers' God, too, was bare and impersonal. It was not the maker of the world (which was itself eternal). It was a perfection which had need of nothing beyond itself and the contemplation of itself, for whom no activity was worthy except the contemplation of the knowledge of its own perfection, and in imitation of which all things aspired; it was the principle of life, the *anima mundi*, which in moving itself, or so Plato believed, set in movement all other things, or, as Aristotle had thought, set living things in motion by exciting desires within them while remaining unmoved itself. Man, then, was but a kind; and the mortal body and soul of each individual was but part of the succession of individuals through which this kind, like all kinds of the sublunary order, might achieve the immortality, that quality of God, which all things strove to imitate. Possessing an intellect, however, meant that the highest activity of Man was to seek knowledge, again in imitation of the perfect being. And since he also possessed language and was able to perceive good and evil, and to determine what was just and unjust, it was also evident that the individual man was meant for association. But association, too, was of a kind of which family was also a part, and both were (in Aristotle's teleological world) part of a tendency towards the polity – the best of the kind. It was also because of this teleology that the polity preceded the individual man, the family, and the association not in time but in order of nature. The individual was of, and existed for, the polity and mankind.

The uncertainty of the individuality, the perishability of the soul, and the eternal nature of the world, the impersonal perfection of God, and Man's existence for the polity, were views not easy to square with Christian beliefs. Indeed, despite the efforts of Aquinas (d.1274) it became evident that agreement between Christian teachings, on the one hand, and Aristotle and so many other strains of Greek writing, on the other, was not to be found. A division between the proofs offered in these works and the Churchmen's faith would have to be accepted, and other arguments ventured. Aristotle's own discussion on substance had seemed to focus the mind of the medieval scholars on the question of how individuals of the same species might differ from each other. Duns Scotus' (d.1308) view was that the individual was a higher perfection added to the human species; while Ockham argued simply that a 'species', besides describing a number of similar individual things, had no separate or real existence.

But although there had been a shift in emphasis towards the individual, it could not do without that of the whole: each person was in some way bound to another. The objects of knowledge, argued Augustine, were God's eternal thoughts; and our appreciation of them were part of His design. Duns Scotus, too, despite his elevation of the individual, argued that mathematical objects and other abstractions existed only in God's thought. Even monastic seclusion gave ground to community: if the Christian was to find the joy, hope, love and faith of salvation, he must be united with God through Christ and in Him with his fellow believers. Private prayer and the individual's relationship with God went hand in hand with community worship, and both dimensions were crystallised in our earthly relationships with each other and service to mankind. The early Lutherans and Calvinists were never staunch individualists either; nor were they determined to destroy the Church or question its divine origin, nor dispense entirely with its discipline. They argued that salvation was the gift of God, not of the Church; and they wished to restore the social dimension of the Eucharist. In doing so, in returning the balance to community and individual worship, they were doing no more than returning to the practices of the early Christians.

Descartes' God was not quite that of the Christian's. His was the philosopher's God – an infinite and perfect consciousness. But it was, Descartes argued, through the certainty of this God's existence that the we can see the universe clearly and distinctly. And it was through this God that the Cartesians, if not Descartes himself, had thought that we were all united in another way. Descartes had supposed that the mind was quite separate from the body which belonged to the mechanical world. And yet the mind (the soul) clearly affected and moved the body. How could this be so? Descartes declared the link between the two to be the pineal gland, though some of his followers, particularly Geulinex (d.1669), preferred Occasionalism as their explanation. Whilst there was no interaction between soul and body, God mediated between the soul and body causing us to see and move. Others, notably Malebranche (d.1715), returned the word 'ideas' (which Descartes had understood as representations in the mind of what exists outside it) to its Augustinian sense (that of divine thoughts).

Perhaps it was a consideration of this problem arising from Descartes' separation of soul and body which had led Spinoza (d.1677) to his view that there was only one substance; that there was therefore no distinction between mind and matter, nor between creator and created. Each individual was part of the whole system of material nature which was itself but an extension of a greater whole. Though we might believe that we are individuals with our own free will, this is merely because we are ignorant of that whole. So much so are we at one that when we say 'we love God', it is the same thing as to say 'God loves us'. God's love for Himself is the same as our love for ourselves. There, in his writing, also lay the implication that mathematical and mechanical truths, and works of poetry, art, literature and music, though created by individual minds, become common property, something greater than the individual minds which produced them, and upon which still greater things were built.

For Kant and then Hegel, too, society and its institutions were more than the individuals who comprised them. From the moment we reason, believed Kant, we become aware of the moral law. Reason tells us that people are not a means to an end but an end in themselves and that we each have duties and rights. Reason tell us what we must do, and it is because we know what must be done that we become aware of our freedom of will. Yet this freedom of will and action is not quite as it seems. We have grounds for holding the freedom to be true, but doubt cannot be removed. We are bound to act as though we are free, for otherwise our actions mean nothing. But every act has an antecedent and in this sense all our actions are determined. When seen from the outside by another, or when we look back upon our past actions, our actions no longer appear free. Our faith in freedom may be necessary for moral choice, but it is not proven. The same could be said of God. Conscious of the moral law and of unconditional obligations, it is as if the world is ruled by a supreme moral intelligence.

Hegel saw in these arguments doubt over what was real and what was not. For him, the world as it really is waits to be discovered by the mind through opposing arguments, each gradually adjusted against the other until the truth is reached. And in coming to know the world, so the mind also comes to know itself, for the principles of nature are also those of the mind. The history of society, worked out through dialectics, is nothing less than an expression of the unfolding of the mind; and the mind is nothing less than the product of experiences, knowledge and traditions far broader and deeper than any to which a single individual could lay claim. All the thoughts the individual mind possesses it owes to society.

Neither could the libertarians do without the whole and a force of some kind. Since something could not be conceived to have come from nothing, reasoned Locke, then something must have existed from eternity, something powerful and knowing enough to be the source of all energy and knowledge. Bound also were we by the law of God (or natural law) which gave to each of us inalienable rights to life, limb and property, and to the freedom necessary if the social contract was to mean anything; a law made all the more abstract because it was left more implicit in social conduct. The unintended consequences which followed from the transactions of individuals each pursuing happiness and profit were of such regularity, universality and benefit that Smith gave the force which guided these consequences the name 'invisible hand'. No less powerful, thought Hume, was the self-interest and sympathy (the origin of the moral motive) innate in man and which led to common conclusions. And such was the power of the laws in Mill's world, such was the unity they brought to nature and to man, that the individual could do no other than desire pleasure and happiness.

Even those for whom the individual was almost everything seemed to require the whole. Schopenhauer (d.1860) had argued that the desires of the will, the only reality, could never be satisfied by living. Only in the very quality of reason through which the will attempts to satiate what cannot be satiated can the will find relief from the tyranny of itself. Only through reason – and therefore in the realisation that life is vanity, that all its forms are but expressions of one will, and that individuality is an illusion – can salvation be found. Nietzsche (d.1900), too, had need of the whole if only to explain the religious origin of tragedy, and to serve as the antitype which the individual must struggle against and then overcome if he is define himself as a superman.

But if the individual could not do without the whole and the principles it implied, then neither could the whole do without the individual. Aristotle had not discounted the individual; and, as we noted earlier, in his inquiry into substance, he raised in the minds of the medieval scholars the question of difference among individuals of the same species. As for the fate of the individual soul, Plato had not discounted the possibility of its survival. Though he classed the matter one of myth, which need only avoid conflict with what was known about the nature of Ideas, he suspected that the individual soul may pass through a series of reincarnations. And whilst the Stoics did not believe in free will, the early Christians, as we have said, believed that the individual might have a special place in God's design; and, like the Cynics, the Stoics regarded the subsumation of the individual's life in the customs of the city as a kind of tyranny, preferring to see themselves as citizens of the world. In this, perhaps, the early Christians saw the revolutionary, iconoclastic spirit which they also saw in themselves. In Spinoza's world, too, the individual was not, at least by implication, defunct, for how could it otherwise be suspected that he was but part of something much greater? And must not each mind be different enough to make different contributions to that store of knowledge greater than can be held by any individual? Kant had a faith in individual freedom; and neither the individual nor the whole could be conceived of by Hegel without the other, for each was part of the same dialectic. It was also individuals who might senselessly criticise and reject the tradition; and who in fact appropriated and used for political self-interest Hegel's own philosophy. Even the Marxist held high, and yet simultaneously depersonalised, the individual. In society's institutions, laws and morality the Marxist saw justification and support for the dominant relations of production which made puppets of both master and slave. Only by denying private property would individuals, no longer alienated from one another, experience true freedom.

Our haunted minds

Lying within – or, as some might argue, stirring the very heart of – this dispute between the individual and the whole is a debate about the nature of that mysterious thing – I, me, myself, the soul – if indeed it is a thing at all. Is it a spirit that can exist independently of the body (and its brain)? Or is it something material which is intimately connected to, but quite distinct from, the body? These beliefs are strong and always have been, perhaps because they seem to be confirmed by our everyday lives. I know that I am. I know that I feel sensations and emotions. I know that I have beliefs, desires, intentions and ambitions. I know that I think. I feel myself to be in control of this body and its brain (for I can decide whether to think about this or that, or to let myself wander through my day-dreams). It is as if I am the pilot of a ship or the ghost in a machine. I am irreducibly me, and I can only guess, from my own experiences, my own imaginings, at what it is like to be you. I can, in my mind's eye, place myself in your shoes; but I will never truly know what it is like to be in those shoes.

Because I know myself, I can also doubt all that I am. I can argue that my sense of being me, that 'I', is an illusion, a consequence of the working of my body. When we refer to our mental states we are doing no more than describing, in coded terms, our behaviour. I say that I am in love. I feel a yearning for another person. But when I say that I am in love I am merely describing, or rationalising, my pre-disposition to behave in a certain way. The feelings I have, and the things I do, are merely the by-product, or the mechanisms, of my programmed behaviour. And if it is true that our emotions, sensations and behaviour can be explained by the workings of our bodies, then perhaps that sense of 'I' is also better understood in this way? Could it be that one part of the brain is capable of scanning its other parts? Or is it that our brain comprises an integrated neural network in which each cell is connected with every other, such that self-monitoring circuits are created? If so, then mechanisms like these must be determined by our genes; and our genes and the particles through which they exert their influence must be subject to fundamental physical and biological laws. Much of what we are, we must assume implicitly or explicitly, and much of what we do, is predetermined. Our feelings, interpretations, ideas, beliefs, and sense of 'self', we must believe, are but the effects or rationalisation of programmed behaviour. When a mother gives her life for, or fights ruthlessly to protect, her child, any feelings of affection, love, attachment and anger are but descriptions of complex electrical, chemical and biological reactions controlled by her genes and, ultimately, by fundamental physical laws. She is propelled by her genes into a course of action necessary to protect and pass on that genetic material. Any feelings she experiences are by-products of, or necessary stimuli for, such behaviour. If this is true, then it would also seem to follow that our thoughts, including modern science, must be fixed in our physical make-up. Since our brains have, by way of natural selection, evolved around the natural world, then, given that there must be order in the natural world to allow our existence, it is hardly surprising that we are coming to know something of that world. Our science, like our other thoughts, must be a product of natural selection.

There is another kind of doubt, too, or is it the hope that we might free ourselves from our introspection? If I am able to reason and if I live among others who do likewise then surely it is inconceivable that what I feel, think and desire, and the problems I see and the solutions which occur to me, cannot be felt, thought, desired, perceived, understood and arrived at by 'you', and vice versa. Could it not be that 'I' am of the 'public'? No matter how private my feelings, thoughts and desires may seem to me, no matter how much they seem to well up from within me, I am able to formulate them, reflect upon them, and communicate them only because I do so in a public language. And if they can be referred to in a public language, then they must be known to other people. 'You' 'know' what 'I' feel, think and desire; and were I able to transfer those feelings, thoughts and desires to 'you', then 'you' would recognise with immediacy, without any doubt, confusion or hesitancy, what I feel, think and desire, just as I would be able to comprehend with immediacy 'your' states of mind. I may be a thinking and rational individual, but this I owe to the public. This is a notion which requires us to step outside the first person for a moment, and to put away my sense of 'self': I must see 'me' from the third person, and accept that what I feel to be me is that person which other people see and with whom they form their relationships. Once I do so, then it becomes easier to accept that my sense of self, my sense of isolation, and my desire to seek relief from that isolation, all stem from the public. Easier, too, is it to understand that it is my very sense of self which insulates me, such that I cannot experience with immediacy and without doubt that of which I know myself to be a part – the public.

Yet despite my doubts the puzzle remains. I know that I am me. I know what it is like to be me, and I know that it is absurd to suggest that I do not. I also know that I can only guess at what it is like to be you. Even if I do not believe that there is this ghost in this machine, I have an overwhelming sense that I am here, that I am me. No matter how much I try to imagine away that sense of 'me', and think of the sensations and emotions which I feel as being unbound by self or as mere descriptions of my predisposition to behave in certain ways, I am still here. Perhaps I am wrong in thinking that my mental states are known only to me. Perhaps it is true that my sense of self is bounded only by those among whom I live, whose language I share. Perhaps it is true that when I say I am in love I am only describing and rationalising instinctive biological mechanisms. Perhaps it is true that everything that I know myself to be can be reduced to, and explained by, the interaction of fundamental laws. But none of this denies that I know what it is like to be me. If my sense of self is an illusion, then to whom is this illusion being played? Who is it that is experiencing this illusion, even though this is what they know it to be? If I decide quite voluntarily to move my little finger, from where does that initial decision arise? If I listen to music that moves me, who is it that finally interprets those chemicals and electrical impulses as sadness or beauty? Always we are left with one more step to make. Always we are led back once again to what may seem absurd – the mind, the thinker behind the thoughts. Whatever explanation we devise to replace 'the mind' or the 'soul', that sense of self is always present, no matter how I doubt it. If I convince myself that I am an illusion, then to whom is it illusory? If I convince myself that my consciousness is reducible, then how do I account for that initial decision, and that final subjective interpretation? How can its parts come together to create, or to interpret, that sense of 'I' unless I am already there? Always a voice whispers to me: 'but I am here!'

Are there, then, other possibilities that we might consider? Perhaps our consciousness is indeed rooted in our genetic make-up, its evolution and natural selection; but maybe there exists between these phenomena and processes a more complex and less direct relationship that we have assumed so far. Our ability to reason, our thoughts, and our consciousness may perhaps represent a retreat from conditioned or determined behaviour. Is it that as the organism becomes more complex, the genetic codification of every nuance of action and behaviour is made more difficult? Or is it that there is no advantage in a rigid and deterministic link between the behaviour and the complex physical genetic coding of an organism? Are not those organisms best suited to survive those which possessed a repertoire of behavioural patterns and could respond to, or even change, their surroundings in different ways? By 'selecting' particular strategies for survival, an organism could 'choose' (in a very limited sense) their environment and thus influence the outcome of natural selection. The wider the choice open to the organism, the more efficient natural selection would prove to be; the more rigidly prescribed its behaviour, the more difficult it would be for natural selection to produce new adaptations. Human consciousness, suggest Popper and Eccles (1977), marks an evolutionary summit;[1] our thoughts and ideas, our debates and arguments, and the application of our ideas through trial and error, represent a continuation of natural selection at another, higher plain. If we accept this, then does not the fact that the evolutionists can see a reason for our behaviour which arises out of an insentient process, requires admission that either they are interpreting in the light of their beliefs or that reasoning by a sentient being is itself enough to explain that behaviour? May we not reason that modern science, like the other galleries of our thought and behaviour, is in no sense built into us. It must have developed from, and is still founded upon, unregulated, chaotic, unmethodical and intuitive ways of thinking which because of their lack of form allows all kinds of possibilities to be explored. It is in the expression of this fog of nonsense and truth that we have learnt to discipline ourselves, such that possible explanations – even those which we instinctively prefer, and which seem to confirm our beliefs or prejudice or common sense – can be eliminated until we are left with what must be; and then subjected again to doubt, to the possibility that while our observations and explanations may hold true here and now, they may not hold true at all places or at all times, to the possibility and that such laws or regularities may be no more than anthropomorphic superstitions.

Perhaps it may be that natural science is even now uncovering a still more plastic and uncertain physical world, and an absence of connexions between, on the one hand, our genetic make-up and, on the other, our thought, our behaviour, our decisions and the social world that we create around us? By tracing the hardwiring of our minds, and our genetic, endochrinal and other biological systems, such that we are able to explain in detail how our bodies work, we may also have explained to us how a being has retreated from a programmed existence, and how choice, feelings and the conscious shaping and redirection of thoughts, desires, intentions, beliefs, values and behaviour are left outside the command of those systems and processes. Thus we will have explained to us scientifically why there can be no truly scientific explanation of human society. Whilst many see great wonder at the emergence of a sentient being with the capacity to understand the blind, unknowing, unfeeling, natural world from which it emerged, there is perhaps greater wonder to be found in what it is that modern science may be *unable* to tell us about ourselves.

Or perhaps we might even question the notion of natural selection itself? Let us begin by accepting what we are told – that, as a consequence of random mutations, blind chance and blind circumstance, only those living things which happened to be best suited to environment and to competition with other living things survived and perpetuated their lines. Of this process, all living things are the product; and our brains, in their complexity and dominance over all other living things, mark an evolutionary summit. The possibility that this is so, we could add, is strengthened by two questions which might at first sight appear to imply criticism of natural selection. First, if what exists is best suited to that existence, then what conceivable advantage has the animate over the inanimate? (This is a question which presumes that we are not prepared to accept that the existence of living things is somehow different from the existence of the inanimate, and, therefore, that natural selection only applies to living things.[2]) Second, if what lives is best suited to living, then what advantage does the complex organism have over the simple? In answer to both questions, and possibly in response to any obstacle that we might wish to set up to natural selection, we need only look at the fact of our existence. The complexity and dominance of the human brain, and its manipulation of the material world, amply demonstrate that complex living things are the best (though not perfect) evolutionary strategy. Unlikely though it may seem that life in all its extraordinary complexity could be the result of a random, blind, and unknowing process, the very fact of complex life with all its imperfections declares the extraordinary power of that process.

But now let us ask if there is not something teleological, even mystical, in all this? Evolution, through the process of natural selection tends, blindly, randomly, unknowingly, towards the best (though not to perfection). The human brain, by virtue of its complexity and dominance, is the best. It was therefore towards the human brain that things have been moving, and the existence of the brain may be taken as confirmation of this. The human brain is first, not in time, but in the order of things. To understand living things we must understand them in the light of the existence of that which now contemplates them. All interpretations of the qualities of other living or extinct organisms are now shaped into an explanation which, naturally enough, places what it is (the mind) that understands them at the centre of that understanding. Strip away that teleology, however, and we have only, say, a mathematical tendency to complexity from which emerge many lines of organisms. Some of these are perpetuated, and some are not. What we see here today and in such remnants as we have preserved in fossil records, is not the totality of the pattern of that mathematical tendency, but fragments of it. We cannot know or prove what it was that led to the extinction or survival or one or other line. We can never be sure that the link we make between the qualities of an organism and its existence (no matter how obvious and strong the association might seem to be) is anything more than an interpretation, an invention, made in the light of our own existence which itself is the product of this mathematical complexity. It is, we must assume, only our imperfect knowledge of the total pattern and of the process of the mathematical tendency which brought that pattern about, and the importance which we attach to our consciousness because we are conscious, that leaves us with the impression that the qualities of living things are shaped by anything other than this mathematical tendency. We should look, then, not to natural selection to understand ourselves and our place among other living things but to that tendency towards mathematical complexity; to the internal dynamics of the particles of living things; and to the transmission of those particles within and, presumably, even across what we have classed as genus and species. What might then emerge, perhaps, are still more complex, uncertain and unpredictable interconnections among the particles of living things, between these particles and the organism as a whole and its evolution (for the argument is against natural selection, not evolution), and between the physical make-up of the organism and its actions. Of this uncertainty which stems from this mathematical tendency to complexity, consciousness is the exemplar. Perhaps, then, there are indeed other things at work of which we are not yet aware – perhaps, as Chalmers (1996) has posited, various kinds of as-yet-undiscovered psycho-physical laws?

Or do we need to do no more than accept that consciousness is just what it seems – an irreducible thought, a thought that invades all others, a thought which emerges in the early part of our lives with our reasoning. If, or when, 'this' thing, event or action – the most common and therefore the most important being those which stem from the people around us – appears to lead, or is in some way related to, 'that', there is, in this connexion, imagination, supposition and rationalisation. And if it is being perceived that 'this' may lead, or is in some way related, to 'that', then, by following that same line of reasoning, there must also be a connexion between what is being perceived and the fact of that perception: 'I' must 'be'. Always I am brought back to 'me', this ghost in the machine, this reasoned conclusion which is my consciousness. With this emerging self-awareness comes emotion, drive, desire, intention and instinct, for without 'I' there can be no feeling, no sense that 'I' am being driven, or pressed, or influenced by something from within or without, no attempt to rationalise, redirect, control, or harness those emotions, desires and impulses, no sense of wishing, yearning, ambition, design, planning, or choice. With the realisation that 'I' must 'be', and with the emergence of 'my' emotions, desires, drives and intentions, there comes an intimation of 'you' and 'we', of how 'I' affects 'you' and 'them', and of how 'you' and they' may affect and influence 'me'. But then what is the nature of our reasoning?

Or perhaps we must face the truth that we can never know what consciousness is. Was von Hayek (1952) right when he argued that the workings of the human brain could be explained only by a structure of still greater complexity?[3] Or is it that the very nature of our consciousness creates a paradox in any explanation, leaving a knowledge of its true origin just out of our reach? If what we feel ourselves to be is to be explained (causally) by the origin of our consciousness, then surely we cannot truly see the world for what it is, nor see ourselves for what we are. All that we see, do and think must be tainted and conditioned by our origins, such that even the explanation that we give for the origin of our consciousness must be suspect: our 'reason' may be faulty, and 'evolution' or 'the public' may limit and distort our outlook. All may be illusion. If, on the other hand, I declare that my explanation is correct, then for my assertion to be true must I not be free of my origins? But if I am free of my origins, if that causal link between my consciousness and its origin is now broken, then how can I ever be sure that the origin of my consciousness is as I say?

Culture, institution and the wider world

Clearly, my earlier suggestion that we can see an emphasis on the individual strengthening as we look back through the twentieth and nineteenth centuries, did over-egg the pudding somewhat, as did my suggestion that social science today is dominated by the whole. There was in the past much of the individual in the whole, and much of the whole in the individual, just as there is today: the distinction between communitarian and individualist, and their populist labelling as left or right, are most unsatisfactory. Where, for instance, can we place Scruton's doubts (1997) about the self, his emphasis on community and institutions, and his criticisms of both the libertarian and the socialist?

Could not a case be made that Derrida's determination that the self and a single truth or meaning is a fiction, or Foucault's apparent view that institutions equate with power and its acquisition, be construed as justifications for an intensely self-centred, individualistic world? And what of Rawls' philosophical justifications of the welfare state, seen by some as libertarian and the socialist? Indeed, the centuries-old debate over the nature, sphere and implications of negative and positive rights, but part of the still-older debates on the individual and the whole, has long-since removed any simple distinction between individual and community if such a distinction ever existed.

But this only makes still more striking both the heavy burden carried by cultural and institutional explanations so common in the social sciences and also the limitations which this imposes upon our outlook. For there is, in our discussions on the whole and the individual, and in all our uncertainty about the nature of 'I', 'you', 'they' and 'us', much to agree and disagree with, and many possible lines of thought to be seen, any one of which, it seems to me, is at least as interesting as any continued reliance on culturalist-cum-institutionalist interpretations of our social world.

We might begin, for instance, by arguing that there is in the strict view of the 'individual' and the 'whole' something of a contradiction. If it is suggested that there are only the individuals and associations of individuals, then whilst we can call the sum a 'society', there is, except in this descriptive sense, no such thing. Society, institutions, practices, customs are but passive expressions of individual will and purpose. And it is only individuals who affect other individuals. Similarly, if it is argued that society and its institutions, values, beliefs, patterns of behaviour are more than the sum of its parts (the individual), then whilst we can talk of the individual, the individual can only be understood as an extension of the whole.

We might suggest, however, that both views are unsatisfactory. The strictly individualistic point of view seems to go against experience. My language is not my own; I cannot claim that my conclusions – my ideas, beliefs, values, practices, patterns of behaviour and so on – are my own; and if they are expressed in this public language, and if, when stripped of imperfect expression, they can be understood by others, then surely they cannot be my own? And must not the fact that I reason mean that all those who reason may arrive at, or have long-since arrived at, the very same conclusions which I have reached? I also have a need for expression, confirmation and affirmation, for is it not in the expression, sharing and disputation of ideas which makes them real and of interest to me? If I am isolated and there is no contradiction, no confirmation and no affirmation, then how can I be sure of anything that I think? And how does the strict individualist explain that common behaviour which holds individuals and associations of individuals together, and appears to gives them direction without implying some force of some kind (such as rationality and pursuit of happiness and profit) to be present within or without the individual – a force which itself implies a deeper unity?

But so too, if I declare individual will to be a fiction or an illusion, and make society supreme, then this also seems to deny what I know to be me. It also suggests that while I think I know, I do not, and can never, know anything for certain. If I am not allowed seclusion and always seek confirmation, affirmation and contradiction, then how can I let my thoughts roam free, experiment and in this way develop? And again, by what force do individuals initially create institutions capable of governing; and by what force do those institutions govern and shape individuals?

We can make the case, then, that whilst the individual and the whole seem to exclude each other, the one cannot do without the other. We might now, in response, try to meld the two together in some way, creating a dialectic or form of recursive relationship. But in doing so the problems only intensify. Whether the individual is emphasised, and society admitted an influence, or whether the emphasis is on society, and individuals are allowed to alter only in some small way the whole by which they are shaped, we must now turn to some force which we must assume exists both within and without the individual. We must explain many individuals' common initial behaviour and cohesion, and then explain how and why institutions capable of exerting influence were first created and how and why they exert the influence that is indeed exerted. We might, for instance, call upon socialisation, enculturation, drift, conduction or convection. The notion of culture adds further to the problem: our concern is no longer to identify universals, but to describe the forces which shape patterns held to be distinctive of, or even unique to, a particular group, though here again there is the implication that a deeper, generic force underlies this multi-cultural world.

We seem, then, to be faced then with two ideas – the individual and the whole – both of which repel each other, both of which are yet so interdependent that when the one is marginalised or denied, it must, for the sake of the other, be substituted for by the invocation of forces. And infusing this vast debate is an intense concern with our relationships. One implication to be taken from this, surely, is that the individual and the whole represented in our discussions reflect not two corporeal things nor even two different ideas, but the same ideas as it is pulled in various directions? That is – and I shall elaborate upon this shortly – we have but a single common idea of being which arises out of, and is interpreted through, our relationships and thus assumes different forms and purposes. This at least is a suggestion which also follows on from, and now leads us into, a more explicit consideration of, the central arguments which underlie this book.

The personal and the absolute

Our reasoning and sense of being, I have intended to imply in these pages, derive from, or are at least initiated in, our relationships with each other, and that it is on account of our reasoning that we strike towards our relationships attitudes which I have described as being more, or less, personal or absolute. These attitudes have profound implications for the quality of our lives not least because it is from our social relationships that our institutions procedures, practices of our bureaucratic, political and economic and social life are translated.

To choose the personal is to view the networks of relationships we stitch together as the symbol and measure of wealth (by which I mean our understanding of status, power and prestige – social and political). They are material for manipulation, the means for realising personal ambitions and of protecting oneself from the ambitions of others. If that ambition grows, and if it is to be satisfied, then individuals must reach far and wide, draw in competing networks, and gather them into their hands. And if this new empire is to hold together, then greater predictability and stability must be brought to relationships which are inherently uncertain. Images which reinforce that personal authority, so important when so much depends upon such fragile relationships, take on still greater significance. The leaders become the embodiment of all that is held to be right and good and strong. Their authority is unquestioned and reason enough to demand that their followers defer to the culture they now represent. With their authority and in the name of the culture they cajole, persuade, organise, inspire and coerce, and thereby secure their position. Implicit in this culture is the idea of the whole, the aggregate: a tangible, indisputable truth to which each member of that culture belongs. Artists, sculptors, writers, musicians and technicians must read well the ambitions which the culture serves and – in its accepted styles (the symbols of unity) – impress the sense of these ambitions upon their work; then may their leaders' greatness, like that of Ozymandias, be felt even among the crumbling monuments in ages still to come. The gods, too, are transformed into the nymphs of earthly ambitions, for their will, anger and favours are channeled through the leader as if with him they are as one. Strengthening these images of the whole is the leaders' control over the procurement and distribution of goods, either directly through the necessary institutions, or by binding merchants to the leaders' will. It is upon the control of the materials that production depends, and it is with these materials that opportunities and favours may be granted and obligations established in others. Each individual belongs to the whole and so with righteous justification may be directed legitimately with fierce prejudice, and may have imposed upon them such policies and criteria of excellence and perfection of government, administration and morality as its leaders see fit by virtue of their self-proclaimed insight, understanding, vision and good intentions, and by virtue of their position as representatives of that 'oneness'. But such images are only illusions, and the complex of institutions of administration and government are only fragile shells. The leadership must rely upon their ability to handle the tides of our relationships: as the tide shifts, as events unfold, as new combinations of relationships come together, and as old ones fray and dissolve, the shells crumble, images are dispelled, and opportunities are left open to those with sharper ambitions.

To choose the absolute is to perceive and treat relationships more as something pure and profound in their own right. It is to distance them from the conduct of professional life and the realisation of ambitions. The institutions, laws and procedures of state with which we are faced, and in which we work, though fashioned from our relationships, are viewed as discrete entities which, though subject to considered debate and measured change, should be treated as if absolute, to whose benefits all are entitled and to whose authority all are subject. And if it is believed that certain rights are inherent in all individuals, and apply equally to all, and that justice and fair play are universal sentiments, and that neither these rights or sentiments or the principle of the rule of law are bound or determined by culture, and if we act upon those beliefs, then the interpretation of values, rights, institutions, patterns of behaviour, conventions, limits of authority, and the determination of what is acceptable and unacceptable must be subject to debate, to advocacy, to argument, to a gulf-stream of criticism, to the test of trial and error, to examination, and to considered change. There is no-one who may claim with legitimacy to know what is or should not be, for there is no-one who may claim with legitimacy to be capable enough, or to have the right, to judge who is above, or who is below, what is held to be common to all, or to enforce or to impose those interpretations. Government and administration acts to weigh and balance the interests of individuals, groups, minorities and majorities, and to protect individuals from the overbearing sanctity of the mass. Policies are shaped less by the 'visions' or 'plans' of governments and by their attempts to engineer what they believe should be, than by individuals as they pursue interests, desires, fulfilment, and a sense of worth, each according to their own values and beliefs; by the practical and psychological need for expedient absolutes; and by common humanitarianism. Society is not thought of as a 'whole', nor is the individual considered an ideology – as concepts to be understood by reference to theoretical and conceptual allegories, as concepts to be engineered and shaped by the seer. Now the gods need no shamans, kings or emperors; art and technology become expressions of their creator's will. The purpose of governance and administration is understood to be the management of expedient absolutes and their evolution as the beliefs, interests and values of individuals, and their sense of self-worth and fulfillment, change or appear to change in meaning as the wider context alters; and to manage that evolution without centralising power and authority to the extent that the concept of the 'whole' is made incarnate.

Though I have presented here what is in effect a common, practical choice between the personal and the expedient absolute (or, for the sake of convenience, just 'absolute') which each one of us, and so each society, faces, this 'choice' is perhaps better presented as shifts in emphasis which derive from our own interpretation of our immediate knowledge in the light of our attitude towards our relationships. By this immediate knowledge I mean every individual's knowledge of their own sensations and emotions or states of mind, which, no matter how much we might think of as illusory, are nevertheless keenly felt. The implication here is that we interpret and rationalise our undifferentiated emotions and sensations in the light of attitudes towards relationships, such that those emotions and sensations are now felt and communicated more precisely and with greater intensity. This immediate knowledge, seen through the personal, constitutes a powerful sense of self. The personal attitude is confirmed and strengthened by return; and even the idea that the individual will is an illusion is transmuted into a justification for the pursuit and satisfaction of transitory pleasures. Interpreted through the absolute, however, we begin to mould from those same raw undifferentiated emotions a need to be not only in a community, but *of* the community; and the more we attempt to control and manipulate others, the more alienated from that community we feel.

Put another way, the personal and the absolute are not mutually exclusive. Within each of us and among us all there is an awareness of other interpretations of our emotions and sensations. With the personal comes a powerful sense of self. Yet there is an awareness of the absolute, of a sense of community, a sense sharpened in opposition. On this account alone we may begin to interpret our immediate knowledge through the absolute. And, vice versa, where the absolute dominates, an awareness of the personal, of that sense of self, may begin to intensify in opposition; and so we begin to interpret in the light of the personal.

I have argued, then, that there is an intimate association between our relationships, our reasoning, our attitudes, our interpretations of our own emotions, and our sense of self and of the whole. Each follows from and strengthens the other. I have also suggested that there is in the shifts between the personal and the absolute much spontaneity. But there are also, I have implied, strong practical considerations at work from which the personal and the absolute as well as the shifts between them may emerge, in part, as practical, reasoned responses. There are, for instance, the practical concerns stemming from a need for general stability. Whether the individual is a fiction or not, it is necessary to believe in its substance as if it were real. If we were to regard it simply as an illusion then how could we be sure that we know anything? And without the individual, without the certainty that our knowledge is more than an illusion, might we not behave as if nothing matters except the satisfaction of our own transitory pleasures, and as if other people are little more than material for manipulation in our own personal, imaginary world. So, too, if we were to regard individuals as pure absolutes, as supreme and unassailable, each with perfectly equal and, necessarily, absolute rights and responsibilities, then might not the individual become inflexible? In this perfect world of equal spheres of negative rights, would we not be unwilling to allow our own diminution, to give way to altruism and self-sacrifice, and to accept the imperfections and weaknesses in ourselves and others qualities so necessary in the practical conduct of our lives? Transformed thus into a rigid ideology which if rigidly applied would create a frozen impractical world, the notion of the individual is more open to manipulation: it becomes an artifact, a means of legitimating, a means to an end, a means of undermining and manoeuvering around the frozen world it has been used to create, valuable only in the pursuit of ambition at another's expense. In the same way, our patterns of behaviour, conventions, beliefs, values, practices, procedures and institutions, whether seen merely as composites of calculating individuals or as pure absolutes, as something quite separate from the individual, are transformed into material for self-centred manipulation, a means to the fulfilment of personal desires.

If, however, the concepts of the individual and whole are treated *as if* absolute – that is, treated as absolute for immediate practical reasons yet always subject to debate and considered change, always open to finely judged allowances, and always the possibility of imperfection and weakness acknowledged – then they take on other qualities. Individuals are now treated as if real, yet their rights and responsibilities are made flexible, altruism and self-sacrifice admitted, imperfections and failings allowed for. The concept is now made substantial but not pure and inflexible. Institutions, values, practices, procedures and patterns of behaviour, too, are now treated as real but subject to considered debate and change which must be broad and inclusive if they are not to be presented by some as pure absolutes to others. Substantial, but not pure, neither concept is easily manipulated for personal interest; both concepts are now more susceptible to being treated as ends in themselves.

But perhaps the most vital practical consideration from which may emerge shifts in attitude from the personal to the absolute is commerce. The simple everyday working of businesses, in particular, demands a gradual shift in attitude as a balance is struck between the manipulation of relationships, such that they facilitate the workings of economic organisations, and the need within the mind to 'distance' social relationships from relationships within the firm or connected to its dealings. Such distancing is necessary in order to free the firm from the tensions, diversions and unpredictability which the manipulation or relationships would otherwise generate. Provided that the number of people working in or with businesses is sufficient, it is likely that the distancing of relationships that are social from those which are professional becomes so widespread that it becomes unacceptable, even outside the firm, to treat social relationships as material for manipulation and ambition. Our sense of worth, too, shifts its attention from the everyday politicking that is the essence of the personal, to profit-making, to creating, doing and providing things that are desired by others. Material things and their acquisition begin not only to symbolise our wealth or sense of worth, but to be valued more and more in themselves; and our strengthening notion of 'taste' becomes more than just a marker of social and political prestige and pretensions. And as relationships are distanced further from economic life, as the economy brings greater material comfort and material power, as the treatment of relationships as manipulative instruments becomes less acceptable, as things and actions take on an aesthetic value in themselves, so the need to rein in the power and influence of the ambitious may become more evident. With the absolute, then, comes an interest in art, music and literature as activities in themselves, and in emotions and ideas and relationships which, now released from the service of narrow political and economic concerns and interests, may be treated as subjects in themselves and found interesting in themselves. And with this, we might also suggest, comes a frame of mind in which it is easier to entertain the possibility of a natural world of absolutes operating independently of human concerns and considerations. In these ways the division between social, economic, political, institutional, scientific and aesthetic spheres of our lives sharpens.

Commonality of being?

There is in all this the implication of a commonality among individuals derived from the fact that we each reason. It is, in other words, because we reason and on no other account that we arrive at common conclusions – at common sets of solutions, practices, responses, arguments, values, beliefs, institutions and behaviour. For instance, and most fundamentally, it is on account of our reasoning that we see a need – in view of our physical nature and in the immediate knowledge of our sense of separateness and individuality – to live and work with each other, and also to seek solitude. It is reasonable that we should manipulate and translate our relationships into complex institutions and practices. It is reasonable that we should create all manner of kernels (such as kinship, place of origin or language) around which relationships may be formed and institutions shaped. Reasonable it is that we should strike certain common attitudes to those relationships. And it is reasonable that we should interpret our immediate knowledge in the light of these attitudes and in this way construct for ourselves common purpose, direction, ambition and notions of prestige. This commonality derived from our reasoning also logically extends, or so it would seem, to technical solutions. This being so, then independent invention may often be more significant than is sometimes assumed.

A further implication which arises from this discussion – and it is one which has already been alluded to above – is this: just as more specific emotions and sensations may be considered as extensions of a more undifferentiated immediate knowledge, so the more complex and the more specific mediums of reasoning (art, literature, philosophy, music, social organisation and the handling of relationships) may be considered as extensions of less differentiated, simple forms of reasoning. A common conclusion may be arrived at independently by the child and by the philosopher: in its simple form by the child; the philosopher, meanwhile, cascades the simple through all the earlier ideas and reasoning, through the personal and the absolute, through our immediate knowledge, through the more precise emotions and sensations, layering conclusion upon conclusion, until it emerges in a more complex form, and may do so as easily through the medium of music, art, social organisation, or mathematics and science as through the medium of words. The ideas which any one of us produces and through whatever medium, I am arguing, are being, or have been, or will be, in their essence, constantly produced by many other individuals at some time or other.

It is, then, on account of our reasoning that we reach broadly common conclusions; and it is in the light of our reason that we translate, through our attitudes, our relationships into institutions, practices and procedures. It is also on account of our reasoning that we transmit, accept, agree with, feel obligated to, impose, or are determined to argue and revolt against, and reject, ideas, practices, institutions and behaviour. That we should interpret as spirit structures or forces apparent trends in what are but aspects of our commonality of being owes much to those very attitudes which also endow the social world with its most essential qualities. Interpreted through the absolute, we permit ourselves, to some degree, and for the sake of stability and predictability, to behave towards the ideas, precedents, conventions, institutions, practices and procedures which we create as if they were absolute and as if they possess a life of their own. Interpreted through the personal, we see, and create, a world vacillating between fuzzy institutions, uncertain networks of community, flint-like authoritarianism, and steel-like images set upon unstable sands.

To describe, as we have done, the turning or translation of common relationships and attitudes and interpretations in varied, though common ways, to varied, though common ends is simply to say that we, our relationships and the social world we shape, possess many dimensions. Our social relationships – the give and take layered with emotions and values interpreted through the personal and absolute – remain the same in all walks of life. It is only within the mind something of a distinction or distancing emerges in our relationships. What we see and feel as distinct are but different aspects of the same relationships. It is precisely this multidimensional quality which oils our professional relationships. It is also this multidimensionality that helps us to understand the nature of our apparent differences. As the intentions and perceptions of those who participate and those who observe alter, and as individuals come and go, so those dimensions begin to rotate. The arbitrary extraction of institutions and behaviour, practices, procedures, values and beliefs, and their presentation as a fixed unidimensional pattern which is held to be distinctive or unique to a particular group, is 'the culture' – a common, reasoned technique for legitimating authority, knowledge and cohesion. It is one often born out of a common, well-reasoned fear: in the realisation of similarity lies the realisation that the particular cultural images which have been accepted hitherto and may now be questioned.

The 'reason' which I am envisaging, and through which we reach common sets of conclusions, is not, I would suggest, to be equated with rationality. What I am asserting is that the conclusions which any of us might reach, have been, or are being, or will be, reached in their more simple or complex forms (and expressed through varied mediums) at countless other times and places by other people. When seen in this broader view, then even the apparently outlandish, fresh, rational, irrational, superstitious, ludicrous, brilliant, mad, despised, hated, original or admired no longer appear as once they did. I am also asserting that there is no context of slowly altering structures and forces within which our reasoning must operate, such that our conclusions, as if in some version of Herskovits' and Sapir's 'drift', are conditioned. Although the 'context' which we sense is itself of our common conclusions and may therefore be seen in very similar ways, those conclusions, and any subsequent conclusions which may be reached, represent fluid possibilities rather than certainties: it is likely that any specific conclusion in a specific form and medium reached by one mind will be reached at other times by many other minds; but there is no guarantee that it will be acted upon or given expression by sufficient people. Any context which we might sense may also alter with the individual's attitudes and states of mind. Of this ever-changing, multidimensional complex that is our social world we each see only a small part. Of the rest we can imagine only the most vague and distorted outline of what that world might be if it could be held and perceived by a single mind.

Social relationships and social science

I implied in the introduction that this book is as much about how all of us – whoever we are and wherever we live – shape our social world as it is about the Nazarenes. Our relationships are, for each of us, the substance of our lives, the delicate, ephemeral connexions, the gossamer of our minds, through which we reach outside ourselves and so create our social world. To understand ourselves and so that world, we must look what it is that we are: at our struggle with that feeling of being separate; at how, through the give and take of favours layered with emotions, sentiments and values, we form relationships; at our apperception and perceptions of others, and at how we use those images; and at how far we allow those images to dominate us. We must look at how we form and re-form, shape and re-shape, these threads into our institutions and patterns of behaviour; and we must look, above all, at our attitudes towards our relationships.

In understanding our commonality of being, there is no need for recourse to structures or forces within us or without. It derives quite simply from the fact that we reason and that we are aware – and have an intimate knowledge – of self and 'you'. It is an understanding of what we and others are, feel, desire and do, understandings that are extrapolated, reconsidered and changed in the light of imagination and experience. These commonalties find expression, I believe, through our technologies, our material symbols, and most fundamentally, our relationships – through 'my' understanding of what it is like to be 'you'. These incorporeal threads, through which our self-awareness and consequential sense of isolation find relief, we 'turn' and 'manipulate' for our own ends; fashion into symbols of peculiarity and uniqueness, sameness and universality, power and subordination; weave to form our institutions; and so make our social world. There, in that turning or translation we lay bare what we believe to be valuable and valued in us, and so reveal the 'personal' and the 'absolute' in ourselves.

Now we can also begin to see that the characteristics of society and its problems are but translations of the most detailed nuances of everyday life; and that the similarities to which I have referred are no mere chance parallels. The differences of culture, of East and West, of North and South, of religion, politics and ideology, which appear so profound, are but the coloured shadows thrown by our true substance – our commonality of being and our common reasoned responses to circumstance. As the observer alters his perspective, or as we turn to other ends our relationships (and so our institutions, values, beliefs, emotions and ideas), or as we deliberately re-present ourselves and our creations as distinctive or unique, so our shadows appear to lengthen, shorten, twist and change their form. Yet if we switch our attention from the shadow to the substance, and allow ourselves within our mind's eye to rotate about that substance, its many dimensions become apparent and our differences may be seen for what they are – distant, ephemeral images. We ourselves and the gossamer of our minds, we with our many dimensions, have remained the same all along. Now it is not the differences but the similarities between one society and another, whatever their cultures and ideologies, that are remarkable.

We can also begin to see why it is so necessary to reconsider how we might approach understanding. Our relationships are so central to our everyday lives that they cannot but have a strong bearing upon how we understand. There is in our writings, and in our reading of them, just as there is in the people we are reading or writing about, much of the personal and the absolute. The value in, say, our discussion on the consciousness, the individual and the whole may lie not in what they purport to tell us about their origin and nature, but in what they tell us about how we think about ourselves and others. If we are able to consider such diametrically opposed views of what we are, if we are able to step outside ourselves and doubt our sense of self, if we can be both intensely private and yet strive to be an immediate part of the public, then do we not in our desire to explain consciousness, whatever that explanation, reflect something of a desire to be of the public, to link this powerful sense of me, here inside this body, into something that we all share and of which we are all a part? Do we not in our in our wondering about what 'I' am and about what it is to be 'you' reflect an intrinsic and intense concern with our relationships with each other? These ideas on consciousness, the individual and the whole may also give us an indication of what it is, or was, that was seen and felt by individuals other than the particular writer. I am thinking here not of a *zeitgeist* (if by that is meant some abstract force), but of our commonality of being, of ideas beliefs, practices and states of mind – emotional, intellectual, scientific, artistic, or social – arrived at independently or transmitted and accepted *because* we reason. I have in mind here, say, the strain of the expedient absolute strong in Kant's work, followed so closely by the full flush of romanticism and the industrial revolution; or the rise of commerce, the emergence of welfare institutions, and the creation of art with romantic qualities during the Sung Dynasty; or the desire to pursue art for art's sake, the sentiment that landscape and nature were in themselves objects of beauty, the strengthening of the Mahayana sect of Buddhism with its emphasis on love and compassion as virtues in their own right, and the contempt for rites and politics that followed the collapse of the Han Dynasty. My contention, then, is that we can see in what is written, ideas that were being arrived at more generally in more or less sophisticated forms and expressed through varied mediums, and which were accepted because they chimed with those other forms and mediums.

It is with this argument in mind that we might look at social science with its implied forces and structures. Now such a natural part of everyday thought and practice in the mature democracies of Europe and America, the view that individuals, their relationships and institutions should be treated *as if* absolutes, has in academic analysis been transposed into pure absolutes – phenomena and forces which though once created by individuals nevertheless exist independently of them and as part of some greater whole. This transposition is not, however, a consequence of writers becoming inured to particular views and practices. The writers are themselves, I would suggest, reaching common conclusions which are also being reached in varied forms and expressed through varied mediums by other people including those who are being described and analysed. In other words, we are seeing in the transposition of expedient absolutes into the pure absolutes of social science manifestations of a shift towards the personal which also finds expression as a lessening of substance and a strengthening emphasis on image, auditing, monitoring, policing, networking, orthopraxy and the creation of manuals of best practice, behaviour and thought in every other sphere of life from the arts and politics to science and business.

The cultural explanation, for instance, with its forces and structures, is more than just an analyses of what is held to be the workings of culture. The explanation is *of* the practices which it purports to explain. By this I do not mean that the forces assumed in that explanation are anything other than imagined; my meaning is only that the explanation in its dependency upon the apathetic fallacy is a representation of, or code for, an underlying or 'raw' explanation which, wrung through the personal, is political and instrumental in nature; just as the interpretation generated by that explanation of practices, and presented to the world, is a representation of the 'raw' practices which are again political and instrumental in nature. And the reasoning which finds expression in those 'raw' practices may be very similar to, or may be of, the reasoning which leads to the raw explanation. The explanation and the practice, though different in the form of expression, are of the same common conclusions. The cultural explanation, then, is, in its reasoning, a common conclusion that is being reached by other people in more or less complex forms and expressed through varied mediums. Globalisation, too, with its imagined structures, does not merely represent a description or analysis of what is held to be globalisation; the writer's analysis is itself one manifestation of common conclusions which are also being reached by others whose very behaviour is being analysed and described by the writer as 'globalisation'. Put another way, the cultural explanation is one expression of the reasoning which also leads to the creation and manipulation of culture; just as the 'globalised' explanation is one expression of the reasoning which also leads to the behaviour being described as 'globalisation'. As the expression of the explanation moves closer in form to the raw practice which is being explained, however, the commonality of the conclusions shared by the explanation and the practice becomes more evident. The writer who furnishes a cultural explanation generates cultural images in the course of that explanation. The writer who furnishes the globalised explanation of ever-widening aspects of life moves closer, in the creation of this truly overarching and all-embracing conception, to the form of the raw practice being explained. Indeed, explanation and practice may quite easily merge. The explanations of culture and globalisation which assign so much importance to the networking practised by those who are being analysed are themselves kernels of association around which like-minded writers may gather. These explanations may also serve as a *point d'appui* around which the writer may establish relationships with those in business and politics. Being of their common conclusions, the writer's explanation is easily drawn into, and there used to give precision and authority to, the merchants' and politicians' rationalisations and justifications for their own actions. Many explanations and understandings of China, for instance, are closely aligned with China's images of itself. To borrow Yeats' words, this was, and still is, like all others, a civilisation 'hooped together, brought under a rule, a semblance of peace by manifold illusion'.

The images created for political purposes were drawn upon by European and American writers, romanticised and, in turn, drawn back into the creation of China's own images as part of an East–West dialectic. And, by the same token, just as scholars (from West and East) have 'bought into' China's images of itself, so they have 'bought into' the West's less flattering apperception – images in whose construction a default comparison with China and, more importantly, the notion of Orientalism have had a hand. I am not denying that Europeans and Americans took hostile, patronising or disparaging views of people outside, or indeed within, Europe and America. My point is only that as conceived by Said (1978): Orientalism – a structure of theory and practice, of enabling socio-economic and political institutions, a dynamic exchange between individual authors and large political concerns shaped by British, French and American Empires, and a sort of surrogate and even underground self against which European culture could set itself off against and gain in strength and identity – is a fiction of social science. It is not a set of structures and institutions 'out there' waiting to be uncovered, shaping and being shaped by individuals and their thoughts, and which, if understood, shows us how 'the West' constructs the 'other'. Orientalism is an idea, a technique of social science, a composite of imagined structures and cultures, which is used to legitimise intensely political images of 'the West', its colonial history, and its baleful influence on the world today. Ideas may now have become throw-away devices in the pursuit of networks of relationships and influence; but in their adoption as explanation, and in the relationships established with merchant and politician, there is for the writer the allure of greater authority and recognition. In a world of many dimensions, the assumption that there exist forces governing what we do has great advantage, as the gods, kings and emperors of old knew.

* * *

How we might understand the social world in the absence of our apathetic fallacy and despite the presence of thoughts and interpretations infused with our relationships and attitudes, has been a question central to this book even if, for the most part, it has been left unspoken The answer, I have argued, is simply to acknowledge that we are indeed of our relationships and that even as we approach our studies each of us carry preconceptions, beliefs, prejudices, emotions, imagination, experience and doubts – qualities and weaknesses that are 'me'. In this there is great value, for we are *of* each other, not because we are subject to some force – mystical, religious, social or genetic – but simply because we are, each of us, conscious and reasoning. There, in that play between our own qualities and failings, and what each of us sees, imagines and experiences, we build our thoughts and our understandings of ourselves and others; and so we create the world around us – a broad expansive place of brilliant colours and many dimensions where we see in doubt not weakness but the freedom of possibility and tolerance. To pretend otherwise, to hide what we are, and so to deny empathy, is to pretend that I am separate from 'you' and it is to say that 'you' can only be understood by calling upon something removed from the one or both of us (such as structure or culture) and which I say, *ipse dixit*, explains your nature, your actions, your behaviour and decisions. It is to say that you can only be understood intellectually. You then become the servant of my intellect, subject to what I imagine and desire unrestrained by empathy. Ideas, protected by the privilege of my intellect and my knowledge of what explains you, become political instruments. Should we, on the other hand, admit empathy, then the arguments and interpretation we present are no longer privileged: they are *of* the social world, infused with our relationships and attitudes; they are necessarily self-reflective and self-critical; and even those ideas presented to us with the claim of privilege are easily seen for what they are. My proposition, then, is very simple. We should be content to accept that the scope of our competence is a consideration of that unseen world which we form within our minds, and of the social world which we create from that substance. To understand these worlds we must look at our commonality of being from which emerge striking similarities overlain with thin, illusory representations of difference; at our common constraints; at our common reasoned responses made in the light of circumstance; at our attitudes towards our relationships with each other; and at our capacity to doubt even that which we believe ourselves to be.

Notes

Introduction

1 I say a kind of dialectic because it does not involve true opposites, as we shall see in Chapter 4.

1 Manananggot

1 A purok is a subdivision of a barangay. A barangay is a kind of political ward.
2 Armed Forces of the Philippines

2 Making politics

1 Pertierra 1988; Cohen 1981, 1974; Meskill 1970; See 1981; Hsieh, 1977.
2 Based on the number registering each month with the Department of Trade and Industry, 1996–98.
3 This is a term which I use to include governors, vice-governors, mayors and vice-mayors in cities and municipalities.
4 Office of the President 1997; Commission on Elections 1998a and 1998b; Gutierrez 1994.
5 Freedman 1958; Sahlins 1961.
6 Sidel 1997, 1998; McCoy 1993; Putzel 1992
7 By which I mean director and all lower grades.
8 Grade 22 and above.
9 These figures included couples who had married after they had joined the service.
10 I use 'Education' to include state colleges and universities as well as state schools. In fact, colleges and universities are funded separately and directly.
11 The commissioner of the Bureau of Internal Revenue, for example, could examine the bank accounts of decendants and of taxpayers who claimed to be financially 'incapable'.

3 Making relationships pay

1 Commission on Elections 1998 a and b; Office of the President 1997; Securities and Exchange Commission 1996 and 1997; Securities and Exchange Commission files [Manila and Davao City] 1998; Department of the Interior and Local Government 1995; Davao City Chamber of Commerce 1998; Business Bureau 1998; Gutierrez 1994.

2 Nowak and Snyder 1974; Hollnsteiner 1963; Machado 1978.
3 1995
4 Haynie 1995.
5 Linantud 1998
6 Thompson 1995
7 Casper 1995
8 Pinches 1997; Pertierra 1995; Sison and Palma-Angeles 1997
9 Over the last 8 years or so, somewhere between 600,000 and more than one million Filipinos at any one time have been working overseas most especially in the Middle East, Asia, Europe (mostly in Italy), and the Americas, or on board foreign ships. Around half of these migrants have received a college education. In 1997 alone, overseas Filipinos remitted more than $US 5 billion to the Philippines.
10 Satakc 1998; Rodriguez and Tecson 1998
11 Sicat 1998
12 Together with a small number of those companies which form part of those networks peripheral to the primary core in Davao.
13 As measured by the volume of their sales nationally.
14 These accounted for a steadily increasing share of all companies (including sole proprietorships) registering larger sales. Of all enterprise (including sole proprietorships) registering sales between P250,000 and P4,999,999 20 per cent were partnerships or corporations. This share rose to 90 per cent of all companies registering sales between P10 million and P49.9 million.
15 Business Bureau 1998
16 Securities and Exchange Commission files (Davao)1997
17 National Statistics Office files (Davao)1998.
18 No more than an average variation of a few percentage points in most activities, and an average variation of around 10 per cent or so in manufacturing, wholesaling and retailing.
19 National Statistics Office 1998
20 The term 'cellular' has also been used to describe self-sufficiency and the duplication of activities created by areal administrative barriers and responsibilities in China.
21 If defined as companies employing between 10 and 99 workers, then the number of SMEs in the Philippines is smaller than in many other countries in Asia (Rodriguez and Tecson 1998).
22 Securities and Exchange Commission 1997; National Statistics Office 1998.
23 Bureau of Internal Revenue 1998; Bureau of Internal Revenue Annual Project Team, 1998; National Statistical Coordination Board 1997.

4 Between two worlds

1 Popper and Eccles 1977.
2 Popper and Eccles, however, have suggested that the notion of natural selection might be applied to unstable elements.
3 von Hayek 1952, p. 182.

Bibliography

Albert, M., Becker, T., McCrone, P., and Thornicroft, G. (1998) 'Social Networks and Mental Health Service Utilisation – A Literature Review', *International Journal of Social Psychiatry* 44: 248–66.

Amante, M.S.V. (1997) 'Converging and Diverging trends in HRM: the Philippines' "Halo-Halo" Approach', *Asia Pacific Business Review* 3: 111–32.

Amoyen, N.D., Angeles, T.N., and Lacuesta, M.C. (1992) 'A Profile of the Urban Poor in Davao', *Tambara* XI: 95–124.

Amyot, J. (1973) *The Manila Chinese: familism in the Philippine Environment*, Manila: Institute of Philippine Culture (IPC) Monograph No.2.

Anderson, B. (1995) 'Cacique Democracy in the Philippines: Origins and Dreams', in V.L. Rafael (ed.) *Discrepant Histories: Translocal Essays on Filipino Culture*, pp. 3–47, Philadelphia: Temple University Press.

Bailey, F.G. (1959) 'For a Sociology of India?', *Contributions to Indian Sociology* 3: 90.

Barbieri, P. (1997) 'Il Tesoro Nascosto. La Mappa del Capitale Sociale in un'Area Metropolitana', *Rassegna Italiana di Sociologia* XXXVIII: 343–70.

Barker, Sir E. (trans.) (1948) *The Politics of Aristotle*, Oxford: Clarendon Press.

Bowie, A. and Unger, D. (1997) *The Politics of Open Economies: Indonesia, Malaysia, the Philippines and Thailand*, Cambridge: Cambridge University Press.

Budd, M. (1985) *Music and the Emotions*, London: Routledge and Kegan Paul.

Bureau of Internal Revenue (Republic of the Philippines), Revenue Accounting Division (1998) Various Reports, Davao City.

Bureau of Internal Revenue (Republic of the Philippines), Annual Project Team (1998) *1997 Annual Report*, Manila.

Business Bureau (Republic of the Philippines) Davao City (1998) *License and Permit System*, Davao City.

Carino, T. (ed.) (1985) *Chinese in the Philippines*, Manila: De La Salle University, Chinese Studies Programme.

Casper, G. (1995) *Fragile Democracies: The Legacies of Authoritarian Rule*, London: University of Pittsburgh.

Celoza, A.F. (1997) *Ferdinand Marcos and the Philippines: The Political Economy of Authoritarianism*, London: Praeger.

Chalmers, D.J. (1996) *The Conscious Mind: In Search of a Fundamental Theory*, Oxford: Oxford University Press.

Clunas, C. (1991) *Superfluous Things: Material Culture and Social Status in Early Modern China*, Cambridge: Polity Press.

Cohen, A. (1974) *Two Dimensional Man*, Berkeley: University of California Press.

—— (1981) *The Politics of Élite Culture*, Berkeley: University of California Press.

Commission on Elections (1998a) *Master List of Local Officials* (Regions XI and XII), Davao City.

—— (1998b) *List of Winning Candidates* (Regions XI and XII), Davao City.

Corcino, E. (1945) *Davao, its Land and People*, Davao: Souvenir Book of Davao Fair and Exposition.

Corcino, E. (1998) *Davao: History*, Davao: Philippine Centennial Movement, Davao City Chapter.

Crook, J.H. (1980) *The Evolution of Himan Consciousness*, Oxford: Clarendon Press.

Cullinane, M. (1995) 'Patron as Client: Warlord Politics and the Duranos of Davao', in A.W. McCoy (ed.) *Anarchy of Families: State and Family in the Philippines*, Quezon City: Ateneo de Manila University Press, pp. 163–242.

Davao City Chamber of Commerce (1998) *Davao Trade and Industry Directory*, Davao City.

—— (1998) *Small and Medium Enterprise Data Bank*, Davao City.

Davis, W.G. (1973) *Social Relations in a Philippine Market*, Berkeley: University of California Press.

Department of the Interior and Local Government (Republic of the Philippines) (1992) *Rules and Regulations Implementing the Local Government Code of 1991*, Manila.

—— (1995) *Roster of Local Government Officials*, Manila.

Devarajan, S. and Hossain, S.I. (1998) 'The Combined Incidence of Taxes and Public Expenditure in the Philippines', *World Development* 26: 963–77.

Dewey, A. (1962) *Peasant Marketing in Java*, Glencoe: Free Press.

Dumont, L. (1970) *Homo Hierarchicus: The Caste System and Its Implications*, Chicago: University of Chicago Press.

Dumont, L. and Pocock, D. (1957) 'For a Sociology of India', *Contributions to Indian Sociology* 1: 9.

East Asia Analytical Unit. (1995) *Overseas Chinese Business Networks in China*, Canberra: Department of Foreign Affairs and Trade.

Elias, N. (1994) *The Civilizing Process*, trans. Edmund Jephcott, Oxford: Blackwell.

Freedman, M. (1958) *Lineage Organisation in Southeast China*, London: London School of Economics, Monograph on Social Anthropology, No.33.

Fried, M.H. (1953) *Fabric of Chinese Society: A Study of the Social Life of a Chinese Country Seat*, New York: Octagon Books.

Fukuyama, F. (1995) *Trust*, New York: The Free Press.

Gardner, H. (1983) *Frames of Mind: The Theory of Multiple Intelligences*, London: Heinemann.

Geertz, C. (1963) *Peddlers and Princes: Social Change and Economic Modernisation in Two Indonesian Towns*, Chicago: University of Chicago Press.

Glick Schiller, N., Basch, L. and Blanc-Szanton, C. (eds) (1992) *Towards a Transnational Perspective on Migration*, New York: New York Academy of Sciences.

Goody, J. (1996) *The East in the West*, Cambridge: Cambridge University Press.

Gutierrez, E. (1994) *The Ties that Bind: A Guide to Family, Business and Other Interests in the Ninth House of Representatives*, Manila: Philippine Centre for Investigative Journalism.

Haynie, S.L. (1995) 'Resource Inequalities and Regional Variations in Litigation Outcomes in the Philippine Supreme Court, 1961–1986', *Political Research Quarterly* 48: 371–80.

Hayek, F.A. von (1952) *The Sensory Order,* London: Routledge and Kegan Paul.

Henessy, P. (1990) *Whitehall*, London: Fontana.

Herrera, O.M. (1990) *Remedial Law: Volume I, Civil Procedure*, Quezon City: Rex.

Hodder, R. (1996a) 'A Philippine Town in Chinatown?', *Southeast Asia Research* 15: 103–25.

—— (1996b) *Merchant Princes of the East: Cultural Delusions, Economic Success and the Overseas Chinese in Southeast Asia*, Chichester: John Wiley and Sons.

—— (2000) *In China's Image: Chinese Self-Perception in Western Thought*, London: Macmillan.

Holland, J. (1998) 'Does Social Capital Matter?' *IDS Bulletin* 3: 65–71.

Hollnsteiner, M.R. (1963) *The Dynamics of Power in a Philippine Municipality*, Quezon City: University of the Philippines.

Hsieh, J. (1977) *Internal Structure and Socio-Cultural Change: A Chinese Case in the Multi-Ethnic Society of Singapore*, PhD thesis, University of Pittsburgh, Michigan: University Microfilms International, Ann Arbor.

Hunt, C. and Walker, L. (1974) 'Marginal Trading Peoples: Chinese in the Philippines and Indians in Kenya', *Ethnic Dynamics*: 93–127.

Hutchcroft, P. (1991) 'Oligarchies and Cronies in the Philippine State: The Politics of Patrimonial Plunder', *World Politics* 43: 216–43.

—— (1994) 'Booty Capitalism: Business-Government Relations in the Philippines', in A. MacIntyre, (ed.) *Business and Government in Industrialising Asia*. New York: Cornell University Press, pp. 216–43.

Jacobs, J.B. (1979) 'A Preliminary Model of Particularistic Ties in Chinese Political Alliances: *kan-ch'ing* and *kuan-hsi* in a Rural Taiwanese Township', *The China Quarterly* 78: 236–73.

Jantsch, E. and Waddington, C.H. (1976) *Evolution and Consciousness: Human Systems in Transition*, Massachusetts: Addison-Wesley.

Kolenda, P. (1976) 'Seven Kinds of Hierarchy in *Homo Hierarchicus*', *Journal of Asian Studies* 35: 581–96.

Kuo, C.T. (1995) *Global Competition and Industrial Growth in Taiwan and the Philippines*, Pittsburgh: University of Pittsburgh Press.

Landé, C.H. (1965) *Leaders, Factions, and Parties: The Structure of Philippine Politics*, Yale University: Southeast Asia Studies, Monograph Series No. 6.

—— (1996) *Post-Marcos Politics: A Geographical and Statistical Analysis of the 1992 Presidential Election*, Singapore: St. Martin's Press.

Lewis, M.W. (1991) 'Elusive Societies: A Regional-Cartographical Approach to the Study of Human Relatedness', *Annals of the Association of American Geographers* 81: 605–26.

Lim, L. and Gosling, L. (eds) (1983) *The Chinese in Southeast Asia*, 2 vols, Singapore: Maruzen Asia.

Linantud, J.L. (1998) 'Whither Guns, Goons and Gold? The Decline of Factional Election Violence in the Philippines', *Contemporary Southeast Asia* 20: 298–318.

McCoy, A.W. (ed.) (1993) *An Anarchy of Families: State and Family in the Philippines*, Madison: University of Wisconsin.

McGuire, P. (1995) 'The Non-Partisan League and Social Democracy in the United States: Social Networks, Class Power, State Occupancy, and Embedded Class Biases', *Political Power and Social Theory* 9: 61–87.

Machado, K.G. (1978) 'Continuity and Change in Philippine Factionalism', in F.P. Belloni and D.C. Beller (eds) *Faction Politics: Political Parties and Factionalism in Comparative Perspective*, Santa-Barbara: ABC-Clio, pp. 193–217.

Mackie, J. (1992) 'Overseas Chinese Entrepreneurship', *Asian-Pacific Economic Literature* 6: 41–64.

McVey, R. (ed.) (1992) *Southeast Asian Capitalists*, New York: Cornell University Press.

Marcel, A.J. and Bisiach, E. (eds) (1988) *Consciousness in Contemporary Science*, Oxford: Clarendon Press.

Mercado, L.N. (1975) *Elements of Filipino Theology*, Tacloban: Divine Word University.

Meskill, J.M. (1970) 'The Chinese Genealogy as a Research Source', in M. Freedman (ed.) *Family and Kinship in Chinese Society*, Stanford: Stanford University Press, pp. 139–61.

Mulder, N. (1997) 'Filipino Images of the Nation', *Philippine Studies* 45: 50–74.

Murray, G. (1989) 'New Zealand Corporate Class Networks', *New Zealand Sociology* 4: 115–63.

National Statistical Coordination Board (1997) *Philippine Statistical Yearbook 1996*, Manila.

National Statistics Office (Republic of the Philippines) (1996) Various Files, Manila.

Nissé, J. (1999) 'Sony Enters the Next Century', *The Times (Business Life)*, March 13: 26–7.

Nolledo, J.N. (1995) *The Comprehensive Agrarian Reform Law of 1988 As Amended* (revised edition), Manila: Philippine Graphic Arts.

—— (1996) *The Revised Administrative Code of 1987*, Caloocan: National Books.

—— (1997) *The New Central Bank Act* (reprint), Caloocan: Philippine Graphic Arts.

—— (1997) *Banking Laws of the Philippines* (reprint), Caloocan: Philippine Graphic Arts.

—— (1998) *Statistical Variables*, Davao City: National Statistics Office.

—— (1998) *The 1987 Constitution of the Philippines with Highlights of the New Constitution* (reprint), Caloocan: Philippine Graphic Arts.

Northrup, D. (1978) *Trade Without Rulers*, Oxford: Clarendon Press.

Nowak, T.C. and Snyder, K.A. (1974) 'Clientelist Politics in the Philippines: Integration or Instability?', *American Political Science Review* 68: 1147–70.

Nurge, E. (1965) *Life in a Lyte Village*, Seattle: University of Washington Press.

Omohundro, J.T. (1977) 'Trading Patterns of Philippine Chinese: Strategies of Sojourning Middlemen', in K.L. Hutterer (ed.) *Economic Exchange and Social*

Interaction in Southeast Asia: Perspectives from Prehistory, History, and Ethnography, Michigan: Michigan Papers on South and Southeast Asia, No.13, Ann Arbor, pp. 113–36.

—— (1981) *Chinese Merchant Families in Iloilo: Commerce and Kin in a Central Philippine City*, Athens, Ohio and Manila: Ohio University Press and Ateneo de Manila University Press.

—— (1983) 'Social Networks and Business Success for the Philippine Chinese', in L. Lim and L. Gosling (eds) *The Chinese in Southeast Asia, Volume I*, Singapore: Maruzen Asia, pp. 65–85.

Office of the President (Republic of the Philippines) (1997) *Directory of Government Officials*, Manila.

Palanca, E.H. (1997) 'The 1990 Top Corporations in the Philippines', *Philippine Studies* 45: 547–74.

Pertierra, R. (1988) *Religion, Politics and Rationality in a Philippine Community*, Honolulu: University of Hawaii Press.

—— (1995) *Philippine Localities in Global Perspective*, Quezon City: Ateneo de Manila University Press.

Pertierra, R. and Ugarte, E.F. (eds) (1994) *Cultures and Texts: Representations of Philippine Society*, Quezon City: University of the Philippines.

Pinches, M. (1997) 'Élite Democracy, Development and People Power: Contending Ideologies and Changing Practices in Philippine Politics', *Asian Studies Review* 21: 104–19.

Popper, K. (1974) 'Scientific Reduction and the Essential Incompleteness of all Science', in F. Ayala and T. Dobzhansky (eds) *Studies in the Philosophy of Biology*, London: Macmillan, pp. 259–84.

Popper, K. and Eccles, J. (1977) *The Self and Its Brain*, Berlin: Springer International.

Portes, A. and Böröcz, J. (1989) 'Contemporary Immigration: Theoretical Perspectives on its Determinants and Mode of Incorporation', *International Migration Review* 23: 606–30.

Putzel, J. (1992) *A Captive Land: The Politics of Agrarian Reform in the Philippines*, Quezon City: Ateneo de Manila University Press.

Pye, L. (1985) *Asian Power and Politics*, Cambridge, Mass.: Harvard University Press.

Pye, L. (1995) 'Factions and the Politics of *guanxi*', *The China Journal* 34: 35–54.

Rafael, V.L. (ed.) (1995) *Discrepant Histories: Translocal Essays on Filipino Cultures*, Philadelphia: Temple University Press.

Rank, O. (1932) *Art and Artist: Creative Urge and Personality Development*, trans. Charles Atkinson, New York: Tudor Publishing Co.

—— (1945) *Will Therapy; and Truth and Reality*, trans. Jessir Taft, New York: Alfred A. Knopf Inc.

Redding, S.G. (1990) *The Spirit of Chinese Capitalism*, Berlin: Walter de Gruyter.

Republic of the Philippines (1989) *Rules Implementing the Code of Conduct and Ethical Standards for Public Officials and Employees, and Republic Act No. 6713*, Quezon City: Civil Service Commission.

—— (1991) *Republic Act 7581. Price Act*, Manila: Congress of the Philippines.

—— (1991) *Republic Act No. 3019. Anti-Graft and Corrupt Practices Act*, Manila: Senate.

—— (1991) *Foreign Investments Act of 1991: As Amended by RA 8179*, Manila: Department of Trade and Industry.

—— (1993) *Southern Mindanao Region Development Plan, 1993–98*, Davao City: Regional Development Council XI.

—— (1995) *Philippine Exporter's Manual, Volume I*, Makati City: Department of Trade and Industry.

—— (1997) *The Tax Reform Act of 1997*, Republic Act No. 8424, Manila.

—— (1997) *Executive Order No. 3. An Order Establishing Guidelines for the Effective Implementation of Various Training and Career Development Programs*, Davao: Office of the City Mayor.

—— (1997) *Yearbook of Labour Statistics*, Manila: Department of Labour and Employment

—— (1997) *Migrant Workers and Overseas Filipinos Act of 1995*, Mandaluyong City: Anti-Illegal Recruitment Branch, Philippines Overseas Employment Administration, Department of Labour and Employment.

—— (1997) *1996 Southern Mindanao Development Report*, Davao City: Regional Development Council XI.

—— (1998) *Tariff and Customs Code of the Philippines: Harmonised Commodity Description and Coding System*, Manila: Tariff Commission.

—— (1999) *Mindanao 2000 Development Framework Plan*, Davao City: Mindanao Economic Development Council.

Rodriguez, E.R. and Tecson, G. (1998) 'Liberalisation and Small Industry – Have Manufacturing SMEs in the Philippines Benefited?', *Small Enterprise Development* 9: 14–22.

Sahlins, M.D. (1961) 'The Segmentary Lineage: an Organisation of Predatory Expansion', *American Anthropologist* 63: 322–45.

Said, E.W. (1978) *Orientalism*, New York: Pantheon Bools.

Sajor, E.E. and Resurrecion, B.P. (1998) 'Constellations of Power: Philippine Ecopolitics Re-examined', *Alternatives* 23: 213–43.

Samson, A. (1962) *Anatomy of Britain*, New York: Harper and Row.

Satake, M. (1998) 'Cottage, Small and Medium-Scale Industries', *Philippine Studies* 46: 215–35.

Schweitzer, T. (1996) 'Reconsidering Social Networks: Reciprocal Gift Exchange Among the !Kung', *Journal of Quantitative Anthropology* 6: 147–70.

Scruton, R. (1997) *Modern Philosophy: An Introduction and Survey*, London: Arrow.

Securities and Exchange Commission (Credit Information Bureau. Inc.) (Republic of the Philippines) (1996) *Ratings Guide*, Manila.

Securities and Exchange Commission (Republic of the Philippines) (1995) *Philippines 5000*, Manila.

Securities and Exchange Commission (1998) *Philippines Top 2000*, Manila.

See, Chinbin (1981) 'Chinese Clanship in the Philippine Setting', *Journal of Southeast Asian Studies* 12: 224–47.

—— (1988) 'Chinese Organisation and Ethnic Identity in the Philippines', in J.

Cushman and G.W. Wang (eds) *Changing Identities of the Southeast Asian Chinese Since World War II*, Hong Kong: Hong Kong University Press, pp. 319–34.

Shimuzu, H. (1991) 'Filipino Children in the Family and Society: Growing Up in a Many-People Environment', in Department of Sociology-Anthropology (ed.) *SA21: Selected Readings*, Quezon City: Office of Research and Publications, Ateneo de Manila University, pp. 106–25.

Sicat, G. (1998) 'Southeast Asia's Economic Crisis', *ASEAN Economic Bulletin* 15: 290–6.

Sidel, J.T. (1997) 'Philippine Politics in Town, District and Province: Bossism in Cavite and Cebu', *Journal of Asian Studies* 56: 947–66.

—— (1998) 'The Underside of Progress: Land, Labour and Violence in Two Philippine Growth Zones, 1985–95', *Bulletin of Concerned Asian Scholars* 30: 3–12.

Simons, A. (1995) *Networks of Dissolution: Somalia Undone*, Boulder: Westview Press.

Sison, A.J.G. and Palma-Angeles, A. (1997) 'Business Ethics in the Philippines', *Journal of Business Ethics* 16: 1519–28.

Skinner, G.W. (1996) 'Creolized Chinese Societies in Southeast Asia', in A. Reid (ed.) *Sojourners and Settlers: Histories of Southeast Asia and the Chinese*, St Leonards: Allen and Unwin, pp. 51–93.

Smart, A. (1993) 'Gifts, Bribes and *guanxi*: A Reconsideration of Bourdieu's Social Capital', *Cultural Anthropology* 8: 388–408.

Smart, J. and Smart, A. (1991) 'Personal Relations and Divergent Economies: A Case Study of Hong Kong Investment in South China', *International Journal of Urban and Regional Research* 15: 216–33.

Solinger, D. (1984) *Chinese Business Under Socialism*, California: University of California Press.

—— (1992) 'Urban Entrepreneurs and the State: The Merger of State and Society', in A.L. Rosenbaum (ed.) *State and Society in China: the Consequences of Reform*, Boulder, Colorado: Westview, pp. 121–42.

Steinberg, D.J. (1994) *The Philippines: A Singular and a Plural Place*, 3rd edn, Boulder: Westview Press.

Tan, A.S. (1972) *The Chinese in the Philippines, 1838–1935*, Quezon City: R.C. Garcia Press.

Thompson, M.R. (1995) *The Anti-Marcos Struggle: Personalistic Rule and Democratic Transition in the Philippines*, New Haven: Yale University Press.

Timberman, D.G. (1991) *A Changeless Land: Continuity and Change in the Philippines*, New York: M.E. Sharpe.

Toynbee, A.J. (1949) *Civilization on Trial*, London: Oxford University Press.

Tria Kerkvliet, B.J. (1995) 'Toward a More Comprehensive Analysis of Philippine Politics: Beyond the Patron-Client, Factional Framework', *Journal of Southeast Asian Studies* 26: 401–19.

Vos, J. and Yap, J.T. (1996) *The Philippine Economy: East Asia's Stray Cat?* London: Macmillan.

Wang Gungwu (1995) *The Chinese Way*, Oslo: Scandinavian University Press.

Watson, J.L. (1993) 'Rites or Beliefs?', in L. Dittmer and S.S. Kim (eds) *China's Quest for National Identity*, Ithaca: Cornell University Press, pp. 80–103.

Webb, C.C.J. (1937) *A History of Philosphy* (twelfth impression), London: Thornton Butterworth.

Weber, M. (1958) *The Protestant Ethic and the Spirit of Capitalism*, New York. Scribner.

—— (1968) *Economy and Society: An Outline of Interpretive Sociology*, New York: Bedminster Press.

Weightman, G.H. (1985) 'The Philippine Chinese: from Aliens to Cultural Minority', *Journal of Comparative Family Studies* 16: 161–79.

Werner, C. (1998) 'Household Networks and the Security of Mutual Indebtedness in Rural Kazakstan', *Central Asian Survey* 17: 597–612.

Williams, H.A. (1998) 'There are No Free Gifts! Social Support and the Need for Reciprocity', *Human Organisation* 54: 401–9.

Wilpert, C. (1992) 'The Use of Social Networks in Turkish Migration to Germany', in M. Kritz, L.L. Lim, and H. Zlotnik (eds) *International Migration Systems: A Global Approach*, New York: Oxford University Press.

World Bank (1992) *The Philippines: Domestic Resource Mobilization and Management*, Report No. 10056-PH, Washington DC.

Yang, M.M.H. (1989) 'The Gift Economy and State Power in China', *Comparative Studies in Society and History* 31: 25–54.

—— (1994) *Gifts, Favours and Banquets: The Art of Social Relationships in China*, New York: Cornell University Press.

Yengoyan, A.A. (1983) 'The Buying of Futures: Chinese Merchants and the Fishing Industry in Capiz, Philippines', in L. Lim and L. Gosling (eds) *The Chinese in Southeast Asia, Volume I*, Singapore: Maruzen Asia, pp. 117–30.

Young, M. and Willmott, O. (1957) *Family and Kinship in East London*, London: Routledge and Kegan Paul.

Index